The RNZ Cookbook

A treasury of 180 recipes from New Zealand's best-known chefs and food writers

The RNZ Cookbook

Edited by David Cohen and Kathy Paterson

MASSEY UNIVERSITY PRESS

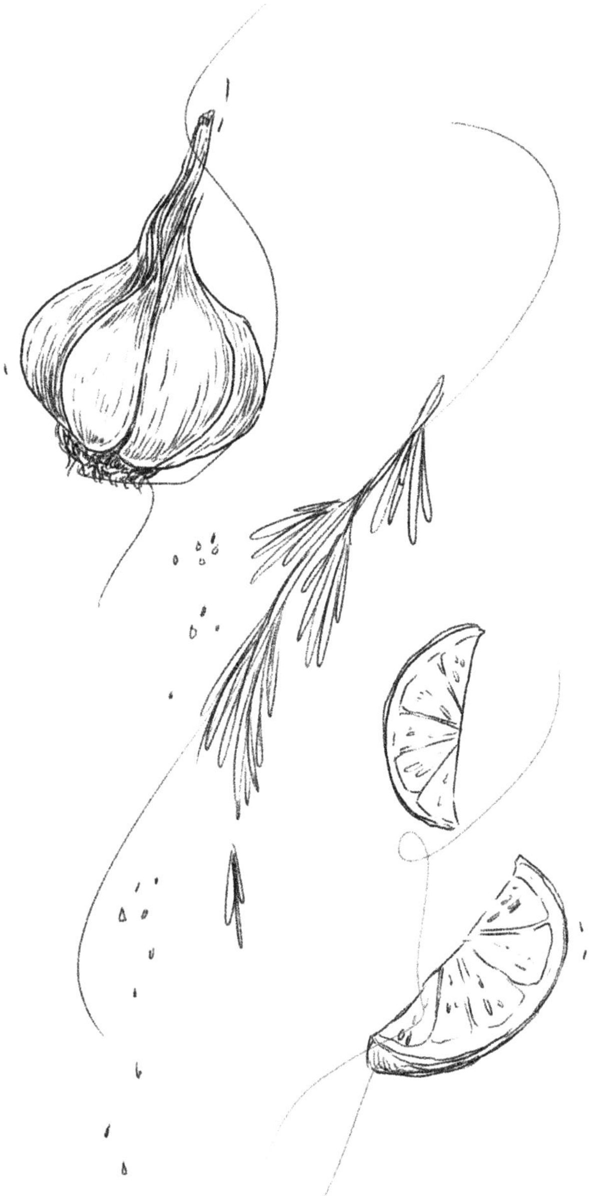

Contents

Foreword

The guilty secret among RNZ presenters is that some interviews are easier than others. As we scan the three to four hours of airtime ahead of us, any opportunity to take a deep breath and perhaps sip a cup of tea shines out in the schedule. Sometimes all you need for that extra burst of energy when interviewing, say, the Minister of Finance on Budget day is the knowledge that, straight afterwards, you're booked in with some international correspondent who can, as my producer Melita likes to say, 'talk underwater with marbles in her mouth'.

When I joined RNZ National's *Afternoons* show in 2015, I thought food interviews would fit in this 'put-your-feet up' category. I'm a restaurant reviewer who loves food, I reasoned, raised by two ex-hippies, an early tofu adopter, a long-form, slow-burn, project-cooking food nut who, under 'hobbies' on his dating profile, used to list 'eating'. These interviews ought to come ready made. You say hello. You ask what the chef's been up to. They tell you what they've been cooking lately and then share a recipe. I shouldn't even have to worry too much about the details of the item they share because listeners can always be pointed to the published version on the website if things start to sound too complicated. It ought to be as easy as poaching fish in a barrel.

How quickly I learnt otherwise. Chefs are quirky. Each has their own set of psychological reasons and circumstances for shunning a sensible nine-to-five job in favour of spending their working hours in a hot kitchen cooking for ungrateful strangers. More than any other kind of guest, in my experience, they're likely to surprise you with the way they answer a question, giving you an answer that requires some unpicking. Often they are stressed, having found their 10 minutes for you in between shifts and deliveries, or they haven't had time to prep for the segment. More than once I've seen authors frantically flicking through their own cookbooks when I ask them to share a recipe.

Then there is the audience. If you thought they were going to sit back and enjoy listening to a few minutes of food porn, well, you'd be wrong. As soon as the interview begins, they start texting in questions: What does a cup of peanut butter *weigh*? Where can I buy Aleppo pepper? Is chicken an acceptable substitute for pheasant? And please warn people before they eat Jerusalem artichokes!

If only New Zealanders were as exercised about, say, local body politics as they are about what sort of eggs to use in a pavlova. (Room temperature, seven days out of the hen, for the record.)

So, broadcasting food is no picnic. But it *is* rewarding. In our regular Friday afternoon food slot we showcase dozens of new recipes each year, from chefs who are either already household names or have become so thanks to the irresistibility of their cooking and charm. On our show, and on the brilliant programmes presented at other times of the day and week, we meet chefs at the height of their powers, often sharing a recipe or idea they've only just created — and we are delighted to be their test kitchen: a creative space for them to drop in on between cookbooks.

Though I have an administrative job to do with these visiting chefs, I tend to treat them as a reverent listener would: marvelling at their imaginations, salivating at their latest creations and, occasionally, thinking, *I could do that.* And deciding to give it a go.

I often wonder how many listeners actually try the recipes we share. Although I don't think it matters. The idea that you could attempt this or that if you want is the appeal. But it's no small thing to enter your kitchen to try something new. As with clothing, most grown-ups have their favourites. Auditioning anything new is a major decision. You wait for the feedback from those around you, and then bump an old regular of perhaps fading fashion to make way for the interloper. If you're lucky, an interviewee might introduce you to an entirely new ingredient along with several different ways to cook it. Though I beg you . . . be cautious with Jerusalem artichokes.

Among the scores of incredible chefs, cooks and pundits featured in this book, it would be unprofessional of me to tell you my favourite.

Okay, it's Julie Biuso. Julie often arrives in studio with a recipe you think you already know how to make and then proceeds to give you the little prep tricks and tips that will mean that your kitchen benchtop does not end up looking like the site of a small tornado. In her recipe for rib-eye roast on page 130, for example, she tells you exactly how to manage the juices from the meat once you lift it from the roasting dish and onto a board for resting and then slicing: by tucking paper towels around the edges of the board to absorb them.

Food culture changes fast: if it tastes good, tradition and politics don't tend to get in the way of progress. When comparatively recently, local chefs learned they could create acidity using not just citrus but also fermented foods, it changed our menus forever. Kimchi, kefir and kombucha are no longer mistaken for lost Kardashian sisters but welcome additions to our New Zealand food culture. More than one chef has attempted a step-by-step guide on the radio to creating these ferments in the home kitchen, and I think Kelly Gibney's sauerkraut (page 205) is as close to a fool-proof guide as you'll find.

But I will admit it's the classics (and special versions of the classics) that I gravitate to in this collection. Having tried Lauraine Jacob's muffins, made with an entire orange blitzed with dates and brown sugar then folded into some simple dry ingredients, would you ever bake anything else again? Is it possible for a dish to sound more delicious than Nadia Lim's Indian lamb shank curry?

In my experience, the straightforward dishes are the ones that resonate with our listeners too, and although there is certainly a place for fine-dining chefs on the radio, it's hard to adapt what a team of kitchen staff does over 12 hours into something people can try at home ('Before we begin, I'm going to tell you how to dehydrate your feijoa skins then turn them into a powder,' I distinctly remember one chef telling me as the live country music duo lined up to play next in studio sighed and put down their instruments). Asking a molecular culinary ninja to come up with a simple crowd-pleaser can feel like asking Jackson Pollock to teach you how to draw a cat. Still, some of them manage it, and you'll see some famous names in this book, to whom we're intensely grateful for meeting us at our level.

Thanks to you for picking up this book — and thanks to the contributors who've devoted their time, art and expertise to creating its delicious contents. I hope you'll enjoy reading through and recreating these recipes. And if you have any questions, well, I know from enjoyable experience you won't be shy about asking.

Jesse Mulligan
Host, *Afternoons*

Introduction

It's early in the afternoon and I'm rustling up some tzatziki to go with a lamb recipe for the family to have for dinner while I head out to work. You know the drill. First spoon some creamy yoghurt over a peeled and diced cucumber in a small bowl. Then add olive oil, fresh garlic, lemon juice and kosher salt. Plus herbs. I'm feeling a bit reckless so I go with dill and mint. Finally — and this is important for me at least — the trick is to mix the ingredients oh-so-gently-gently to the sound of RNZ in the kitchen.

Cooking and listening to the radio are two things I do every day of my life. These past few months they have also constituted an enjoyable job brief as I've scoured the RNZ archives for fabulous recipes with everyday appeal for everyday people.

In the following pages you'll find 180 gems garnered from the country's best cooks, chefs, bakers, farmers, environmentalists, kitchen monarchs and local food heroes. They've been grouped into various menu suggestions, along with snacks and other essentials for the pantry. There's a democratic split between meat and poultry dishes and vegetarian (and vegan) ones, and between sweet and savoury, and there's a bit of street food along the way. Wherever possible, the lineup includes dishes by Māori and Pacific Island chefs and food writers.

Without getting all existential or pretentious about it, the selection also keeps an eye out for recipes that capture something of the elusive essence of who we are as New Zealanders, for the tasty, easy, homey food that brings people together in a land where people don't always have a lot of other common symbols or even experiences to draw from. That's a working brief not unlike that of our national broadcaster.

Most of their ingredients are widely available. Even the slightly obscure stuff is reasonably easy to source. That's as it ought to be, really, given the subject. New Zealand is doubly blessed by being a land of immigrants, who invariably bring with them exciting new ideas for meals, as well as being a land that yields so much of what's needed to put those ideas on the table.

As one of our most quintessentially Kiwi chefs, Al Brown — who also happened to be the first to agree with alacrity to his work being featured in this collection — says of the local style: 'Our ace of cards in the culinary deck are our four distinct seasons, fertile soils, and our distance from the source — be it from the sea or the land.' All of these offerings easily work to that observation, which in turn rather suits the country's major public broadcaster's chartered requirement to provide for a broad church.

RNZ shares with its wider audience just such an easygoing love of food. The two fit together like peas in a pod. Or rather, to be a little more precise, peas in a salad: of broad beans, feta cheese, chillies, and a handful of coarsely chopped mint, all of which makes for a scrumptious meal whether served with a rack of lamb or simply as a standalone lunch. (The chef Hester Guy's recipe for this succulent dish, along with instructions on preparing her own tzatziki dressing, can be found on page 143.)

The chapters here run along similar lines to RNZ's own media menu — breakfast eaten to a radio background of *Morning Report*, lunch with *Midday Report*, snacks with *Afternoons*, dinner with *Checkpoint*, and so on. But if the structure was a no-brainer, making the actual selections proved no piece of cake.

Indeed, the difficulty in whittling down such an exhilarating list is that there are more than 3000 recipes to choose from on the RNZ website alone. That's counting only the appearances chefs and food writers have made on the platform over the past 20 or so years. It's interesting to track their careers against the website: some came on air to share a recipe while talking about a new book, a new restaurant or some new project. Many recipes featured what was then a novel ingredient, and the discussion of it with the radio host was an invaluable aid to home cooks wondering what it was and how they could use it.

Well-established figures — Dame Alison Holst, for example — featured regularly early on, and rising stars — Nadia Lim, Monique Fiso — appeared later. As such, an archive of our food history was created. But *The RNZ Cookbook* is not the work of a food historian. That would have meant pages given over to items such as curried eel, roast black swan and something called braised pukeko pie, the last of which sounds like something you might cook in a gumboot for 10 hours before throwing the pūkeko away and eating the gumboot. Decent books already exist along those scholarly lines, a personal favourite being David Burton's illuminating *Two Hundred Years of New Zealand Food & Cookery*. Nope, I'm simply an enthusiast lucky enough to have lived in a country and worked in an industry during a time when the joys of food were also being discovered in a big way.

When I got into journalism in the late 1980s, celebrity chefs were just emerging on to the scene: you saw them featured in publications like *Metro*, and the number of places where you could dine out was rapidly expanding. Back then I quickly staked a small claim to the subject I had already become passionate about. I wrote about dining and travel, did restaurant reviews and profiled chefs, that sort of thing. In the early 1990s, I went to Tel Aviv, learnt how to make shakshuka, and in time became a full-fledged Middle Eastern food nut. Later I put in some more research doing food tours or attending cooking classes in places like Dubai, Soweto and Cape Town, Buenos Aires, Dublin, Milan and Venice, and Nice. A few years ago I co-authored a cookbook on Levantine cuisine.

RNZ's relationship with the subject goes back much further, and runs deeper. The state-owned corporation's food story opened when it was barely a decade old, really, with Aunt Daisy, or Maud Ruby Basham, who worked happily for the New Zealand Broadcasting Corporation in Wellington, where she sometimes cooked meals for herself and colleagues in the dingy basement underneath the old studios on Waring Taylor Street.

In 1929, after her husband lost his job as an engineer, she took a career-swerve into radio, landing a full-time announcer role on the 2YA station, initially to 'fill up' Wednesdays, a day on which the station previously had not broadcast. A couple of years on, they fired her. The station had become nationalised and public service rules decreed that only one female was allowed to be employed at each station. Partly, one supposes, the 'jobs for the boys' edict had to do with the straitened times, but it also reflected a view of women — and of cooking for that matter. But if a woman's place really was 'in the kitchen', Aunt Daisy upended the prejudice by taking it at its word, and taking her own recipes to the then privately owned ZB network.

Thus the mother of the food nation was born, dispensing recipes, cooking advice and handy kitchen hints as she went, all in a rapid-fire voice that quickly won over a huge following.

She offered comfort during the excruciating Depression years and the war that followed. In 1944, as part of her own war effort, Basham visited Washington on a trip entirely funded by the proceeds of cookbooks, which were already beginning to sell well and would for many decades hence. She famously sipped tea with Eleanor Roosevelt, passing on personal messages to her from some of the American troops stationed back in New Zealand. But her bigger passion remained in sharing an on-air cuppa with the listeners back home. There she worked almost up until the day she died, on 14 July 1963.

Sharon Crosbie, the broadcaster who went on to become a chief executive with the corporation, was one of the first to keep the oven on in her own popular morning show. As did many of her successors, up to and including the current foodie-in-chief, Jesse Mulligan, who presents *Afternoons*. A quarter of a century ago Kim Hill put together a book of recipes called *Sounds Delicious*, the name of the cooking slot on what is now *Nine to Noon*.

These days the operation is more a sound and vision affair. Half a million of us listen to it live every week, yes, but RNZ is a multimedia platform: on-air, online and on-demand, with plenty of clips and snazzy food photos to show for it. Only somebody who grew up in some far-flung time might sometimes think of it a little more wistfully as simply the wireless.

I grew up in suburban Wellington in a house where the National Radio served as an organising principle around which life and food were planned. Breakfasts were set to the crackly pip-pip-pips of the BBC cable news on what used to be called 2YA. Evening meals appeared to the orchestral sounds of 2YC, or what's now RNZ Concert, to a show called *Dinner Music*, an orchestral version of a classic rock show in which the evergreens were Puccini, Schubert and Bach. In the weekends, brunch-style, there were request shows. (Did people actually post handwritten letters asking to hear such-and-such a David Bowie song, and then wait a week to hear it play over lunch? Oh, yes, they certainly did.)

The music was a blast, but the food — and here I mean no disrespect to my late immigrant Irish mother — wasn't terribly flash. Whose was in those days? The great spices in our pantry, like most Kiwi pantries, were salt and pepper. The quality of most meals would have caused seasoned guests to leap out a window.

Still, progress was happening. In the wider culture, a small revolution was taking place. Tony Simpson writes so well in his marvellous book *A Distant Feast* about living in Europe during the same period and coming back to New Zealand in the 1980s with dread and foreboding to a land that had never been, putting it mildly, a mecca for gourmets. You could have knocked him over with a plastic spoon. In the space of a few short years, the country had 'ceased to be the virtually restaurant-less food wilderness of my recollection and had become instead a nation of diners-out'. Suddenly there were all these restaurants everywhere, not only in Wellington, Auckland and Christchurch but even . . . Clyde. Home cooking was even becoming a bit of a thing.

Partly this had to do with changing demographics — the country was starting to welcome more people than ever before, especially from parts of Asia. And the widespread elimination of most tariffs made it easier for importers to bring in the kind of ingredients that had previously been a huge hassle for local cooks to sauce — sorry, source.

And guys were getting in on the act, too, far more than even a decade earlier. In 1974, the marvellous Alison Holst (also featured in this collection) produced her own *New Zealand Radio & Television Cookbook*, a collection of recipes sent in by listeners and viewers. Holst's description of the typical contributor was revealing: 'Farmers' wives and city women; those who cook for one or two, and the mothers of large families . . . women who buy just what they fancy and those who watch their food budget carefully; young cooks and women with years of cooking behind them . . . What they have in common is their interest in food!' Indeed, but you didn't need to be an exasperated feminist to notice a certain glaring omission from the roll.

In my case, I'd like to think there was also a genetic component kicking into my own burgeoning enthusiasm. My paternal great-grandparents were brought together by immigrant food — in their case fish and chips, which many regard as a quintessential British (and later, Kiwi) favourite, but whose origins are in fact continentally Jewish. Rachael Karamelli was a cook in a fish restaurant in the East End of London; Sam Levy worked, in the vernacular of the era, as a 'potato monger'. They made a dishy couple. The eatery where they met was part of a 40-strong empire of fish-and-chip restaurants established by another far-flung relative of mine called John Jacobs.

With all this in mind, I particularly enjoyed working on the section inside this book having to do with the various 'ethnic' dishes other newcomers have brought to this country. It may also explain my ever-so-slight bias in favour of fish recipes.

Which brings us to the spot customarily reserved for editors to go on about how this was really a team effort — the without-whom-none-of-this-would-be-possible bit. Well, this happens to be true. *The RNZ Cookbook* may have been conceived on my lonesome, but, like the best programming, everything else has been a collaborative effort in which I sometimes only played a relatively small part. I feel a bit like a radio presenter, actually, the strength of whose work is totally reliant on a team of set-up producers, executive editors and technical folk in the offing.

Nicola Legat, the publisher at Massey University Press — who in a previous journalistic life was a restaurant judge and wrote many of those early food articles I read in *Metro* and *North & South* and has published many cookbooks — guided the subsequent work, running a cliché detector over the initial drafts. Many times I asked her if something read well, and many times she suggested ways it could read better.

The two of us initially pitched the idea to RNZ's editor-in-chief, Paul Thompson, who reckoned it to be a feast in the making. The subsequent project was superbly managed by Emily Goldthorpe, a former food-truck owner, expertly edited by well-known food writer and caterer Kathy Paterson and illustrated by Pippa Keel. Many of the recipes were road-tested by one or other of them along the way. My wife, Pamela, helped in a number of ways, in particular by lending an American perspective in conversations about what constitutes distinctly local cuisine.

None of this would have been possible without the creators of the recipes giving their permission for their reuse in this book. We are so grateful to them, both for this but also for being this nation's food champions down the years. (There's more about each of them at the back of the book.)

The publisher and RNZ wanted to give something back, and that is why a portion of the royalties from the sales of this book will go to the food charity founded by Nick Loosley in 2017, Everybody Eats.

Most of the selections that made the final cut originally aired on one or other of the RNZ shows (or went straight on to the website) after the year 2000. The self-imposed guideline of sticking with 2003 for the recipes may seem a little arbitrary, but that's the way it is with self-imposed guidelines. On the other hand, the choice of chefs is spread across more than 40 delicious years, and a few have been with us even longer than that.

I need to excuse myself now and tidy up the kitchen before heading out for another evening of it. Among my other media activities, I am a senior producer on *Morning Report*. I work out of the RNZ headquarters in Wellington, alongside Martin Gibson and the crew, a wider editorial and technical complement of more than 300 people, and sometimes — or so it seems late at night, when the place empties out and the studio light is dimmed — the ghost of Aunt Daisy.

David Cohen

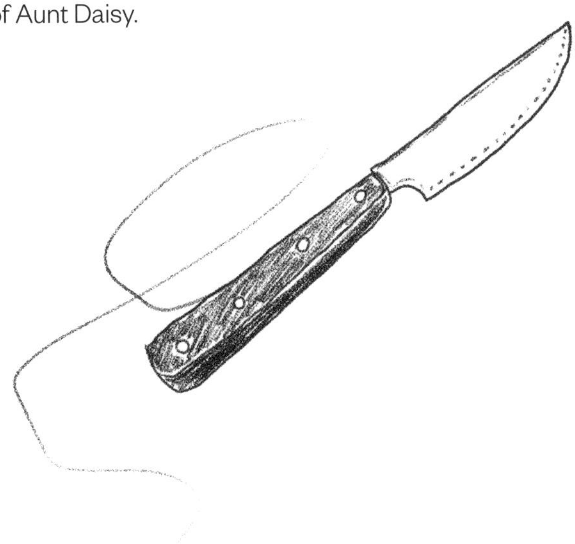

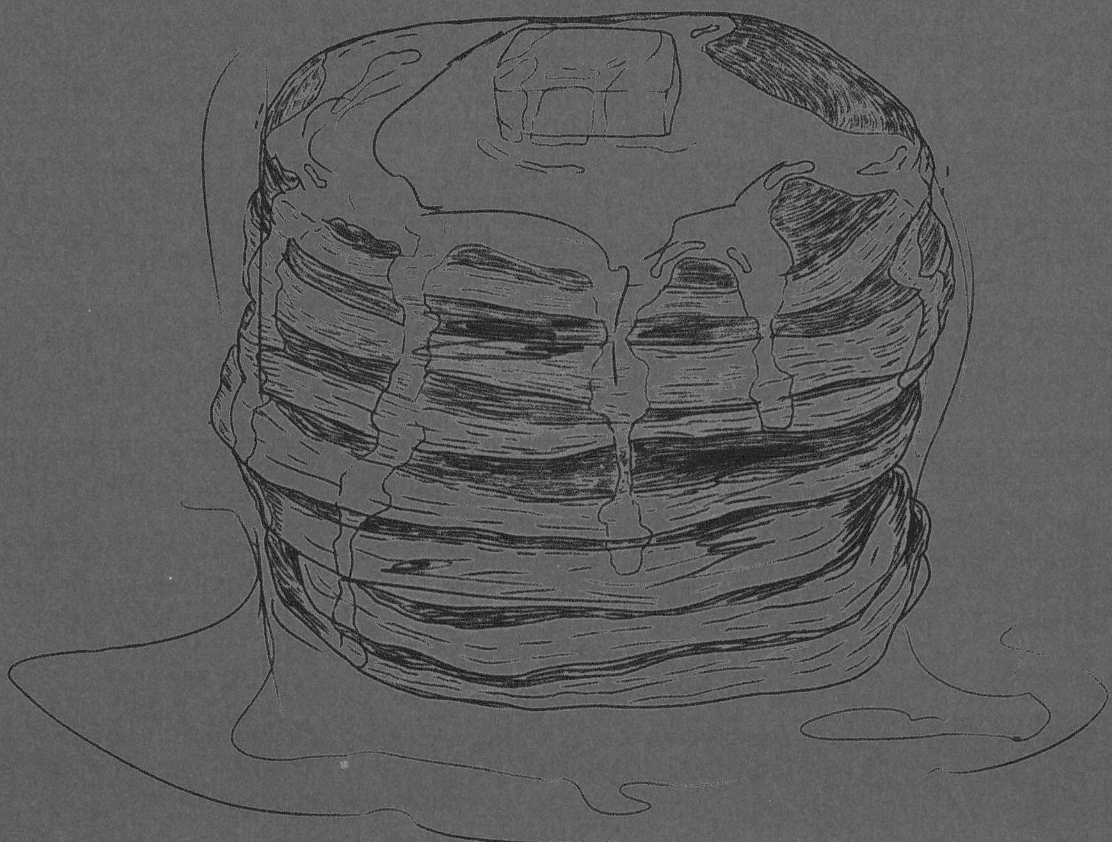

Morning Report

Morning Report, RNZ's flagship current-affairs show, routinely enjoys the highest number of listeners of any of the regular programmes. Almost everybody who is anybody in broadcasting seems to have worked for it at one time or another.

If sometimes its early-morning guests sound a little grumpy, it's possibly because they've just rolled out of bed. These breakfast recipes are for them as much as the hundreds of thousands of Kiwis who tune in each morning.

Buttermilk pancakes

Serves 6

Maple cinnamon butter
125g unsalted butter, softened (but not melted)
1 tablespoon maple syrup
1 teaspoon ground cinnamon

Pancakes
3 free-range eggs, separated
1½ cups buttermilk
½ teaspoon baking soda
1⅓ cups plain flour
1 teaspoon baking powder
½ teaspoon salt
1 tablespoon sugar
2 tablespoons melted butter, plus extra for cooking

Buttermilk kickstarts baking soda into action and helps to break down strands of gluten. This Al Brown recipe from 2012, the year his landmark eatery Depot won *Metro*'s Supreme Restaurant of the Year Award, was broadcast on *Summer Report*.

To make the maple cinnamon butter, mix all the ingredients together. Dollop the flavoured butter down the centre of a piece of baking paper. Fold the paper over and roll into a sausage shape, then twist the ends of the paper in opposite directions to further shape the butter. Put in the fridge to firm up, then slice as needed.

To make the pancakes, place the egg yolks in a large bowl with the buttermilk and baking soda. Sift in the flour, baking powder and salt, then add the sugar. Whisk until you have a smooth batter. Stir in the melted butter.

In a clean bowl, whisk the egg whites to medium peaks (the peaks should have a curl). In batches, fold the whites into the pancake batter.

Heat a large frying pan over medium-low heat. Grease the pan with a little butter. Ladle about ¼ cup of the batter into the pan for each pancake, leaving space between pancakes. Cook until bubbles appear on the surface and the batter is no longer glossy, then flip to cook the other side for 1 minute. Remove and keep warm while you cook the remaining pancakes.

Serving idea — layer pancakes with grilled bacon and maple cinnamon butter, and top with maple syrup and fresh cherries. Serve pancakes hot so the butter melts lusciously between them.

Raisin bread with ricotta, honey and barbecued peaches

Serves 6

3 ripe freestone peaches
70g thinly sliced prosciutto
good knob of butter
small raisin or fruit loaf, sliced, or sliced fruit bread
100g ricotta
maple syrup or runny honey for drizzling
fresh thyme sprigs for garnishing

Julie Biuso explained how to make these sweet toasts in 2009, the year she published her barbecue cookbook *Never-ending Summer*. They can also be made with croissants or sliced brioche.

To prepare the peaches, halve, remove stones and slice into quarters. Wrap each peach quarter in a little prosciutto.

Heat a barbecue hotplate or a large frying pan over medium heat. Add the butter, and when sizzling add the prosciutto-wrapped peaches and cook until they take on some colour.

As the peaches are cooking, toast the bread then arrange on plates and top with teaspoonfuls of ricotta. Remove the peaches and serve on top of the ricotta, drizzled with a little maple syrup or honey. Garnish with fresh thyme sprigs.

Vine-ripened tomatoes with fresh ricotta

Serves 4

8 large and 12 small tomatoes, use a variety of colours and shapes
2 tablespoons extra virgin olive oil
1 teaspoon balsamic vinegar
flaky sea salt and freshly ground pepper
1 sourdough baguette
300g fresh firm ricotta
a few basil leaves, to garnish

This recipe by Catherine Bell, founder of The Epicurean Workshop, co-founder of *Dish* magazine and chair of the Garden to Table Trust, which works in schools to teach children to grow and then cook their own fresh produce, was shared with *Nine to Noon* listeners in 2012.

Slice the large tomatoes thickly and cut the smaller ones in half.

Combine the olive oil and balsamic vinegar and season with salt and pepper. Pour over the tomatoes, toss gently to coat and leave for 15 minutes to half an hour.

Cut 4 elongated diagonal slices from the baguette and toast or grill them. Generously spread with ricotta, season with salt and pepper and place each one on a plate.

Spoon the tomatoes over the ricotta and drizzle with a little of the dressing. Garnish with basil and serve immediately.

Breakfast apple crumble

Serves 1

3 tablespoons butter
2 apples, finely diced
2 tablespoons brown sugar
2 tablespoons rolled oats
2 tablespoons wholegrain oats
2 tablespoons sunflower seeds
1 teaspoon ground cinnamon

In January 2014 Laura Vincent appeared on *Summer Nights* to talk about comfort food and share this recipe. She had come to fame as the author of the food blog *Hungry & Frozen* — she was one of New Zealand's earliest food bloggers, starting in 2007 — and the cookbook of the same name had been published a few months prior. These days she's vegan and would make this recipe with coconut oil.

Heat 1 tablespoon butter in a frying pan and add the diced apples. Cook gently, stirring, for 5 minutes or until the apples have softened slightly but not collapsed into mush. Place in a serving bowl, then melt the remaining butter and the brown sugar together in the same frying pan. Once sizzling, add the remaining ingredients and stir to toast everything slightly and coat in syrup. Once the mixture is looking browned and crisp, spoon it over the apples.

Raw chia Bircher muesli

Serves 1

1 tablespoon coconut chips
1 tablespoon dried goji berries
1 tablespoon sultanas
1 tablespoon Brazil nuts, chopped (or use almonds, walnuts, hazelnuts or cashew nuts)
1 teaspoon chia seeds
1 teaspoon pumpkin seeds
1 teaspoon sunflower seeds
½ cup almond milk (or other plant-based milk, or freshly squeezed apple juice, or coconut water)
¼–⅓ cup coarsely grated fresh pear

To serve
fresh or dried fruit
coconut chips
bee pollen
mix of chopped nuts

This super-healthy muesli mix by naturopath, nutritionist, medical herbalist and plant-based food blogger Buffy Ellen was shared on *Nine to Noon* in 2019.

Combine the coconut chips, goji berries, sultanas, nuts and seeds in a bowl. Pour over the almond milk, then cover and leave to soak overnight in the fridge.

In the morning, add freshly grated pear and extra almond milk or water if you want a thinner consistency.

To serve, top with your favourite combo of fresh or dried fruit, coconut chips, bee pollen and chopped nuts.

Hot-smoked salmon with sorrel, poached eggs and crispy pancetta

Serves 4

4 rashers pancetta (or free-range streaky bacon)
olive oil
4 very fresh medium-sized free-range eggs, at room temperature
splash of white vinegar
8 slices toasted bread or sliced baguette
butter, softened for spreading, plus extra for cooking
4 small handfuls of baby sorrel leaves, washed, dried and trimmed
100g hot-smoked salmon, skinned and flaked
black pepper

Sorrel has a fresh, clean, lemony bite which cuts through the richness in this dish. This Julie Biuso recipe from 2015, the year she published her cookbook *Julie Biuso at Home*, was discussed on *Afternoons*. It would also work just fine without the pancetta.

Sizzle the pancetta or bacon in a small frying pan in a little hot oil. Drain the rashers on paper towels and set aside.

Have ready a wide, but not deep, saucepan of simmering water with a good splash of white vinegar (*not* white wine). Make a little swirl in the water with the end of a wooden spoon (the movement of the water will help the egg white wash over the egg yolk as it spins around, forming a neat little shroud), and lower in the eggs, encouraging the egg white to fold over the yolks. Lower the heat immediately and poach until the whites are firm but still feel soft and spongy. Lift the eggs out of the water with a large slotted spatula or spoon and mop the underside with paper towels or a folded cloth.

While the eggs are poaching, butter the toast and put it on 4 warmed plates. Heat 1 large tablespoon of butter in a frying pan and add the sorrel leaves. Toss the sorrel in the butter for 10–15 seconds until slightly wilted. Spoon on to the toast.

Divide the salmon between the plates. Trim the eggs if necessary and place 1 egg on each toast stack, grind over black pepper, then top with crispy pancetta or bacon. Serve immediately.

Foundation breakfast dahl

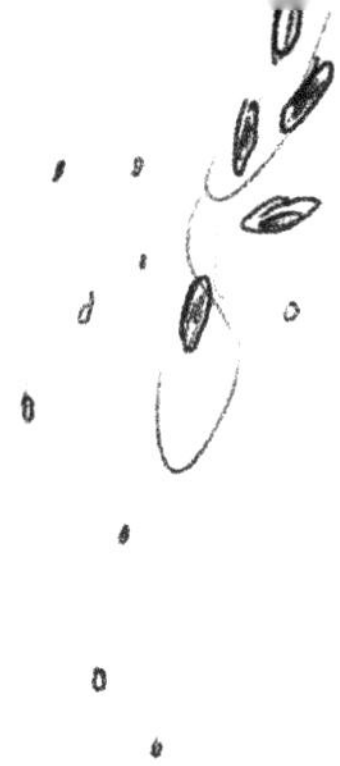

Serves 4

1 tablespoon olive oil
5cm piece of fresh ginger, peeled and finely chopped
2 cloves garlic, peeled and finely chopped
3–4 small stems (about 15g) coriander, leaves picked, stalks finely chopped
1 teaspoon cumin seeds
1 teaspoon ground coriander
1 teaspoon ground turmeric or 5cm piece of fresh turmeric root, peeled and grated
300g split red lentils, rinsed
1 litre hot water
salt and pepper
juice of 1 lemon
splash of white vinegar
4 very fresh free-range eggs, at room temperature

To serve
plain unsweetened Greek-style yoghurt
feta for crumbling
cumin seeds, toasted
fresh chilli, thinly sliced
roti

Lentils for breakfast? Why not? They abound in plant protein and fibre and offer a break from the more usual cereals, eggs or yoghurt. Plus they have been part of the human diet for over 10,000 years. Christchurch chef Ruth Trevella shared this recipe on *Afternoons* in 2020.

Heat the oil in a large saucepan over low heat. Add the ginger and garlic, then the coriander stalks (reserve the leaves for garnishing) and cook, stirring frequently, until the edges of the garlic colour a little.

Add the cumin seeds, ground coriander and turmeric and cook for a minute or so to let them toast and release their oils. Add the lentils and stir to coat in the oil.

Add the hot water and a pinch of salt. Stir well and simmer on low heat for 20–30 minutes, or until the lentils are well cooked and the mixture has thickened. Add the lemon juice and season with salt and pepper.

Put a wide saucepan of water on to simmer. Add white vinegar, then poach the eggs until the egg whites have set. Remove with a slotted spoon and drain off any water on a folded cloth. To serve, divide the dahl between 4 warmed bowls and top each with a poached egg, a dollop of yoghurt, crumbled feta, coriander leaves, toasted cumin seeds and a little thinly sliced fresh chilli. Serve with roti.

Upma

Serves 2–3

1 cup semolina
2 tablespoons vegetable oil
1 teaspoon black mustard seeds
1 teaspoon cumin seeds
1 teaspoon split chickpeas
½ teaspoon split pigeon peas
1 dried red chilli
6 curry leaves
½ onion, finely chopped
2 green chillies, finely chopped
1 teaspoon peeled and finely grated or chopped fresh ginger
3 cups water
½ teaspoon sugar
½ teaspoon salt
knob of butter
juice of ½ lemon
1–2 small stems fresh coriander, finely chopped

High-carb, silky tasting and popular in its South Indian home setting as a traditional breakfast food, this dish works as great comfort food. This recipe from Sammy Akuthota, whose family runs Auckland's famous Satya restaurants, and who then set up the Satya Chai Lounge in the Auckland suburb of Sandringham, was broadcast on *Nine to Noon* in 2018.

In a large pan, dry-roast the semolina over a low heat for 2–3 minutes. Remove from the pan and set aside to cool completely.

In the same pan, heat the oil over a low heat and add the black mustard seeds, cumin, split chickpeas, split pigeon peas, dried red chilli and curry leaves. Cook until the mustard seeds pop. Add the onion and cook on a low heat until soft, about 5 minutes. Add the green chillies and ginger and cook for about 1 minute.

Pour in the water and bring to the boil. Stir in the sugar, salt and butter. Over low heat, slowly add the roasted semolina to the pan, stirring continuously to prevent any lumps forming. Cover and simmer for 5 minutes or until the upma is cooked.

Stir through the lemon juice and fresh coriander. Serve either plain or with chutney.

Shakshuka

Serves 4

2–3 tablespoons olive oil
1 onion, roughly chopped
4 cloves garlic, crushed
fresh red chilli, finely chopped, to taste
8–10 ripe tomatoes, cut into wedges
4 merguez sausages
8 very fresh free-range eggs, at room temperature
salt and freshly ground pepper
fresh bread for serving

This fiery North African egg and tomato dish is a menu staple at Auckland chef Yael Shochat's restaurant, Ima Cuisine. When she explained how to make it Tel Aviv-style on *Nine to Noon* in 2015, the year before she published her *Ima Cuisine* cookbook, she suggested using merguez, or spicy beef, sausages, but it works just as well as a vegetarian dish without them.

Preheat the oven to 200°C.

You will need a pan that is about 30cm in diameter, large enough to hold all your ingredients in one layer, and has a tight-fitting lid. The pan needs to be able to go in the oven too. (If not, then transfer the onion and tomato mixture to a small roasting pan for its 10 minutes in the oven.)

Heat the oil in the frying pan over a medium heat. Add the onion and cook, stirring regularly, until golden, then add the garlic and chilli and cook for a further 2 minutes. Add the tomatoes and continue to cook for 3–5 minutes, then transfer the pan to the oven for 10 minutes.

While the shakshuka is cooking in the oven, pan-fry or char-grill the sausages, ensuring that they are well browned all over. Transfer to a board and cut into chunks.

Remove the shakshuka from the oven. Add the sausage chunks and return the frying pan to a medium heat. Crack the eggs into the frying pan in such a way that they are evenly spread around the pan, not at the edge of the pan as they will cook too quickly. Reduce the heat and cover.

The shakshuka is ready when the whites of the eggs are set but the yolks are still runny. Season with salt and pepper. Serve with plenty of fresh bread.

Eggs, avocado and smoky bean wraps

Serves 4

Chickpea wraps
250g chickpea flour
350ml warm water
1 teaspoon sea salt
½ teaspoon black pepper
1½ tablespoons coconut oil or ghee
2 tablespoons za'atar

Filling
15g butter or ghee
1 tablespoon tomato purée
1 teaspoon smoked paprika
400g can red kidney beans, drained and rinsed (or use pinto or black beans)
1 avocado, thinly sliced
4 very fresh free-range eggs, at room temperature
sea salt and black pepper

To serve
jalapeño salsa
small handful of fresh coriander leaves, roughly torn
1 red chilli, finely sliced or diced

This hearty breakfast recipe was broadcast on *Nine to Noon* in 2018, when British food writer and sustainability champion Melissa Hemsley had just published her best-selling cookbook *Eat Happy*. Hemsley is but one of many international food writer and chef guests who have appeared on RNZ to talk about their new cookbooks and share recipes from them. If you are serving this for more than four it would be easier to scramble the eggs.

To make the wraps, place the chickpea flour, water, salt and pepper in a bowl and whisk together. Leave to sit for 10 minutes. Melt 1 teaspoon of the oil/ghee in a medium-sized frying pan over high heat. Add 3 tablespoons of the batter to the frying pan, swirling it around to cover the base, and cook for 1½ minutes. Sprinkle over a little za'atar, then flip and cook on the other side for another 30 seconds. Repeat to make 8 wraps.

On each of 4 plates, put 2 chickpea wraps, slightly overlapping each other. Set aside.

For the filling, heat a frying pan over medium heat. Add half the butter/ghee, the tomato purée and the smoked paprika and cook for 1 minute. Stir in the beans and heat through for 2–3 minutes. Season to taste with salt and pepper, then spoon over the wraps. Top with sliced avocado.

Wipe out the pan and return to the heat. Add the remaining butter, and when sizzling crack in the eggs and cook over a medium-high heat until the whites are becoming crisp around the edges but the yolks are still runny. Season with salt and pepper to taste, then add an egg to each of the wraps and drizzle over the salsa. Serve sprinkled with fresh coriander and chilli.

Nine to Noon

If *Morning Report* is RNZ's front-news page, then *Nine to Noon* serves as a magazine accompaniment, taking a couple of steps back for a longer look at news events, with jauntier analyses and less flinty interviews. But, first on the watch of Sharon Crosbie and then Kim Hill, the show has also acquired a long-standing reputation over the years for sharing recipes and talking food. The current host, Kathryn Ryan, also has a dedicated food spot on Mondays. Which makes perfect sense given the time of day.

Lemon coconut biscuits

Makes about 36

250g butter, softened
1½ cups sugar
finely grated zest of 2 lemons
2 free-range eggs
1¼ cups plain flour
1 cup self-raising flour
2 cups desiccated coconut

Listeners to this easy Allyson Gofton recipe detailed on *Afternoons* in 2009 no doubt felt like going directly to the kitchen and baking them.

Preheat the oven to 180°C. Lightly grease 1–2 baking trays or line with baking paper.

In a large bowl, beat the butter, sugar and lemon zest together until light and creamy. Add the eggs, one at a time, and beat well after each addition.

Sift the flours together and add to the bowl with the coconut and mix gently.

Place large teaspoonfuls of the mixture onto the prepared trays and press down with the tines of a floured fork.

Place the trays in the oven and bake for 12–15 minutes until golden brown, rotating the trays during baking if needed. Transfer to a wire rack to cool. Once cold, store in an airtight container.

Ginger crispies

Makes about 30

125g butter, softened
½ cup sugar
1 free-range egg
1¾ cups self-raising flour, sifted
1 cup finely chopped crystallised ginger
1 cup cornflakes, crushed

Allyson Gofton was a regular on *Afternoons* in 2009. Here she shared another reliable recipe from her baking repertoire.

Preheat the oven to 180°C. Lightly grease 1–2 baking trays or line with baking paper.

In a medium-sized bowl, beat the butter and sugar together until light and creamy. Add the egg and beat well.

Stir in the sifted flour and the ginger.

Roll teaspoonfuls of the mixture into balls. Roll each ball firmly in the crushed cornflakes, pressing the cornflakes onto each one. Place on the prepared trays and press down with the tines of a floured fork.

Place in the oven and bake for 15–20 minutes until firm and golden. Leave on the tray for a minute before transferring to a wire rack to cool. These biscuits will crispen as they cool.

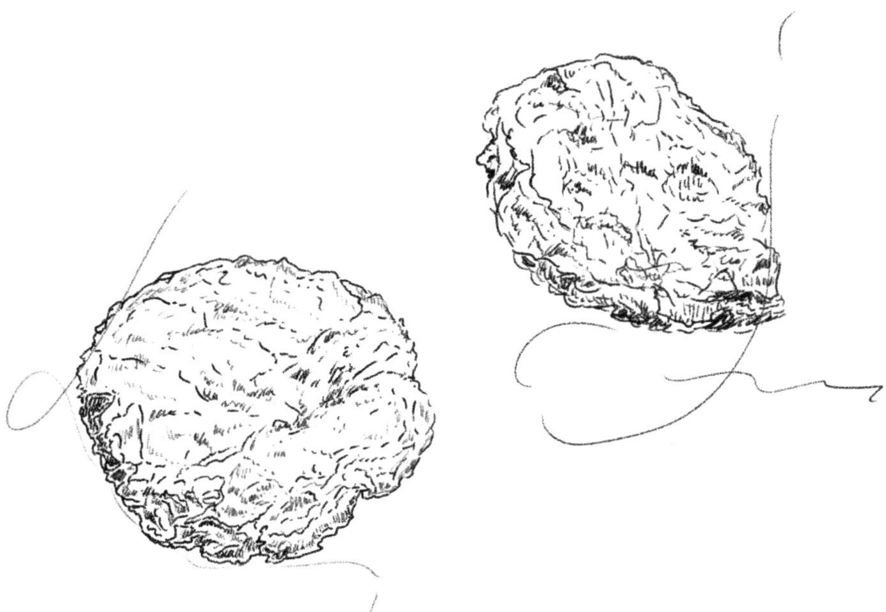

Earl Grey tea cookies

Makes about 30 cookies

- 115g butter, softened
- 40g icing sugar
- 150g plain flour
- 1 tablespoon finely ground good-quality Earl Grey tea leaves
- ½ teaspoon salt
- 1 teaspoon finely grated lemon zest

The innovative Auckland baker Jordan Rondel had just published her first cookbook, *The Caker*, in 2013, when she explained how to make these biscuits on *Nine to Noon*.

In the bowl of an electric mixer, beat the butter and icing sugar together until pale and fluffy.

Add the flour, ground tea leaves, salt and zest, and combine.

Wrap the dough and place in the fridge to chill for at least an hour.

Preheat the oven to 180°C fan-bake. Line 2 baking trays with baking paper.

Lightly flour a surface and roll out the dough to a thickness of ½ cm. Using a cookie cutter of your choice, cut out as many cookies as possible. Place on the baking trays 3cm apart.

Bake for about 15 minutes until the bottoms are just golden. Let the cookies cool and firm on the baking sheet for 10 minutes before transferring to a wire rack to cool.

Store in a cool, dry place in an airtight container or cookie jar for up to a week.

Lemon and almond biscuits

Makes about 20 biscuits

1½ cups blanched almonds, very finely ground
1 cup caster sugar
½ teaspoon ground cinnamon
finely grated zest of 1 lemon
2 free-range egg whites

Dunedin food writer and food-tour guide Judith Cullen, who had just published *Dinner in a Basket*, explained this recipe on *Nine to Noon* in 2008.

Preheat the oven to 180°C. Line a large baking tray with baking paper.

In a bowl, combine the ground almonds and the sugar. Add the cinnamon and lemon zest.

In a separate bowl, beat the egg whites until they form soft peaks. Fold into the almond mixture.

Place teaspoonfuls of the mixture on the baking tray. Place in the oven and bake for 10–15 minutes until the edges start to brown. Cool on a wire rack. Store in an airtight container.

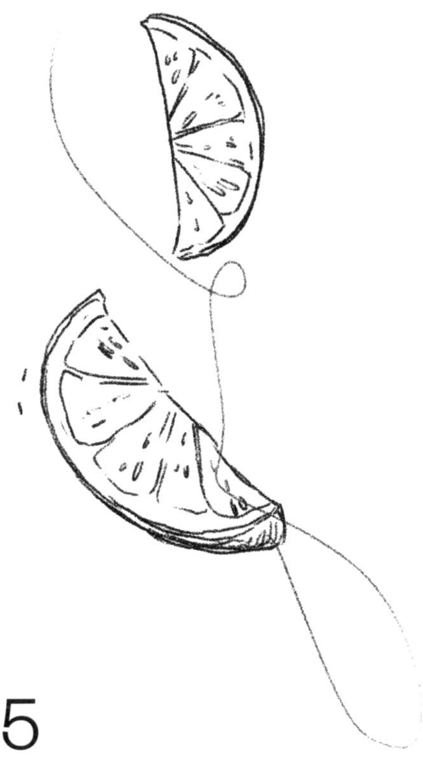

Sablé biscuits

Makes 36 biscuits

225g plain flour
100g icing sugar
25g cornflour
200g cold butter, diced
3 free-range egg yolks
36 blanched almonds

Sugar syrup

1 cup caster sugar
2 cups water

Shaun Clouston, longtime head chef and part owner of Wellington's Logan Brown, explained how to make this delicately crumbly shortbread biscuit from Normandy on *Afternoons* in 2009, the year Logan Brown won the coveted *Cuisine* Restaurant of the Year award.

Place the dry ingredients in a food processor and process for 10 seconds, to sift. Add the cold butter and process until the mixture resembles breadcrumbs.

Add the egg yolks and process to just combine, being careful not to over-process. Remove from the food processor and bring together — the dough should be smooth. Divide the dough in half and with floured hands roll each into a log about 3cm wide. Wrap and chill in the fridge for half an hour or so.

For the sugar syrup, place the sugar and water in a saucepan over a low heat, gently stirring until the sugar is dissolved. Increase the heat and boil for 5 minutes or until syrupy. Set aside.

Preheat the oven to 130°C. Line 2 baking trays with baking paper.

Remove the dough from the fridge and cut each log into 18 thin slices, placing on the prepared baking trays. Press down on each one to slightly flatten. Brush with sugar syrup and place an almond on each. Brush once more with sugar syrup.

Place in the oven and bake for 15 minutes or until golden. Remove from the oven and cool on a wire rack before storing in an airtight container.

Peanut butter and chocolate cookies

Makes 20–24 cookies

- 1 cup peanut butter (check it's gluten-free)
- 1 free-range egg
- ¾ cup brown or raw sugar
- ½ teaspoon baking soda
- 85g dark chocolate, chopped into chunks (check it's gluten-free)

Niki Bezzant walked *Nine to Noon* readers through how to make this gluten-free recipe in 2010, the year she was named Editor of the Year in the New Zealand Magazine awards for her work at the helm of *Healthy Food Guide*.

Preheat the oven to 180°C. Line a large baking tray with baking paper.

Combine the peanut butter, egg, sugar and baking soda in a bowl and mix well. Add the chocolate chunks and stir to combine.

Roll small teaspoonfuls of mixture and place on the baking tray, about 5cm apart.

Bake for 10–12 minutes, until lightly browned on top. Cool on the tray for a few minutes before removing to a wire rack to cool. These cookies have a soft, chewy texture.

Louise cake with lemon curd

Makes 24 pieces

Base
130g plain flour
½ teaspoon baking powder
pinch of salt
75g butter, softened
45g caster sugar
2 free-range egg yolks
¾ cup lemon curd, apricot jam or strawberry conserve

Topping
2 free-range egg whites
120g caster sugar
60g desiccated coconut

It was peak lemon season when Julie Biuso shared this take on Louise cake with *Afternoons* listeners in 2020. In her mind, the lemon curd filling is a magnificent alternative to the standard raspberry jam of yore.

Preheat the oven to 160°C. Line a small (roughly 25cm × 16cm) Swiss roll tin with baking paper.

Sift the flour and baking powder together with a pinch of salt. Put the butter in a smallish warmed bowl and beat with an electric beater until soft and loose. Gradually beat in the sugar, and beat until light and creamy. Beat in the egg yolks, then fold in the dry ingredients. The mixture will be on the dry side and will be difficult to combine, but this is how it should be, and it will form a stiff paste with a bit of elbow grease.

Press the mixture into the prepared tin and spread generously with the lemon curd or jam.

Beat the egg whites until stiff. Gradually add the sugar and beat until stiff and glossy. Carefully stir in the coconut.

Spread the coconut meringue topping evenly over the curd or jam layer, making sure all the curd or jam is covered.

Bake for about 15 minutes, or until the coconut meringue is lightly coloured and the curd or jam is bubbling underneath. Cut the Louise cake into 24 slices while still warm, then transfer to a cooling rack. Store in a container, separating the pieces with waxed paper.

Tip — If you want to get some preparation done in advance, make the base, press it into the paper-lined tin and freeze. Once frozen, remove from the tin and transfer to a sealable freezer bag and freeze until required.

Jonny Schwass's mum's mum's ginger slice

Makes about 20 squares, depending on how large you cut them

Base
125g butter, softened
½ cup sugar
1½ cups self-raising flour
1 teaspoon ground ginger

Icing
170g butter
2 tablespoons golden syrup
3 teaspoons ground ginger
2 cups icing sugar

Well-known Christchurch chef Jonny Schwass shared this family recipe with the *Afternoons* audience in 2014. Its method instructions are completely charming.

Preheat the oven to 180°C.

Lightly grease and line a slice tin with baking paper and set aside.

Have a weak cup of tea and do the across section of the daily crossword.

Cream the butter and sugar together until fluffy. Sift the flour and ginger together then mix into the creamed mixture. Press the mixture into the prepared slice tin.

Sneak a piece of crystalised ginger.

Put in the oven and bake for 20 minutes. Remove from the oven.

Meanwhile, make the icing. In a small saucepan over a low heat, or in a heat-proof bowl in the microwave, heat the butter, golden syrup and ground ginger until the butter has melted. Sift in the icing sugar and mix well, then pour the icing over the hot base.

Allow to cool, finish the down section of the crossword, remember you left your cup of tea at the mailbox when you collected the mail, return to the kitchen to discover someone has baked you a lovely ginger slice, smile, slice and be happy.

Chocolate fudge slice

Makes about 24 bars

- 250g packet plain biscuits, such as wine biscuits or malt biscuits
- 1½ cups desiccated coconut
- 1 cup raisins or sultanas
- 395g can sweetened condensed milk
- 2 tablespoons cocoa powder
- 150g butter
- 1 teaspoon vanilla essence

Icing

- 1½ cups icing sugar
- 3 tablespoons cocoa powder
- 3 tablespoons butter, at room temperature
- 2 tablespoons hot water
- ½ teaspoon vanilla essence
- hundreds and thousands, to decorate (optional)

Sophie Gray, The Destitute Gourmet, is another of this country's fine baking-recipe writers. In 2021, she shared this recipe that requires no oven time with *Summer Times* listeners.

Grease a Swiss roll tin or slice tray and line with baking paper.

Crush the biscuits in a sturdy bag or pulse in a food processor, then combine with the coconut and raisins or sultanas in a large bowl.

Place the condensed milk, cocoa powder and butter in a small saucepan. Heat until bubbling, stirring frequently to prevent scorching. Remove from the heat and add the vanilla.

Stir the hot mixture into the dry ingredients until thoroughly combined. Press into the prepared tin, then refrigerate or slip into the freezer until cooled and firm.

To make the icing, place all the ingredients except the hundreds and thousands in a bowl and beat together until smooth. Spread over the cooled slice using a spatula or palette knife. Sprinkle with hundreds and thousands, if using. Chill to set the icing before slicing into bars.

Tip — If coconut allergy is a problem, substitute rolled oats; my sister always made this with oats as her kids simply didn't like coconut.

Scott's Farewell Square

Makes 16 substantial squares

115g butter, softened
170g brown sugar
2 teaspoons golden syrup
1 free-range egg
170g plain flour
pinch of salt
1 teaspoon baking powder
1 tablespoon cocoa powder
85g desiccated coconut, plus extra for sprinkling
55g walnuts, roughly chopped
4 Weet-Bix, crushed
115g pitted dates, roughly chopped
55g raisins

Chocolate icing
120g icing sugar, sifted
2 tablespoons cocoa powder
15g butter, melted

On *Nine to Noon* in 2016, Alexa Johnston explained that this slice should sustain a traveller on a long, cold journey, since it was created in honour of the great explorer Robert Falcon Scott, who sailed from Dunedin for Antarctica in November 1910 on his ill-fated journey to the South Pole. Take it next time you go tramping, Alexa says, in memory of the heroic age of Antarctic exploration.

Preheat the oven to 190°C. Grease and line a shallow baking tin (about 20cm × 20cm) with baking paper.

Cream the butter and brown sugar until light and creamy then stir in the golden syrup and the egg.

Sift in the flour, salt, baking powder and cocoa. Mix to combine and then add the desiccated coconut, walnuts, crushed Weet-Bix, dates and raisins. Stir thoroughly.

Tip the mixture into the prepared tin and spread it out evenly.

Bake for 15–20 minutes. Remove from the oven and put on a wire rack to cool.

To make the icing, combine the icing sugar, cocoa, melted butter and a little hot water, and mix to a spreading consistency.

Spread over the slice and sprinkle with extra desiccated coconut.

Cut into squares when the icing has set and store in an airtight container. Omit the icing if you are planning to carry this in a lunchbox or pack.

Tip — Toast the extra coconut for a few minutes over a gentle heat in a dry frying pan before sprinkling over the iced slice.

Whole orange and date muffins

Makes 12

210g plain flour
1 teaspoon baking powder
1 teaspoon baking soda
large pinch of salt
100g pitted dates
150g soft brown sugar
2 large oranges
110g butter, chopped into small pieces
1 large free-range egg

This recipe by former *Cuisine* and *Listener* food editor Lauraine Jacobs was shared with *Nine to Noon* listeners in 2020.

Preheat the oven to 200°C. Butter a 12-cup muffin tray, or use paper cases in the muffin tray.

Sift the flour, baking powder, baking soda and salt together and put aside.

Pulse half the dates in a food processor with 50g of the brown sugar until the dates are coarsely chopped.

Wash 1 whole orange, cut into 8–10 pieces and add this to the food processor, pulsing until all is finely chopped.

Roughly chop the remaining dates and add to the food processor with the remaining brown sugar, the butter, the egg and the juice of the remaining orange. Blend well.

Add the sifted ingredients and pulse until just mixed, taking care not to over-process.

Divide the mixture between the muffin cups and place in the oven. Bake for about 15 minutes until firm to the touch and lightly browned.

Serve warm with butter.

Banana and blueberry bran muffins

Makes 12 large muffins

1 cup self-raising flour
2 teaspoons ground cinnamon
good pinch of salt
1½ cups bran flakes (or wheat bran)
½ cup sultanas or raisins (optional)
⅓ cup golden syrup
¼ cup grapeseed oil or other vegetable oil
3 large, very ripe bananas, mashed
1 teaspoon vanilla essence or extract
2 free-range eggs
¾ cup dairy or coconut yoghurt
1 level teaspoon baking soda
1 cup blueberries, fresh or frozen (if frozen, defrost and drain well)

In 2017, Nadia Lim had just published her seventh cookbook, *Let's Eat*, and shared this recipe from it on *Afternoons*.

Preheat the oven to 200°C. Line a 12-hole muffin tin with paper cases.

Sift the flour and cinnamon into a medium-sized mixing bowl. Stir in the salt, bran flakes and sultanas/raisins (if using).

In a large mixing bowl, whisk the golden syrup, oil, banana, vanilla, eggs, yoghurt and baking soda together until smooth.

Add the flour mixture to the wet mixture. Fold together with a large metal spoon until just combined — do not over-mix; it's fine if it's a little lumpy (this generally gives lighter muffins). Quickly fold through the blueberries.

Spoon the mixture into paper cases, dividing equally. Bake for 20–25 minutes or until the muffins have risen and the tops are light golden and spring back when lightly pressed. Remove from the oven and leave to stand for 5 minutes before removing from the tin to a wire rack to cool.

Keep in an airtight container for a few days or freeze for up to a month.

Tip — For even more fibre, you can substitute self-raising flour with 1 cup wholemeal flour plus 1½ teaspoons baking powder.

Cheese scones

Makes 9 large or 16 small scones

2 cups flour*
2 teaspoons baking powder
¼ teaspoon cayenne pepper (3 good pinches)
2 cups grated tasty cheese, plus extra for topping
¼ cup milk
¾ cup boiling water
150ml cream

* Myra uses heaped breakfast cups of high-grade flour, and heaped teaspoons of baking powder.

In 2008, Alexa Johnston, who had just published her best-selling cookbook *Ladies A Plate* — which can lay claim to kicking off the modern-day baking revival — told *Nine to Noon* listeners about her scone-making mentor, Myra Lawrie, who taught her, among other things, that cream left in the fridge for a week or so, even if slightly sour, is very good for scone-making. You can use full cream milk or buttermilk instead, in which case rub in 2 tablespoons (30g) butter before adding the liquids.

Preheat the oven to 200°C. Sprinkle a baking tray with flour.

Sift the flour and baking powder into a large mixing bowl, lifting the sifter high to aerate the flour as much as possible. Add the cayenne pepper and grated cheese and lightly mix.

Place the milk in a heatproof jug and add the boiling water.

Make a well in the centre of the flour and pour in the cream, then half of the milk and water mixture, and stir together with a table knife. Add the rest of the milk, and water if you need it, to make the dough come together — it should be not too dry and not too wet. Your hands shouldn't stick to the dough.

Tip the dough directly onto the floured baking tray. Pat it down with floured hands into a square about 3cm thick. Flip the whole square over to make sure it is well floured.

Cut into 9 (or 16) squares and top with extra grated cheese.

Place in the oven and bake for 12–15 minutes, until nicely risen and golden, rotating the tray halfway through. Cool on a wire rack.

For date scones, rub 2 tablespoons (30g) of cold butter into the flour, then stir in about 2 tablespoons of sugar. Add 1½ cups of chopped pitted dates (or less if you prefer). Pour in the liquid ingredients and stir with a fork to form a dough before turning out and cutting. Brush the tops with cream and sprinkle with demerara sugar before baking.

Blueberry and yoghurt scones

Makes 9 scones

2 cups plain flour
4 level teaspoons baking powder
3 level tablespoons caster sugar, plus a little extra for sprinkling
80g butter, soft or firm
small cup of blueberries
¼ cup plain, unsweetened yoghurt
¾ cup milk, plus a splash if needed, and a little extra for brushing

The legendary Lois Daish, longtime *Listener* food writer and restaurateur, shared this summery scone recipe with *Afternoons* listeners in 2008.

Preheat the oven to 200°C. Lightly butter a baking tray.

Sift the flour, baking powder and sugar into a large bowl. Add the butter — if it is soft, rub in with your fingers; if hard, grate it in and toss to mix. Add the blueberries. Put the yoghurt in a measuring cup and fill the cup with milk. Gently whisk together with a fork.

Pour the yoghurt and milk into the dry ingredients and use a blunt knife to mix lightly yet thoroughly. Add another splash of milk if the mixture isn't holding together.

Tip out onto a floured bench and form into a square, 2–3cm thick. Brush lightly with a little milk and sprinkle with sugar. Cut into 9 squares.

Transfer the squares to the baking tray and bake for 15 minutes until golden brown, top and bottom. Transfer the scones from the baking tray to a wire rack.

Serve within a few hours.

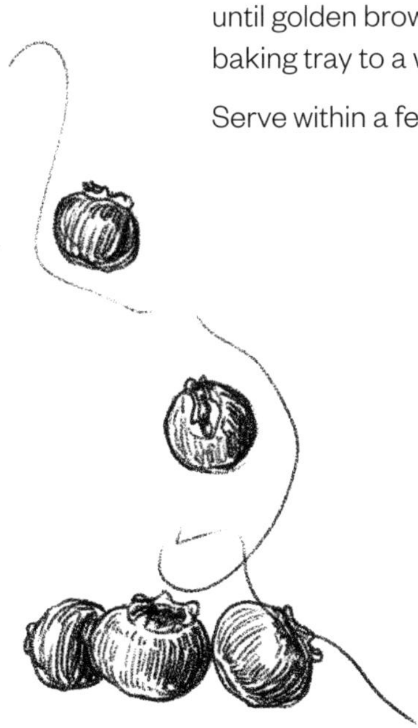

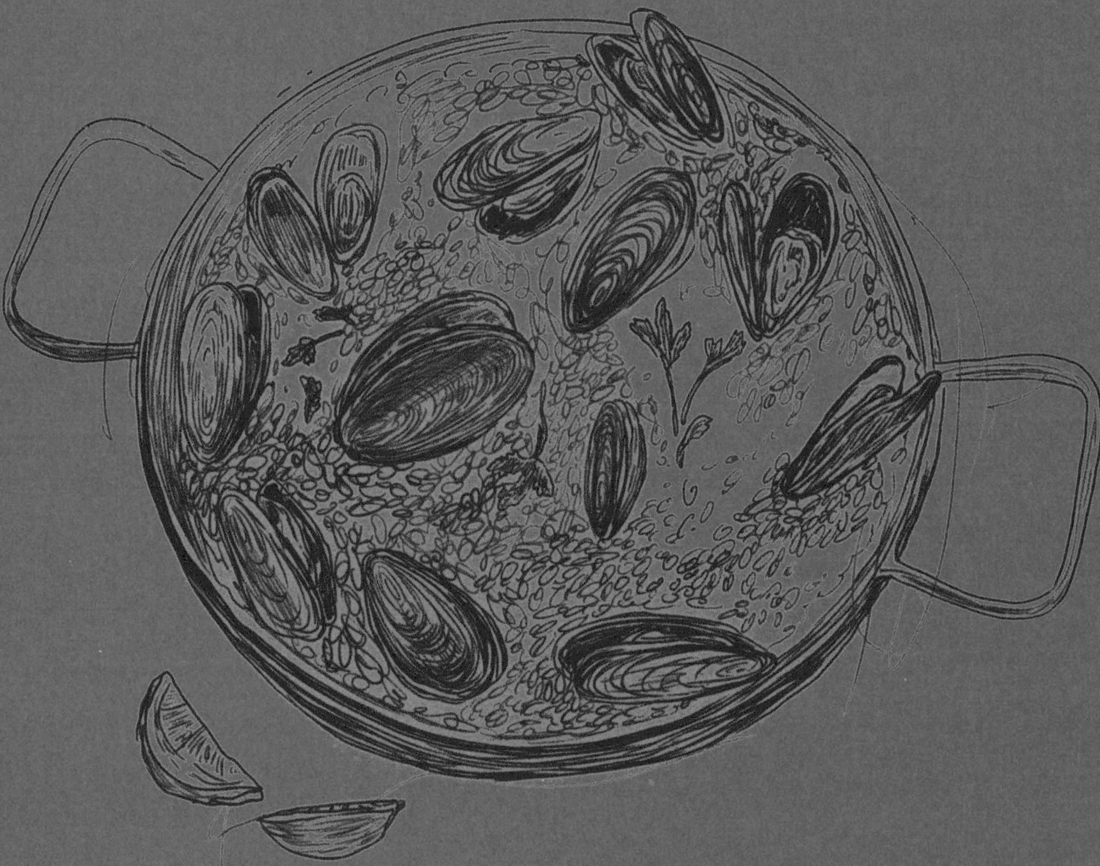

Midday Report

Te Pūrongo o te Poutūtanga Midday Report is RNZ's lunchtime current affairs show, presented by Māni Dunlop (Ngāpuhi), and ranging across business, rural and sports news and the all-important long-range weather forecasts. There's often news from the courts, too. Always lots to chew on over lunch.

French onion soup

Serves 8

125g butter
8 cups thinly sliced onions (large white onions are best here)
3 tablespoons plain flour
3 litres beef stock
salt and pepper
1 cup brandy
1 stick French bread
100g Gruyère, grated
100g Parmesan, grated
olive oil for drizzling

In 2007, then Hippopotamus chef Laurent Loudeac shared this classic French recipe from his homeland with Kim Hill's *Saturday Morning* audience.

Melt the butter in a large saucepan over a low heat and add the onions. Cook, stirring constantly, until they are soft and well caramelised.

When the onions are soft, sprinkle them with the flour. Add 2 cups of the beef stock and stir until the mixture thickens. Now add the remaining stock, then season with salt and pepper. Stir in the brandy and bring to the boil. Cover and simmer for 30 minutes or until well flavoured.

Preheat the oven to 200°C. Cut the French bread into slices 1–2cm thick. Place on a baking tray and toast in the oven for about 15 minutes, turning to toast evenly.

When ready to serve, turn the oven to grill. Sit 8 ovenproof bowls in a large roasting dish. Ladle the soup into the bowls and cover each with a thick handful of Gruyère. Top with a piece of the toasted bread and drizzle with a little olive oil, then sprinkle the Parmesan over the top. Place in the oven and grill until the cheese is golden brown, bubbly and dribbling over the edge of the bowls.

Lentil soup

Serves 6–8

½ cup olive oil
4 large pieces of beef shank, cross-cut
2 carrots, scrubbed and diced
2 stalks celery, washed and sliced
1 large onion, diced
1 leek, trimmed, well washed, and sliced
2 cloves garlic, crushed
salt, to taste
10 black peppercorns, crushed
2 bay leaves
250g brown or verte du Puy lentils, rinsed
beef stock or water, to cover (roughly 2 litres, or 8½ cups)
2 tablespoons curry powder, mild or hot
1 Rookworst Dutch smoked sausage

Sarah Klisser shared the recipe for this classic, thick soup on *Nights* in 2007.

Place around half of the olive oil in a large heavy-based saucepan over a high heat. Brown the beef shank well on both sides, working in batches if necessary to not overcrowd the pan. When the meat is dark and golden remove to a plate and set aside. Discard the used oil and any charred bits, but make sure to keep the remnants that have stuck to the base of your pan.

Add the second half of the olive oil to the pan over a medium heat. When the oil starts to shimmer add the sliced carrots, celery, onion and leek and stir well. After around 4 minutes add the crushed garlic. Cook, stirring, until the onions are translucent and the other vegetables soft and starting to gain colour. Season lightly with salt and add the crushed peppercorns and bay leaves.

Return the meat to the pan, along with the rinsed lentils and the stock, and bring to the boil. Place the curry powder in a cup and add a ladleful of hot stock to dissolve the powder, then add the curried stock back into the soup.

Simmer over a low heat for at least 3 hours, the longer the better. Skim off any foam that rises to the top of the pan. Taste and season again.

Serve with the Rookworst either cooked separately or simmered in the soup for the recommended cooking time. Slice the sausage and remove the beef shanks from the soup. Pull the meat from the bones with a fork, discarding the very fatty bits. Divide the meat and sausage between bowls and pour over the lentil soup. Mustard or horseradish sauce make tasty accompaniments, as do whole gherkins and hot crusty bread.

Tip — When dicing and slicing your onion, leek, carrots and celery it helps to think about how they will need to fit onto a soup spoon. Try to keep all your vegetables the same size and shape.

Butter chicken soup

Serves 6

Marinade
1 tablespoon lemon juice
1 teaspoon ground coriander
1 teaspoon ground cumin
1 teaspoon chilli powder
1 teaspoon finely grated fresh ginger
2 large cloves garlic, crushed

Soup
1 large boneless chicken breast, or equivalent weight of boneless thigh meat
1 tablespoon butter
1 onion, finely chopped
1 teaspoon ground coriander
1 teaspoon ground cumin
¼ teaspoon chilli powder
1 teaspoon finely grated fresh ginger
400g can chopped tomatoes
3 cups chicken stock
¼ cup basmati rice
2 tablespoons tomato paste
1 tablespoon plain flour
2 tablespoons brown sugar
¼ cup cream
salt and pepper to taste
natural yoghurt to serve
fresh coriander to garnish
naan bread for dunking

Sophie Gray chatted about this recipe to Kim Hill on *Saturday Morning* in 2003, the year she published her first *Destitute Gourmet* cookbook. The familiar ingredients of this classic soup are shuffled with an earthy-tasting marinade.

Combine the marinade ingredients in a glass bowl. Cut the chicken into small pieces, or slice thinly, and mix into the marinade. Refrigerate for at least 1 hour.

To make the soup, melt the butter in a medium-sized saucepan and add the marinated chicken and the onion. Cook, stirring constantly, until the chicken is sealed (white-looking) and the onion is soft.

Add the dried spices and ginger, then stir in the tomatoes and stock. When simmering, pour in the rice, stir and simmer for 10 minutes.

Mix together the tomato paste and flour and whisk this, a little at a time, into the soup. Add the brown sugar and cream, and season to taste with salt and pepper.

Serve in soup bowls with a dollop of natural yoghurt and some chopped fresh coriander on top. Provide some torn-up naan bread for dunking.

Pan-fried fish with pāua and tuatua sauce

Serves 4

Sauce

1 tablespoon oil
½ onion, diced
1 clove garlic, very finely chopped
200g pottle minced pāua
½ cup white wine (we use a chardonnay)
16 tuatua, purged of sand and grit
½ cup cream
handful of chopped chives

Fish

½–1 cup plain flour
salt and pepper
4 fresh fish fillets
1 tablespoon butter
1 tablespoon oil

The 2014 MasterChef winners Kasey and Kārena Bird spoke to Karyn Hay via Skype from Maketū in June 2020, not long after New Zealand's first Covid lockdown had ended. Lockdown had forced them to cancel their busy schedule and they had switched to livestream cooking demonstrations. This was one of them.

For the sauce, heat the oil in a frying pan over a low heat, add the onion and garlic and pan-fry for a few minutes until translucent. Add the pāua and cook until just golden.

Pour in the wine and let it bubble up, about 1 minute. Add the tuatua and cover with a lid. Turn up the heat and shake the pan to help open up the tuatua. Once the tuatua are just beginning to open, finish with the cream. Stir in the chives. Set aside in a warm place.

For the fish, place the flour on a flat plate and season with salt and pepper. Dust the fish in the flour, shaking off the excess. Heat a large frying pan over a medium heat and add the butter and oil. When the butter is sizzling, pan-fry the fish for 2–3 minutes on each side, until just cooked through. Serve topped with the sauce.

Quinoa tabouleh

Serves 4

200g quinoa
500ml water
salt and pepper to taste
2 tablespoons olive oil
2 tablespoons lemon juice
½ cup finely chopped parsley
½ cup cooked corn kernels
½ cup diced cucumber
2 cloves garlic, crushed
1 small red onion, diced
6 cherry tomatoes, halved

This recipe by Jan Bilton, author of the classic *New Zealand Kiwifruit Cookbook*, debuted on *Saturday Morning* in 2004. Given the ubiquity of quinoa now, Bilton was ahead of her time. Cold quinoa is a superb salad base when combined with fresh vegetables, fruits, herbs and spices — and it's also terrific warm, as a great accompaniment for casseroles or stews.

Place the quinoa in a strainer and wash well under cold running water. Place in a saucepan with the measured water and bring to the boil. Reduce the heat and simmer for about 12 minutes until translucent and tender. Remove from the heat and drain, then fluff with a fork. Cool to room temperature.

Season with salt and pepper and fold in the other ingredients. Serve as an accompaniment.

Middle Eastern couscous salad

Serves 4

1 red capsicum
1 yellow capsicum
2 courgettes, cut into 1cm-thick slices
1 medium-sized red onion, cut into wedges
1 cup instant couscous
3 tablespoons olive oil, plus ¼ cup to dress the salad
handful of basil leaves
handful of flat-leaf parsley leaves, roughly torn
250g punnet cherry tomatoes
1 bulb black garlic (optional)
juice of 1 lemon
salt and black pepper

This recipe was explained to host Caitlin Cherry on *Summer Report* in 2013 by well-known Wellington restaurateur Paul Hoather, who deployed charred peppers, with their smoky, complex texture and flavour, to add the Middle Eastern touch. That year Hoather had combined running his famous The White House with a new venture, Charley Noble.

Char the capsicums over an open flame to blacken, then put them in a stainless-steel bowl and cover for 15 minutes to let them steam. Peel and deseed the peppers and roughly chop, reserving any juice.

Heat a barbecue grill. Toss the courgettes and onion wedges in 1 tablespoon olive oil, then throw them on the grill and cook until slightly caramelised.

Put the kettle on to boil. Pour 2 tablespoons olive oil into a saucepan, heat, then add the couscous and toast in the oil (similar to making risotto). Slowly add boiling water to the couscous, adding more as it is absorbed. Keep tasting the couscous. It is ready when it has increased in size by roughly two-thirds.

Place the couscous in a serving bowl. Add the capsicum, courgette and red onion, and basil and parsley. Rip the cherry tomatoes apart by hand so the juice and flesh goes into the salad. Add the cloves of black garlic, if using.

Add ¼ cup olive oil, lemon juice and salt and pepper to taste. Toss, taste and season again if necessary.

Insalata invernale (winter salad)

Serves 6

⅓ French loaf, ripped into bite-sized pieces
4 tablespoons olive oil
salt and freshly ground black pepper
6 very thin slices prosciutto
½ small cauliflower, central stem removed, cut into small bite-sized florets
½ small broccoflower, central stem removed, cut into small bite-sized florets
6 sun-dried tomatoes, sliced
1 clove garlic, finely chopped
3 tablespoons chopped flat-leaf parsley
75ml extra virgin olive oil
3 tablespoons white wine vinegar

This bright-tasting salad, courtesy of legendary food writer and MasterChef judge Ray McVinnie, also works well as a crunchy main course. Without the prosciutto, it's also a great vegan standby. He told the *Nine to Noon* audience how to make it in 2008.

Preheat the oven to 200°C.

Put the bread in a roasting pan, add the olive oil, and season well with salt and pepper. Toss well and place in the oven for 10 minutes or until the bread is crisp and browned. Remove from the oven and cool.

Lay the slices of prosciutto on a baking sheet and place in the oven. Bake for about 5 minutes until crisp and sizzling. Remove from the oven and cool. Break into jagged shards.

Drop the cauliflower and broccoflower florets into a saucepan of boiling salted water and bring back to the boil. Boil for 3 minutes, then remove from the heat and drain.

Put the warm cauliflower and broccoflower in a large salad bowl. Add the sun-dried tomatoes, garlic, parsley, extra virgin olive oil, vinegar, bread and prosciutto shards. Season well.

Toss and serve.

Sumac roasted cauliflower

Serves 6–8

Cauliflower
1 cauliflower, cut into large florets
1 tablespoon ground sumac
½ tablespoon ground turmeric
1 teaspoon pomegranate molasses
pinch of sea salt
oil, for drizzling

Pomegranate caper salsa
2 tablespoons currants
2 tablespoons capers
1 handful of mint and parsley, roughly chopped
juice of ½ lemon
¼ cup pomegranate seeds
1 handful of pumpkin seeds, toasted
pinch of sea salt
1 tablespoon extra virgin olive oil
1 small clove garlic, finely chopped

To serve
Tahini yoghurt (see page 204)
6 small handfuls of fresh rocket leaves

In 2021 Rosa and Margo Flanagan, who run a plant-based food cooking school in Christchurch under the name The Two Raw Sisters, had not long published their best-selling new cookbook *Salad* when they detailed this recipe on *Nine to Noon*.

Preheat the oven to 220°C.

Place the cauliflower florets, sumac, turmeric, pomegranate molasses and salt on a baking tray, drizzle with oil and toss everything together. Roast for 8–10 minutes then turn the oven to the grill function and grill for another 8–10 minutes. Remove from the oven and allow to cool slightly.

For the salsa, place all the ingredients in a bowl and mix to combine. Set aside.

To layer the salad, start with a layer of fresh rocket, followed by the roasted cauliflower, salsa and dollops of tahini yoghurt. Repeat for another 1–2 layers.

Leftovers will keep in an airtight container in the fridge for 2–3 days.

Coconut, corn and herb fritters with smoked salmon

Makes 12 fritters

350ml coconut cream
½ cup long-thread coconut
4 spring onions, finely sliced, including some green
½ cup packed coriander leaves, chopped
1½ cups cooked sweetcorn kernels, about 1 large cob
1 large free-range egg, separated
⅔ cup self-raising flour
sea salt and freshly ground pepper
vegetable oil, for cooking
2–4 slices of smoked salmon per person
rocket leaves, lightly dressed with oil and lemon juice or vinegar
sprigs of coriander, for garnishing

Sauce
½ cup crème fraîche
½ cup plain unsweetened Greek-style yoghurt
½ cup packed coriander leaves, chopped
1–2 tablespoons lemon juice

Catherine Bell shared this appealing recipe with *Nine to Noon* listeners in 2006.

Place the coconut cream, coconut, spring onions, coriander, sweetcorn, egg yolk and the self-raising flour in a large bowl. Combine and season well. Set aside for 20 minutes. When ready to cook, beat the egg white to firm peaks and gently fold into the batter. Heat a large frying pan to medium heat and brush with a little oil. Use a ¼ cup of mixture for each fritter and cook until bubbles appear on the surface and the underside is nicely golden. Turn and cook the other side. Place on a wire rack in a warm oven and repeat with the remaining mixture.

To make the sauce, combine the crème fraîche, yoghurt, chopped coriander and lemon juice and season to taste.

To serve, place 1–2 fritters on each plate, top with smoked salmon, a few lightly dressed rocket leaves and a dollop of sauce, then repeat to create another layer. Garnish with a sprig of coriander and serve immediately.

Oven roasted ratatouille with basil oil

Serves 4

about 700g kamo kamo and/or zucchini, chopped into 2cm chunks
about 700g vine-ripened tomatoes, chopped in 2cm chunks
1 red onion, chopped into 2cm chunks
½ cup kalamata olives
¼ cup extra virgin olive oil
2 tablespoons fresh marjoram or oregano (or 2 teaspoons dried)
salt and pepper

Basil oil
handful of fresh basil leaves
1 clove garlic, peeled
squeeze of lemon juice
100ml olive oil

Nelson food writer and teacher Nicola Galloway, author of the *Homegrown Kitchen* blog and cookbook, explained this 'anything goes' dish on *Nine to Noon* in 2021. And she really did mean 'homegrown': kamo kamo are often overlooked but she grows them in her vegetable patch and regards them as a 'heritage cucurbit'.

Preheat the oven to 200°C.

Combine the kamo kamo and/or zucchini, tomatoes, onion, olives, and extra virgin olive oil in a large roasting dish and toss to combine and to evenly coat with the oil. Sprinkle over the marjoram or oregano and season generously with salt and pepper.

Place in the oven for 20 minutes, then flip the vegetables with a spatula and cook for a further 15–20 minutes until tender and fragrant.

To make the basil oil, blend the basil with the garlic clove, lemon juice and olive oil until smooth. Pour into a jar and use within 3 days.

Serve hot or at room temperature, drizzled with basil oil, and with grilled polenta to soak up the juices. Leftovers can be stored in the fridge for up to 3 days.

Miso eggplant

Serves 4

400g eggplant, cut into 2cm × 4cm lengths
2 tablespoons miso paste
1 tablespoon light soy sauce
1 tablespoon sugar
1 teaspoon cornflour
3 tablespoons vegetable oil
200g pork or chicken mince (optional)
1 teaspoon freshly grated ginger
250g sweet vine peppers (or regular capsicums), cut in half lengthwise, deseeded and cut into 3cm pieces
1 tablespoon sake

This simple recipe that works as a vegetarian main for lunch or as side to meat dishes was broadcast on *Nine to Noon* by Auckland food writer Connie Clarkson in 2010. She explained that the mince can be added straight into it. Longer eggplants are easier to chop.

Soak the eggplant in 2 cups of water for 5 minutes. Drain, then pat dry with paper towels.

Mix ½ cup water with the miso, soy sauce and sugar in a small bowl and set aside.

Mix the cornflour with 1½ teaspoons water and set aside.

Heat the oil in a wok or frying pan and brown the mince (if using) for about 2 minutes. Add the ginger, eggplant and peppers, and cook, tossing, until the vegetables are almost tender — about 5 minutes.

Stir in the miso mixture. Stir the cornflour mixture and add it to the wok along with the sake. Continue to cook, stirring, until the sauce thickens, about 1 minute. Serve immediately.

Thai salmon coleslaw

Serves 4

4 cups mixed vegetables, finely sliced
1 red capsicum, deseeded and sliced
2cm piece of fresh ginger, peeled and finely sliced
1 small cucumber, peeled and sliced with a vegetable peeler into ribbons
12 slices pastrami-cured hot-smoked salmon or cold-smoked salmon slices

Dressing
½ red onion, roughly chopped
½ red capsicum, cored, deseeded and roughly chopped
1 red chilli, roughly chopped, seeds removed if you prefer
2 tablespoons caster sugar
1 tablespoon avocado oil
1 tablespoon fish sauce
2 teaspoons cider vinegar
juice of 1 lime

Niki Bezzant campaigned for healthy eating during the years she was the editor of the magazine *Healthy Food Guide*. She shared this recipe with Kathryn Ryan on *Nine to Noon* in November 2009. Audio reveals that it was 28 degrees in Dunedin that day, and Ryan and Bezzant suggested heat-challenged Dunedinites would find this dish perfect for dinner.

Combine all the salad ingredients except the salmon in a large bowl.

For the dressing, place the onion, capsicum and chilli in a blender or food processor and whiz until well combined. Add the remaining dressing ingredients and mix well. Taste and adjust until you have a spicy, sweet and slightly hot dressing.

Add about half the dressing to the salad ingredients and mix well.

Divide the salad between 4 plates. Top each pile of salad with 3 slices of smoked salmon. Drizzle with the remaining dressing.

Roast chicken salad with dates and almonds

Serves 4

1 small to medium cooked chicken (or ½ a large chicken)
5–6 big handfuls of baby salad leaves
¾ cup roasted almonds, roughly chopped
¾ cup pitted dates, halved
1 handful of fresh coriander leaves, roughly chopped

Dressing
1 small clove garlic
½ teaspoon salt
½ teaspoon hot curry powder
¼ teaspoon honey
2 tablespoons freshly squeezed lemon juice
3½ tablespoons extra virgin olive oil

Wellington food writer Lucy Corry's first cookbook, *Homecooked*, had just been published in 2021 when she shared one of its recipes with the *Sunday Morning* audience.

Make the dressing first. Crush the garlic clove with the salt. Put the garlic paste, curry powder, honey and lemon juice in a bowl and whisk to combine. Add the oil and whisk again until emulsified. Set aside.

Cut the chicken into small chunks, discarding any bones (or save them for stock) and fatty pieces of skin. Put the chicken in a bowl and toss with 2 tablespoons of the dressing.

Put the salad leaves in a serving bowl, then add the chicken, almonds and dates.

Pour over the remaining dressing and toss gently. Scatter over the coriander, and serve immediately.

Yoga bowl with roasted carrot, miso and ginger dressing

Serves 2

Dressing

1 large carrot
1 teaspoon melted coconut oil for roasting
2 tablespoons white miso paste
¼ cup light olive oil
juice of 1 lemon
1 teaspoon sesame oil
1 teaspoon finely grated fresh ginger
½ cup water, or more as needed

Salad

½ cup black quinoa
1 cup vegetable (or chicken) stock
½ clove garlic, finely diced
½ small head of broccoli
2 handfuls of watercress or other salad leaves
½ ripe but firm avocado, sliced
1 radish, sliced thinly
2 button mushrooms, sliced thinly
¾ cup sprouts
½ cup sauerkraut
black and white sesame seeds to garnish

In 2017 Auckland food writer Kelly Gibney had just published her first cookbook, *Wholehearted*, and explained this vegan salad to Jesse Mulligan on *Afternoons*. It can be customised with most vegetables. The dressing gives the mix a tangy lift.

Preheat the oven to 180°C.

Peel the carrot and cut into large chunks. Toss with the coconut oil. Roast for 35 minutes or until tender. Place in a blender or use a hand blender to purée along with the other dressing ingredients until very smooth. Add extra water if you need it. (The dressing will thicken quite a lot when it cools.)

Place the quinoa, stock and garlic in a small saucepan. Bring to the boil before reducing to a simmer. Cook with a lid ajar for 15–20 minutes until tender and the liquid has been absorbed. Place the lid on firmly and leave to sit, off the heat, for 5 minutes before fluffing with a fork.

Cut the broccoli into florets and steam until just tender.

Divide the cooked quinoa between 2 bowls or plates. Split the salad leaves, avocado, radish slices, mushrooms, sprouts and sauerkraut between the dishes.

Drizzle with a little of the dressing — thin the dressing with a little water if it has thickened too much. Garnish with black and white sesame seeds and serve with extra dressing on the side.

Tip — Instead of black quinoa, you can use white quinoa or hulled millet.

Warm salad of asparagus with new season potatoes, hazelnuts and poached egg

Serves 4

- 350g Jersey Benne or new potatoes
- 2 large sprigs of fresh garden mint
- 1 bunch of thick asparagus spears, woody ends trimmed
- splash of malt vinegar
- 4 very fresh free-range eggs
- ½ cup toasted hazelnuts, roughly chopped
- 3 tablespoons olive oil
- juice of ½ lemon
- salt and pepper
- 4–5 stalks of Italian (flat-leaf) parsley, leaves only

This recipe by high-profile Wellington chef Martin Bosley was broadcast on *Afternoons* in 2021 and is typical of Bosley's breezy, easy-to-follow approach to cooking.

Scrape the potatoes clean of any dirt and put into a large saucepan covered with lightly salted hot water. Add the mint sprigs to the saucepan and simmer until the potatoes are tender, then drain through a colander and set aside. Meanwhile, put another deep saucepan of lightly salted water on to boil. Lower the asparagus spears into the water and cook for 2–3 minutes, until they are just tender. Drain the spears and wrap in a damp tea towel — this will keep them warm.

Bring a saucepan of lightly salted water to a vigorous simmer and add the malt vinegar. Carefully break each egg into separate breakfast cups then gently slide them into the water, reducing the heat to a gentle roll. Cook the eggs for 3 minutes then remove with a draining spoon to a tray lined with absorbent kitchen paper.

Cut the warm potatoes into quarters and toss with the asparagus in a large mixing bowl. Add the chopped hazelnuts and turn gently through the salad. Add the olive oil and lemon juice and season with salt and pepper. Arrange the salad on 4 plates and top each pile with a poached egg. Scatter parsley leaves over the top and serve.

Gallo pinto

Serves up to 6

1 tablespoon rice bran oil
1 small onion, diced
¼ cup diced red capsicum
¼ cup diced yellow capsicum
2 cups cooked white rice
2 teaspoons Worcestershire sauce
2 teaspoons soy sauce
425g can black beans, liquid retained
salt and freshly ground black pepper
½ cup chopped coriander leaves

Almost every country in Latin America has a rice and bean dish that it insists is its own, and indeed they do have subtle national variations. In 2015, American-Venezuelan chef Grace Ramirez, then living in New Zealand, had just published her cookbook *La Latina*, and shared the Costa Rican version, known as gallo pinto, with *Nine to Noon* listeners.

In a large frying pan, heat the oil over a medium heat, then add the onion and diced capsicums. Gently pan-fry for about 5 minutes, until lightly seared. Add the rice, Worcestershire sauce and soy sauce. Continue to cook for 2–3 minutes to warm the rice.

Lower the heat to medium-low, and add the beans with some of their liquid. Mix together until combined evenly. Season to taste with salt and pepper and add the coriander just before serving.

Kiwi frittata

Serves 4, generously

- 1 tablespoon vegetable or olive oil
- 1 all-purpose potato, peeled and cut into 2.5cm dice
- ¼ onion, finely chopped
- 1 red capsicum, deseeded and cut into 2.5cm dice
- 1 courgette, cut into 2.5cm dice
- 50g butter
- salt and pepper to taste
- 8 large free-range eggs, lightly beaten with 1 tablespoon milk
- 2 tablespoons fresh or frozen green peas
- good handful of grated cheese or slices of Brie

This vegetarian dish from Laurent Loudeac, who was the head chef at Wellington's tony Hippopotamus restaurant in the Museum Hotel when he explained it to the *Nights* audience in 2009, can be enjoyed for breakfast or dinner and even works over a campfire.

Heat a large non-stick frying pan over a low heat. When hot, add the oil and potato and cook, stirring occasionally, for about 15 minutes.

Add the onion, capsicum and courgette and cook for another 5–10 minutes. The potato should be cooked through at this point. Add the butter and salt and pepper, and toss to mix through the vegetables. Pour the beaten egg and milk mixture into the frying pan and cook as you would an omelette, bringing the sides into the centre.

Add the peas. Once the eggs are nearly set, sprinkle with cheese and cook for a further 4–5 minutes until set in the middle and the cheese has melted.

To serve, remove from the heat and flip onto a plate.

Zucchini quiche

Serves 4–6

- 1 batch perfect shortcrust pastry (see page 227), or 2 savoury shortcrust pastry sheets
- 3–4 small zucchini, trimmed
- 3 free-range eggs, at room temperature
- ½ cup cream
- ½ cup milk
- salt and pepper
- 1 cup vintage or tasty grated cheddar cheese (or you could use a mixture, adding crumbled feta or Gruyère)

In 2015 Christchurch food writer Rosie Belton told *Summer Noelle* host Noelle McCarthy how to make this easy to prepare quiche. She explained that it dates back to her 1980s repertoire, and freezes well.

Preheat the oven to 180°C.

Lightly flour the bench. If using pastry sheets, put them one on top of the other. Roll the pastry until 4mm thick and will fit a 23cm loose-bottomed tart tin. Using your rolling pin, put the pastry into the tin, easing it into the corners then trimming the edges.

Line the pastry shell with crumpled baking paper, then weigh the paper down with baking beans or rice. Put in the oven and bake for 10 minutes. Remove the paper and the beans or rice and prick the bottom of the pastry. Return to the oven and bake for a few minutes until the shell has no wet patches. Remove from the oven.

Lower the oven temperature to 160°C.

Coarsely grate the zucchini and put into the pastry shell.

In a bowl, whisk the eggs, cream, milk and season with salt and pepper, then pour the mixture over the grated zucchini and top with the grated cheese.

Place in the oven and bake for 20 minutes or until the filling is just set, golden brown and puffed. Leave to cool before removing from the tin.

Tip — To brown the quiche, you can turn the oven back up to 180°C for a few minutes at the end of the cooking time.

Lamb pomegranate pizza

Makes 2 large pizzas

250g lamb mince
2 tablespoons pine nuts
1 teaspoon ground cumin
½ teaspoon ground coriander
2 tablespoons chopped fresh mint, plus extra to serve
2–3 tablespoons pomegranate molasses
salt and pepper
2 large pizza bases
¼ cup tomato paste
100g cherry tomatoes
½ cup crumbled feta
1 cup grated mozzarella
plain unsweetened yoghurt to serve

Allyson Gofton shared this recipe with Jesse Mulligan in 2010, when she had just published her cookbook *Bake*. Known as lahm bi ajeen in Lebanon, where it's wildly popular, there are versions of this across the Middle East — some tomato-heavy, others with slivers of preserved lemon.

Preheat the oven to 220°C. Grease two baking trays.

Mix together the lamb mince, pine nuts, cumin, coriander, mint and pomegranate molasses. Season well with salt and pepper. Roll into 20 small balls. Set aside.

Place the pizza bases on the prepared trays. Spread each evenly with the tomato paste. Divide the meatballs, cherry tomatoes, feta and grated cheese evenly on top of the pizzas.

Bake one pizza at a time at the top of the preheated oven for about 10 minutes until well browned. Garnish with some additional chopped mint and serve hot, drizzled with yoghurt.

Potato, fennel, feta, olive and lemon tart

Serves 6

500g pre-rolled flaky puff pastry (Paneton or similar brand)
3 large Agria potatoes
1 free-range egg
3 fennel bulbs, sliced paper thin
2 teaspoons fennel seeds
150g crumbly feta cheese
½ cup olives, preferably stones removed
rind of 1 preserved lemon, flesh removed and cut into small dice
freshly ground black pepper and sea salt
handful fresh Italian parsley leaves

A Lauraine Jacobs recipe is a byword for easy deliciousness. This flavourful lunch dish featured on *Nine to Noon* in 2008.

Roll out the pastry to fit a lined 30cm × 40cm oven tray. Place on the tray and rest in the fridge for at least 30 minutes.

Pre-heat the oven to 200°C.

Peel the potatoes and cut into 1.5cm slices. Simmer in boiling salted water until tender. Drain well and leave to cool.

Beat the egg and brush over the surface of the pastry. Spread the potato slices over the egg, and brush with any remaining egg.

Layer the fennel on top of the potatoes and scatter the fennel seeds over. Crumble the feta over the fennel seeds, and then dot the tart with the olives and preserved lemon rind. Season with pepper and salt.

Place in the oven and turn the heat up to 210°C. Cook for about 20 minutes, or until the pastry is puffed and golden brown on the edges and underside. Remove the tart from the oven, scatter over the parsley leaves and cut into generous wedges to serve.

Garden greens, leek and ricotta tart with hazelnut crust

Serves 4–6

Pastry

½ cup hazelnuts, toasted
1⅔ cups plain flour, plus extra for sprinkling
1 tablespoon caster sugar
1 teaspoon sea salt
125g cold butter, cubed
2–3 tablespoons ice-cold water

Filling

3 tablespoons olive oil
2 leeks, well washed and chopped
salt and black pepper
½ teaspoon dried chilli flakes
1½ teaspoons fennel seeds
5 cloves garlic, minced
6 cups spinach (or kale or silver beet), washed, and leaves torn if large
250g ricotta
1 cup grated Parmesan
1½ cups herbs, chopped (e.g. parsley, coriander, basil)
finely grated zest of 2 lemons
2 free-range eggs

Auckland food writer Gretchen Lowe, who has the popular blog *My Weekend Table*, took *Afternoons* listeners through this recipe in 2021.

To make the pastry, put the toasted hazelnuts into a food processor and pulse until fine. Add the flour, sugar and salt, and pulse. Add the cubed butter and pulse until the butter is pea-sized. Drizzle in the cold water and pulse a few times until the dough just comes together.

On a floured surface, shape the pastry into a flat disk, wrap and place in the fridge for at least 30 minutes (or up to 2 days). It freezes well for 3 months, too, if you want to make a few batches ahead of time.

Heat a large frying pan on medium-low and add the olive oil. Add the leeks, plenty of salt and black pepper, chilli flakes and fennel seeds. Cook for about 8–10 minutes or until the leeks are soft. Add the garlic and cook for another minute, being careful not to burn the garlic.

Add the spinach along with a splash of water and continue to cook for another 8–10 minutes. You can cover the pan but make sure the liquid has evaporated before removing from the heat. Set aside to cool slightly.

Meanwhile, place the ricotta, Parmesan, herbs, lemon zest and eggs in a large bowl and mix well. Add the cooled leek and spinach mixture and stir through.

Preheat the oven to 190°C.

Remove the pastry from the fridge 10–15 minutes before using so it's rollable. Meanwhile, cut a piece of baking paper to fit a baking tray, then place the paper on your benchtop. Place the pastry on the baking paper and sprinkle with flour.

Roll the pastry out until 20cm × 30cm in size. Carefully lift the paper and place onto your baking tray.

Place the filling onto the pastry, leaving a 5cm border around the edge. Fold the sides of the pastry up and around the filling, using the paper to help you.

Place in the oven and bake until the pastry is starting to brown, about 25 minutes. Reduce the heat to 160°C and continue to bake until the pastry is fully browned and the filling is set, about 20 minutes.

Remove from the oven and allow to cool slightly before tucking in.

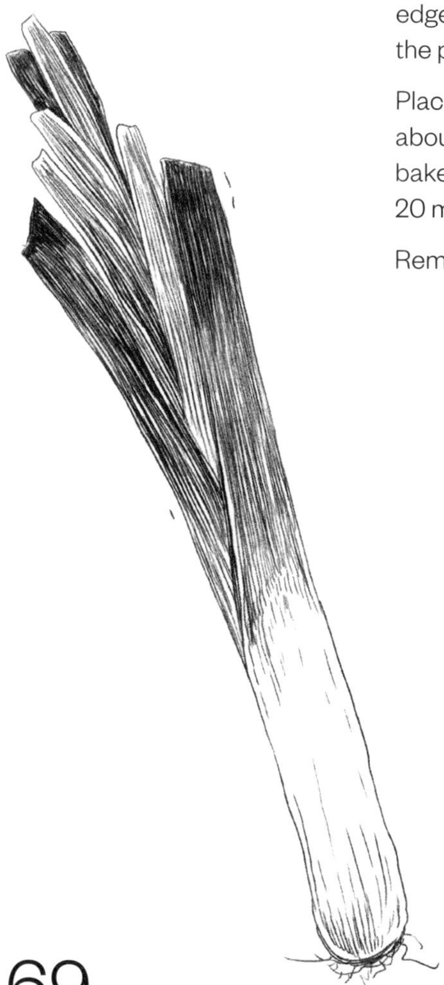

Smoked fish on toast with celeriac remoulade

Serves 4

400g hot-smoked fish
100g unsalted butter
8 slices of bread
200ml mayonnaise
1½ teaspoons wholegrain mustard
grated zest and juice of ½ lemon
1 medium celeriac
salt and freshly ground black pepper

Could anything be more simple or delicious than this recipe for smoked fish on toast, detailed to listeners by Martin Bosley on *Nine to Noon* in 2021? Martin says 'the smoky notes of hoki or moki are blissful with the celeriac. Make a platter of these and share.' Ciabatta has too many holes, so use a baguette, and make sure the fish is brought up to room temperature if you have taken it from the fridge.

Skin the fish, break the flesh into small pieces and place in a bowl. Melt the butter in a frying pan and toast the bread in batches until both sides are golden brown.

Mix the mayonnaise, mustard, lemon zest and juice together in a medium-sized bowl.

Slice the ends off the celeriac and peel away the thick skin with a sharp knife. Split the celeriac in half lengthways and place each half flat-side down on a chopping board and slice into very fine semi-circle slices.

Lay stacks of these slices on top of each other and slice the celeriac into matchsticks. Add the sliced celeriac to the dressing.

Season to taste with salt and pepper and mix well. Spread some of the smoked fish on the toasted bread, then add a layer of celeriac. Top with more smoked fish and serve immediately.

Oven-baked tarakihi with vegetables

Serves 4

- 2 small to medium-sized carrots
- 4 medium-sized tomatoes
- 2 teaspoons olive oil
- about ¼ cup parsley and ginger stock
- 1 tablespoon sweet chilli sauce, or more to taste
- 2–3 skinny slices of preserved roasted red pepper (optional)
- 4 generous fillets tarakihi or other firm white fish, boned
- 1–2 teaspoons plain flour
- salt and pepper
- 2–3 tablespoons buttered breadcrumbs
- 2–3 tablespoons chopped fresh herbs, such as tarragon and parsley, mint and chive, or basil

Parsley and ginger stock

- knob of fresh ginger, peeled
- bunch of parsley

In 2010 *The Press* food editor Kate Fraser discussed a baked fish recipe with Kathryn Ryan on *Nine to Noon*. The original one-pot dish was created from ingredients including braised carrots, cream and wine. Kate has rewritten the recipe for this book; it's lighter, with tomatoes, chilli sauce and a flavoursome stock as key ingredients.

To make the parsley and ginger stock, chop the peeled ginger finely. Finely chop the parsley, including any long stalks. Place in a jug and add 2 cups of boiling water. Cool, cover and refrigerate. The stock will keep well, refrigerated, for a week.

Wash the carrots and, using a mandolin or a vegetable peeler, slice the carrots very finely. Cut the tomatoes into smallish chunks.

Heat the oil in a frying pan over a low to medium heat, add the carrot slices and cook gently, turning often. Add the tomatoes and cook until the vegetables are soft, adding a little of the parsley and ginger stock if the mixture is too dry. Add the chilli sauce and the red pepper, if using.

Preheat the oven to 180°C. Tip the vegetable mixture into a shallow baking dish. Dust the fish lightly with a little flour, season with salt and pepper then place the fillets on top of the vegetables. Add a little more parsley and ginger stock (don't drown the dish), sprinkle over the buttered breadcrumbs and bake, uncovered, for around 12–15 minutes. Scatter with fresh herbs to serve.

Tip — The parsley and ginger stock is great for risotto, braised meats, sauces or stir-fry. Strain before using if preferred.

Marlborough paella

Serves 4

- 1 tablespoon Marlborough olive oil
- 1 onion, finely chopped
- 2 chorizo, cubed
- 1 tablespoon paprika (bittersweet smoked paprika works well)
- 2 cloves Marlborough garlic, sliced
- 250g paella rice
- 850ml vegetable stock, hot
- 36 mussels, scrubbed
- juice of ½ small lemon
- 2 cups chopped fresh vegetables, such as sweetcorn kernels, silver beet, tomatoes, or anything you fancy
- small handful of flat-leaf parsley leaves, roughly chopped

In 2014, Chris Fortune, who got his start working alongside Peter Gordon at the famous Sugar Club in London, discussed this take on the classic Spanish rice dish with Jim Mora on *Afternoons*. The Havelock Mussel and Seafood Festival was due to open the next day and the two were worried about the weather. Fortune advanced this dish as a new Kiwi classic.

Heat the oil in a large, wide saucepan or in a paella pan. Add the onion and cook to soften, 6–7 minutes. Add the chorizo, paprika and garlic, and cook for a further 2 minutes. Stir in the paella rice. Cook for 2 minutes, stirring well to coat.

Pour in the hot stock and bring to the boil. Cover with a cartouche (paper lid) and cook at a gentle bubble for 20 minutes, shaking and rotating the pan periodically until the rice is tender.

Lift the cover and add the mussels, lemon juice and mixed vegetables. Cover and cook for a further 4 minutes or until the mussels have opened and the paella is piping hot.

Serve in warm bowls scattered with the parsley, using the mussel shells as spoons.

Fabulous fancy flounder

Serves 4

- 2 medium-sized flounder, filleted, skin on, frames reserved
- ½ onion
- 6 slices white bread
- 80g cold butter, diced
- 150g white fish fillet, boned
- 1 tablespoon brandy
- ½ teaspoon salt
- grind of black pepper
- 200ml cream
- 1 lemon
- ½ teaspoon fresh thyme leaves
- 4 tablespoons white wine
- 2 tablespoons oil
- flour seasoned with salt and pepper, for coating flounder

Flounder, that unassuming fish, scrubbed up rather well in 2005 when Christchurch food writer and chef Richard Till shared this recipe on *Nine to Noon*. Till turned it into an elegant, understated show-stealer for cooks on a budget.

Ahead of time, put the flounder frames, onion and 1 cup of water in a saucepan. Cover and simmer for 10 minutes. Remove from the heat and leave to cool, then strain and set aside the fish stock.

In a food processor, make breadcrumbs with the white bread and half the butter. Set aside.

Roughly chop the fillet of white fish and place it in the food processor bowl with the brandy, salt and pepper. With the food processor running, slowly add half the cream. Process to a paste.

Lay the flounder fillets skin-side down and spread the paste evenly on the flesh side. Press the breadcrumbs into the fish paste. Pop it into the fridge.

Thinly slice half the lemon.

Preheat the oven to 200°C. Put a flat roasting dish in to heat.

For the sauce, bring the stock to the boil and reduce to ¼ cup, then add the remaining cream and the thyme. Bring to a simmer, then add the white wine and the juice of the remaining lemon half. Reduce to about ¼ cup, and check seasoning.

Heat a non-stick frying pan and add the oil and the remaining butter. The butter should sizzle, but not burn.

Flour the skin of the flounder and cook the fillets, in batches, skin-side down for 1 minute each. When they are all done, transfer the fillets, skin-side up and crumb side down, into the hot roasting dish in the oven and place a slice of lemon on the skin of each fillet. Cook in the oven for 8–10 minutes. Serve with the crisp skin up and spoon a little sauce around each piece.

Afternoons

On RNZ's *Afternoons*, host Jesse Mulligan presides over an upbeat mix of the curious and the compelling, ranging from the stories of the day to the great questions of our time. Mulligan is an enthusiastic foodie, and his show features hundreds of recipes each year. It may be the most critical food segment on RNZ this side of Aunt Daisy's celebrated spots last century.

The afternoon is the time for that most New Zealand of culinary traditions, afternoon tea — the very best of which feature top-notch home baking. These recipes are from some of New Zealand's baking legends.

Chilli, orange and white chocolate brownies

Makes 30 bite-sized pieces

350g dark chocolate (70% cocoa), cut into chunks
350g butter
6 free-range eggs
2¼ cups caster sugar
1⅔ cups plain flour
1 cup good-quality dark cocoa powder
150g white chocolate, roughly chopped
1 teaspoon ground cinnamon
½ teaspoon chilli powder
finely grated zest of 1 orange

Sarah Tuck, who runs the blog *Stuck in the Kitchen* and is the editor of *Dish* magazine, explained how to make these zesty biscuits on *Afternoons* in 2019.

Preheat the oven to 175°C.

Lightly grease a 31cm × 22cm high-sided or deep baking tin (or thereabouts) and line with baking paper.

Place the dark chocolate and butter in a microwave-proof jug or bowl. Heat in 30-second bursts in the microwave on low heat, stirring in between, until smooth and melted.

Beat the eggs and caster sugar together in a bowl until pale and creamy. Stir in the chocolate mixture. Sift in the flour and cocoa powder and stir to combine. Mix through the white chocolate, cinnamon, chilli powder and orange zest.

Pour the mixture into the prepared baking tin. Bake for 40–45 minutes until cooked through. Cool in the tin before cutting.

Spicy fruit loaf

Makes 2 loaves, about 425g each

- 500–550g mixed dried fruit (sultanas, raisins, currants, cherries, dried apricots, mango strips, peaches, nectarines, dried cranberries — use some tangy fruit for best flavour)
- 2 cups water
- 50g butter, cubed
- 1½ cups sugar
- 2 rounded tablespoons golden syrup
- 1 teaspoon salt
- 1 teaspoon ground cinnamon
- 1½ teaspoons ground mixed spice
- ½ teaspoon ground cloves (optional)
- 1 large free-range egg
- 1½ cups wholemeal flour and 1½ cups bread flour (or 3 cups plain flour)
- 1 teaspoon baking powder
- 1 teaspoon baking soda

The doyenne of home cooking and the food personality who was there before almost everybody else, Dame Alison Holst shared this recipe on *Nine to Noon* in 2007, when her publishers had just reissued her best-selling *The Best of Alison Holst*, which included an astounding 1000 recipes.

Preheat the oven to 170°C with a rack just below the middle. Line two 1-litre-capacity loaf tins with two strips of baking paper so the sides and bottom are covered.

Cut the dried fruit into pea-sized pieces using wetted kitchen scissors. Place the water in a fairly large saucepan and turn it on to heat, but don't let it boil vigorously.

Add the fruit, then the butter, sugar, golden syrup, salt and spices, and stir occasionally while the mixture bubbles gently. Let the mixture simmer for 10 minutes, then take the saucepan off the heat and cool the mixture to room temperature by placing the saucepan in a sink of cold water. Stir it occasionally.

While the mixture cools, beat the egg with a fork in a cup or small bowl. Place the flour(s), baking powder and baking soda in a large bowl and mix well with a fork or whisk.

When the boiled mixture is at room temperature, stir in the beaten egg, then add the wet mixture to the flour mixture, all at once, and fold everything together until it is no longer streaky. Do not beat, or the loaves will be tough and have peaks in the middle! The mixture will be fairly soft and rough-looking.

Spoon/tip the mixture into the tins, levelling the tops. Bake for 40–60 minutes or until the centre springs back when pressed, and a skewer comes out clean. Leave to cool on a rack. When cold, refrigerate or freeze in airtight containers.

Tip — To make only 1 loaf, halve the mixture but still use 1 egg. The cooking time will vary with the types and amounts of dried fruits you use. Feel whether the centres of the loaves are firm, and see if a skewer comes out clean, rather than depending on a particular cooking time.

Allergy-free sultana loaf

Makes 1 loaf

25g hulled millet or hemp seeds
250g sultanas
150g brown sugar
325ml milk alternative, such as rice, almond, soy
½ teaspoon salt
¼ cup oil, such as sunflower, grapeseed or olive oil (not extra virgin)
3 tablespoons chia seeds
1 tablespoon ground linseeds or ¼ teaspoon xanthan gum
240g gluten-free flour mix, or combine 80g rice flour, 80g tapioca flour and 80g coconut flour
1 teaspoon ground ginger
1½ teaspoons gluten-free baking powder

In 2007 Ros Campbell had just published the *New Zealand Food Allergy Cookbook* with Jill MacFarlane when she shared this recipe on *Saturday Morning*. She has rewritten it for *The RNZ Cookbook* to make it suitable for all with allergies and wheat and gluten intolerances.

Soak the millet or hemp seeds, sultanas, brown sugar and salt in the milk alternative for 3–4 hours or overnight.

Preheat the oven to 175°C. Line a loaf tin (500g capacity) with baking paper and spray with oil.

Mix the oil, chia seeds and ground linseeds or xanthan gum into the millet mixture.

Combine the flour, ground ginger and baking powder and sift to remove any lumps, aerate the flours and to combine evenly.

Gradually add the flour mixture to the millet mixture and mix well to give a slightly wet but not sloppy consistency (adjust if necessary).

Pour into the prepared tin and smooth the surface. Bake for 50–60 minutes or until a skewer inserted into the centre comes out clean.

Allow the loaf to cool in the tin before turning out onto a wire rack. Ensure the loaf is chilled prior to slicing otherwise it can crumble. Store in the fridge.

Tip — Using a variety of gluten-free flours gives a better flavour and texture. Coconut flour absorbs more liquid than most flours, and offers a sweet, nutty texture that combines well with lighter gluten-free flours. Ground linseeds can be used instead of chia seeds but gives a stronger flavour.

Feijoa shortcake

Serves 6

- 8–10 feijoas
- finely grated zest and juice of 1–2 lemons or 1 orange
- 2 tablespoons caster sugar, plus 1 cup for the shortcake
- 180g butter, softened
- 1 large free-range egg
- 1 teaspoon vanilla extract
- 250g plain flour
- 1 teaspoon baking powder
- 2–3 tablespoons flaked almonds (sometimes known as sliced almonds)

In 2013, well-known Palmerston North caterer Hester Guy detailed this recipe, adapted from an old Jewish cookbook in her collection, to the *Nine to Noon* audience.

Preheat the oven to 180°C. Line the base of a 23cm (or 24cm or 25cm) springform cake tin with baking paper.

Peel the feijoas and slice into rounds 1cm thick. Place in a mixing bowl and sprinkle with the lemon or orange zest and juice and mix in 2 tablespoons sugar. Set aside while you make the base.

Cream the butter and 1 cup sugar until light and fluffy, then add the egg and vanilla and stir to combine. Sift in the flour and baking powder and fold to combine.

Press about three-quarters of the mixture into the prepared tin. Spoon over the feijoa mixture. Break the remaining dough into small pieces and dot casually over the top of the feijoas. Lastly, sprinkle with the flaked almonds.

Place in the oven and bake for 45–60 minutes. Check after 45 minutes, and reduce the oven temperature if the shortcake is browning too much. If you use one of the larger tin sizes, reduce the cooking time accordingly.

Serve warm with lightly whipped cream.

Brioche

Makes 12

150ml warm milk (ideally 38°C)
25g caster sugar
30g fresh yeast or 1 tablespoon active dry yeast
300g plain flour
20g caster sugar
5g salt
3 free-range egg yolks
90g just-melted butter
100g dark chocolate, chopped
1 free-range egg, beaten, for egg wash
icing sugar for dusting

Crème pâtissière

3 free-range egg yolks
100g caster sugar
1 vanilla bean, split, and seeds scraped out
25g plain flour
165ml milk
85ml cream

Jo Crabb, founder of the famous Martinborough café Medici and then of the cooking school Carême, shared the recipe for this French baked classic with *Nine to Noon* listeners in 2014, the year she published her memoir about living in both the Wairarapa and the south of France, *My Two Heavens*.

Mix the milk, first measure of sugar and yeast, and leave for 5 minutes. The yeast should puff up and float. If it doesn't, sit the bowl inside another bowl with some warm water in it until it does. If using dry yeast, make sure it has puffed up well, or you may get bits of yeast through the dough.

Put the flour, second measure of sugar and salt in a bowl and make a well in the centre. Add the egg yolks and the yeast mixture. Mix a little using a wooden spoon. It should not be all mixed through, but look messy. Add the melted butter and mix a bit more. Don't over-mix — a bit streaky is fine. Cover the bowl and leave to rise in a warm place for about 30 minutes or until it looks puffy.

To make the crème pâtissière, whisk the egg yolks, vanilla seeds and sugar until thick and pale, then mix in the flour. Put the milk, cream and scaped vanilla bean into a saucepan over a medium heat. When the milk mixture boils, add a ladle or so to the egg mixture, and whisk well. Then mix the egg mixture back into the milk mixture, and bring back to the boil, stirring with a wooden spoon. Boil for two minutes, continuing to stir constantly. The mixture will seem clumpy, but then turn into a thick custard.

Remove the crème pâtissière from the heat. Cool, then cover and refrigerate. (It will keep in the fridge for 2–3 days.)

Preheat the oven to 180–190°C (depending on how hot your oven runs). Grease a baking tray or line with baking paper.

Turn the dough out onto a floured bench. Roll out until about 35cm × 25cm, trying to keep the corners square. Cut in half lengthwise. Put a line of crème pâtissière down the middle of each half, lengthwise. Top with the chopped chocolate. Fold the sides over to meet on top of the filling and pinch together to secure. Turn over so the join is now on the bottom. Trim the ends and cut each into 6 pieces.

Place on the prepared tray and brush with the egg wash. Leave to sit for 15 minutes or more to rise (this will depend on how warm your kitchen is), then brush once more with the egg wash. Place in the oven and bake for 12–15 minutes until browned. Remove from the oven and leave to cool for 5 minutes. Serve warm dusted with icing sugar.

Tip — Strain the egg wash so you don't get any lumps of white.

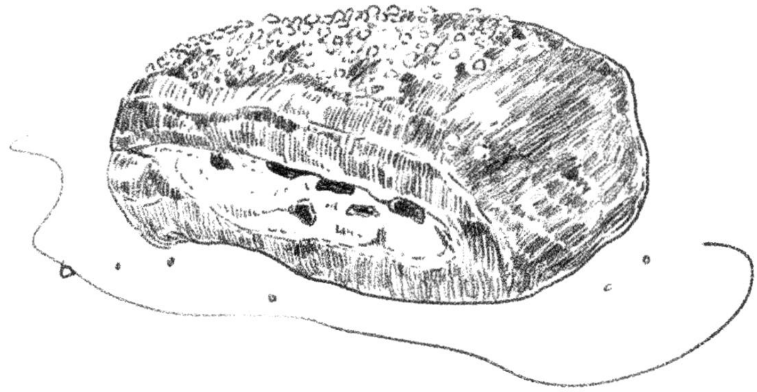

Feijoa and almond cake

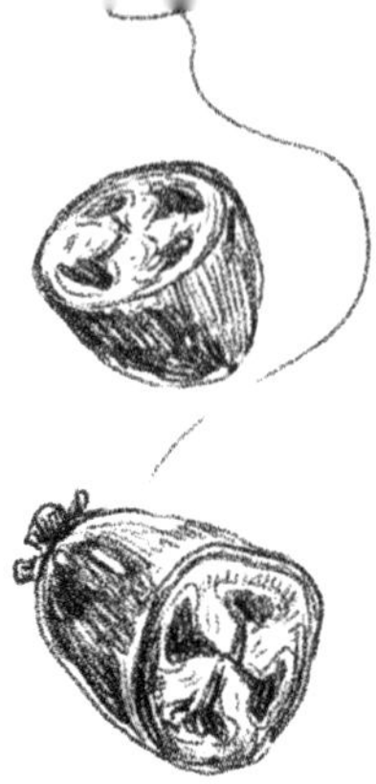

Makes 1 × 22cm cake

130g unsalted butter, roughly chopped and softened
¾ cup caster sugar
2 free-range eggs
1 teaspoon almond or vanilla extract
1⅓ cup plain flour, sifted
2 teaspoons baking powder
pinch of salt
40g ground almonds
225g sour cream
500g ripe feijoas, skinned and cut in half
1–2 tablespoons sugar and 1 teaspoon ground cinnamon, for sprinkling

With this recipe Al Brown gave *Sunday Mornings* listeners in 2020 plenty of reasons to celebrate the feijoa harvest. The whole nation was in lockdown then, so there was plenty of impetus to bake this — if you could find flour. Al based the recipe on one from Annabelle White, and says you can use any fruit in place of feijoas. It's superb with quinces, pears or tamarillos, he advises.

Preheat the oven to 180°C.

Grease and line a 22cm cake tin with baking paper.

Place the butter and sugar in the bowl of an electric mixer and beat until pale and creamy.

Add the eggs one at a time, beating until the egg is incorporated, then add the almond or vanilla extract.

Add the sifted flour, baking powder, salt and ground almonds, followed by the sour cream. Fold into the butter and egg mixture to combine.

Spoon the thick cake batter into the prepared cake tin, then carefully press the feijoa halves halfway down into the batter.

Combine the sugar and the cinnamon and sprinkle over the cake.

Place the cake in the centre of the oven and cook for 50 minutes or until a skewer inserted into the centre of the cake comes out clean. Serve while still warm, cut into slices with dollops of whipped cream or yoghurt.

Simply the best banana cake

Makes 1 × 20cm cake

2½ cups self-raising flour
1 teaspoon baking soda
1 cup caster sugar
4 free-range eggs, lightly beaten
4 old bananas, peeled
1 cup vegetable oil

Cream cheese icing

100g cream cheese, softened
60g butter, softened
3–4 cups icing sugar, sifted
2 teaspoons finely grated lemon zest
juice of ½ lemon

In 2019, just ahead of her appearance at The Food Show in Auckland, food writer Annabelle White brought what she claimed is the best banana cake ever, still warm, into the studio to share with Jesse Mulligan. As he ate it, she explained that the low temperature and long bake time is the secret, as is having good-quality flour. A 'complete novice' at baking could make it, White said.

Preheat the oven to 160°C. Grease and line a 23cm round cake tin with baking paper.

Sift the flour and baking soda into a bowl. In another bowl, place the sugar, eggs, bananas and oil and use a potato masher to thoroughly combine. Add the mashed banana mixture to the flour and mix gently to a smooth batter.

Pour into the tin and place in the oven. Bake for about 55 minutes. Insert a skewer into the centre of the cake, and if it comes out clean then the cake is cooked. Remove from the oven and cool a little before removing to a wire rack. Cool completely before icing.

To make the icing, blend all ingredients together vigorously (I use my food processor). Add more lemon juice if you prefer a sharper, more distinctively lemon flavour. Spread the icing over the top of the cake.

Tip — If you want a deeper cake, use a 20cm round cake tin and bake for about 1½ hours. A simple lemon icing can replace the cream cheese icing for a lighter cake. Using old bananas makes this cake taste even better — even ones that have been frozen can be used.

Beatrice Ojakangas's Norwegian apple cake

Serves 4–6

butter for the cake tin
2 large Braeburn or Granny Smith apples, quartered, cored, peeled and sliced
½ cup (70g) blanched chopped almonds
1 free-range egg
½ cup sugar
1 teaspoon vanilla extract or essence
1 teaspoon baking powder
pinch of salt
1 teaspoon ground cinnamon
½ cup plain flour

Lois Daish shared this recipe on *Afternoons* in 2008, explaining that it was from *The Great Scandinavian Baking Book*, by Beatrice Ojakangas, published in 1988.

Preheat the oven to 180°C. Generously butter a 22cm round cake tin. Line the bottom with baking paper and butter the baking paper. Or you can use a buttered Pyrex pie dish.

Combine all the cake ingredients in a large bowl. Keep stirring with a wooden spoon until thoroughly mixed and starting to slacken. Spoon into the cake tin and smooth the top.

Bake for about 25–30 minutes until golden brown on top. If baked in a tin, leave to cool for 5 minutes before removing. If baked in a Pyrex pie dish, serve straight from the dish.

Plum and toasted hazelnut cake

Makes 1 × 23cm cake

- 100g (1 cup) ground hazelnuts
- 80g (¾ cup) ground almonds
- 110g (½ cup) unrefined raw sugar
- 50g (½ cup) arrowroot or gluten-free organic cornflour (starch)
- 1 teaspoon gluten-free baking powder
- ¼ teaspoon fine sea salt
- 2 large free-range eggs, at room temperature
- 80ml (⅓ cup) extra virgin olive oil
- 60ml (¼ cup) almond, rice or coconut milk
- 1 teaspoon vanilla extract
- 4–6 ripe plums, halved and stones removed

Raglan food writer Emma Galloway, of the blog *My Darling Lemon Thyme*, explained how to make this gluten-free cake to the *Afternoons* audience in 2016.

Preheat the oven to 180°C.

Lightly grease a 23cm round loose-bottomed cake tin and line the base and sides with baking paper.

Combine the ground hazelnuts and almonds in a frying pan over a medium heat and toast for 5–8 minutes, stirring often, until lightly golden and aromatic. Remove from the heat and transfer to a bowl, setting aside for 10 minutes to cool slightly. When cool, add the sugar, arrowroot, baking powder and salt and whisk to evenly combine.

In another bowl, whisk the eggs, olive oil, milk and vanilla extract. Pour into the dry ingredients and mix to form a smooth batter.

Pour into the prepared tin and arrange the plum halves, cut-side up, over the batter. Bake for 45–55 minutes or until a skewer inserted into the centre comes out clean. Remove from the oven and set aside to cool in the tin. This cake stores happily, airtight, for 2–3 days, or in the fridge for even longer.

Tip — If you can't buy ground hazelnuts, simply toast whole hazelnuts in an oven preheated to 180°C for 8–10 minutes until golden. Rub off the skins, cool and grind in a small food processor until fine. If you go this route, skip toasting the ground nuts in a pan.

Almond chocolate cake

Serves 6

200g dark chocolate (64%–72% cocoa solids), chopped
200g unsalted butter
¾ cup raw sugar
6 free-range eggs, separated
200g ground almonds
¼ teaspoon cream of tartar

Chocolate icing
100ml cream
200g dark chocolate (50% cocoa solids), chopped

This recipe was explained by chef and restaurant entrepreneur Mark Gregory on *Nine to Noon* in 2009, the year he was helming the charity DineAid.

Preheat the oven to 175°C. Grease a 25cm round cake tin and line with baking paper.

Melt the chocolate in the microwave or in a heatproof bowl set over gently simmering water, then allow to cool but not set.

Beat the butter and sugar together until light and creamy, then beat in the egg yolks one at a time. Add the cooled melted chocolate and beat vigorously. Fold in the ground almonds.

In a clean bowl, beat the egg whites with the cream of tartar until soft peaks form. Mix one-quarter of the whipped egg whites into the cake batter, then gently fold in the remaining egg whites. Try not to over-mix as lightness and texture might be lost.

Put the batter in the prepared tin and spread evenly. Place in the oven and bake for about 40–50 minutes, until a wooden skewer comes out almost clean but not quite; there should be a little cake mixture adhering to the skewer. Remove from the oven and allow to cool before removing from the cake tin.

To make the icing, simply warm the cream, add the chopped chocolate and stir until velvety smooth. Allow to cool and thicken before spreading over the cooled chocolate cake.

Tropical stained-glass cake

Makes 1 x 22cm cake

125g dried papaya pieces
125g dried pineapple pieces
125g dried mango pieces
125g dried apricots
125g dried dates
100g red glacé cherries
100g green glacé cherries
70g whole Brazil nuts
70g whole blanched almonds
2 free-range eggs
½ cup firmly packed soft brown sugar
1 teaspoon vanilla extract
100g butter, melted and cooled
1 tablespoon dark rum
½ cup self-raising flour, sifted
1 teaspoon ground mixed spice

Auckland food writer Julie Le Clerc explained how to make this visually stunning cake — when cut in very thin slices, the coloured fruit resembles a stained-glass window — to the *Nine to Noon* audience in 2011, not long after her cookbook *Julie Le Clerc's Favourite Cakes* was published.

Preheat the oven to 150°C. Lightly grease a 22cm ring cake tin.

Combine all the fruit and nuts in a bowl.

In a separate bowl, beat the eggs, sugar and vanilla until pale and foamy. Stir in the melted butter, rum, sifted flour and mixed spice. Pour this mixture over the dried fruit and nuts and stir to combine.

Spread the mixture into the prepared tin, making sure the fruit and nuts on the surface are attractively placed.

Press the mixture down firmly.

Bake, uncovered, for 60 minutes. Cover with foil and bake for a further 45 minutes. Stand the cake in the tin for 20 minutes to firm before removing to a wire rack to cool completely.

This cake can last for up to 6 weeks if stored in an airtight container in the fridge. Being fridge-cold also means the cake is easier to cut. Cut in very thin slices to serve.

Carrot, orange and banana semolina cake

Makes 1 × 20cm cake

2 oranges
1 cup plain flour
1 teaspoon baking powder
1 teaspoon baking soda
1 cup caster sugar
1 cup fine semolina
½ cup neutral-flavoured oil
2½ cups grated carrot
1 cup mashed banana
3 free-range egg whites
½ cup dried cranberries
icing sugar for dusting

In 2004, veteran cookbook writer Robyn Martin had just published another of her dozens of cookbooks, full of recipes designed to taste good while going easy on sugars and fats. This cake recipe from that book is a moist classic.

Preheat the oven to 180°C. Line the base of a 20cm round cake tin with baking paper.

Place the oranges in a saucepan and cover with water. Bring to the boil and simmer for 20 minutes or until the oranges are soft. Drain, cool, then cut into chunks, removing any pips. Mash with a potato masher until very fine.

Mix the flour, baking powder, baking soda, sugar and semolina together in a bowl. Add the orange, oil, carrot and banana and mix until combined.

In another bowl, beat the egg whites until stiff. Fold into the cake mixture. Pour the mixture into the prepared tin. Sprinkle over the dried cranberries.

Bake for 1¼–1½ hours or until the cake springs back when lightly touched. Cool in the tin for 10 minutes before turning out on to a wire rack to cool. Serve the cake dusted with icing sugar.

Moroccan honey and mint syrup cake

Makes 1 × 20cm cake

Cake batter

160g butter, softened
310g caster sugar
1½ teaspoons dried or 1 tablespoon chopped fresh mint
6 free-range eggs, lightly beaten
230g desiccated coconut
210g self-raising flour

Mint syrup

200ml water
180g caster sugar
1½ cups roughly chopped fresh mint

Topping

75g butter
180g honey
180g flaked almonds
icing sugar for dusting

This superb cake recipe from Lauraine Jacobs, then food editor of the *New Zealand Listener*, was broadcast on *Nine to Noon* in 2017.

Preheat the oven to 150°C.

Lightly grease a 20cm round springform cake tin and line with baking paper.

Beat the butter, sugar and mint until they begin to change colour. Add small quantities of the egg, coconut and flour, beating well between each addition to prevent the mixture from curdling. Repeat until all the eggs, coconut and flour are incorporated.

Pour the batter into the prepared tin and bake for 1–1½ hours.

Meanwhile, make the syrup. Place the water, sugar and mint in a saucepan and bring to the boil, stirring occasionally to ensure the sugar is dissolved. Remove from the heat and allow to cool for 30–45 minutes. Strain through a sieve and discard the mint leaves.

Check the cake is baked by inserting a skewer in the centre. If it comes out clean, the cake is ready. Remove from the oven and allow it to cool in the tin for 5–10 minutes.

With the cake still in the tin, prick 60–70 holes in the top. Pour the mint syrup evenly over the cake, allowing it to soak in.

Place the butter, honey and almonds in a saucepan and melt together, stirring until well combined. Do not allow to boil. Remove from the heat and immediately spread this topping on the cake.

Place the cake back in the oven and bake the until a light amber colour, about 15 minutes. Remove and allow to cool in the tin for 20–30 minutes.

Carefully remove the cake from the tin then gently remove the baking paper while still warm.

Dust with icing sugar before serving.

Chocolate cake

Makes 1 × 23cm double-layer cake

5 free-range eggs
2½ cups caster sugar
300ml canola oil
¼ cup strong black coffee, preferably espresso
1 teaspoon vanilla essence or paste
250g good-quality chocolate, melted
2 cups plain flour
2 teaspoons baking powder
1 cup cocoa powder
2 teaspoons ground cinnamon
200ml milk

Sugar syrup
1 cup caster sugar
2 cups water

Chocolate ganache
400g good-quality dark chocolate (I use minimum 50% cocoa solids)
1 cup cream

To assemble
1 cup raspberry coulis (see recipe on page 223)
250g mascarpone
½ cup fresh raspberries or edible flowers, to garnish

Auckland café and bakery owner Kim Evans had just published her cookbook *Treats from Little and Friday* in 2012 when she detailed the recipe for this moist, double-layer cake on *Nine to Noon*. She noted that it is best made a day ahead of assembling. Good-quality dark Dutch cocoa and chocolate with a high cocoa content (at least 50 per cent cocoa) such as Callebaut or Valrhona is critical to its success.

To make the cake, preheat the oven to 150°C. Grease 2 × 23cm round tins and line the bottom and sides with baking paper cut to fit exactly.

Using an electric mixer, beat the eggs and sugar at a medium–high speed until the mixture becomes pale and voluminous and falls from the beater in a wide ribbon that holds its form before dissolving back into the mixture.

Keep the beater on medium speed and slowly drizzle in the oil, being careful not to pour too quickly or the mixture will lose volume.

Add the coffee, vanilla and melted chocolate. Use a spatula to scrape the bottom of the bowl and make sure the chocolate is thoroughly mixed in.

Sift the flour, baking powder, cocoa powder and cinnamon into a bowl. Using a large metal spoon, fold one-third of the dry ingredients into the chocolate mixture. When almost combined, add one-third of the milk. Continue in this way until all is combined.

Pour the batter into the prepared tins and bake for 45 minutes, or until the tops spring back when touched lightly and a skewer comes out clean when inserted into the middle of the cakes.

To make the syrup, place the sugar and water in a saucepan on a low heat, stirring until the sugar is dissolved. Increase the heat and boil for 5 minutes or until syrupy.

Pour the hot syrup over the cakes and cool completely in their tins sitting on a wire rack. When cool, turn out by inverting the tins, then turn the cakes upright.

To make the chocolate ganache, gently melt the chocolate and cream in a metal bowl set over a saucepan of simmering water, without letting the water touch the bowl. Stir constantly to form a smooth sauce. Allow to cool and thicken.

To assemble, spread ¾ cup chocolate ganache over 1 cake layer. Spread a thin layer of raspberry coulis over the ganache, then a thick layer of mascarpone, using it all.

Place the remaining cake on top. Spread with the remaining ganache, drizzle with raspberry coulis and garnish with raspberries or flowers.

Tip — You can make as much chocolate ganache as you need (or would prefer) by using the same ratio of chocolate to cream.

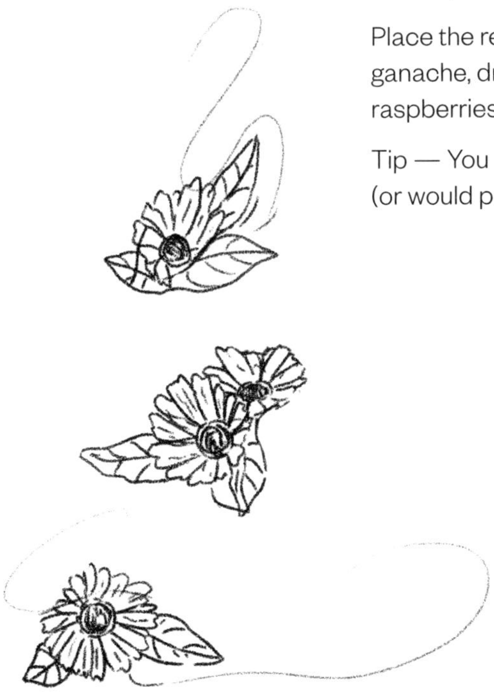

SOY SAUCE

Worldwatch

Rounding off the midday news each weekday, *Worldwatch*'s bulletins of international news plug listeners in to the bigger world out there beyond the Pacific. RNZ's recipe archive features dishes from cuisines across the globe.

Prawn okonomiyaki

Serves 4

1 cup plain flour
¼ cup cornflour
3 free-range eggs
¼ cup sparkling water
1 large onion, finely sliced
2 cloves garlic, peeled and grated
1 thumb-sized piece fresh ginger, peeled and finely grated
2 cups grated carrot
2 cups finely sliced cabbage
1 cup peeled, deveined and diced green (raw) prawns
1 tablespoon sesame seeds
1 teaspoon chilli flakes
vegetable oil for cooking

To serve
Japanese mayonnaise
soy sauce
kecap manis

This simple Japanese pancake recipe is from renowned chef Josh Emett, who discussed it on *Afternoons* in 2020, the year he opened his new Auckland restaurant Onslow.

In a bowl, whisk together the flour, cornflour, eggs and sparkling water to make a batter, then add the rest of the ingredients (except the oil) and stir to combine.

Heat a little oil in a non-stick frying pan, then place enough mix in to just cover the base and gently shape into a pancake shape by pressing flat. You will need to cook in a couple of batches.

Cover and cook on a moderate heat for about 8 minutes, then remove the lid and turn and cook on the other side for a further 5 minutes until crispy.

Place on a plate and top with Japanese mayonnaise, a dash of soy sauce, and kecap manis or other barbecue sauce to serve.

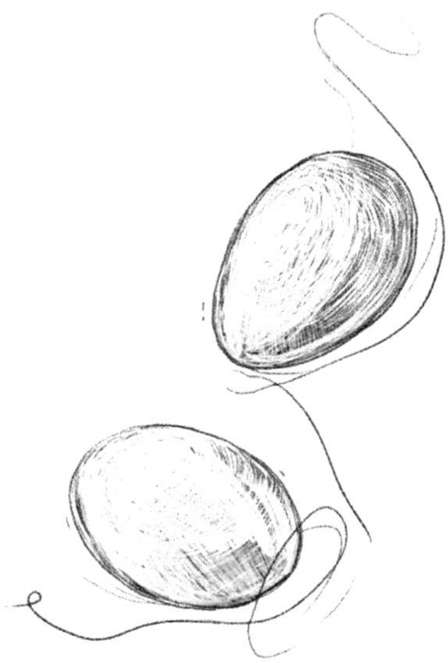

Asian prawn salad

Serves 4

Dressing

- ¼ cup grapeseed or peanut oil
- 1 tablespoon white miso paste
- ½ tablespoon finely grated fresh ginger
- 2 tablespoons mirin
- 1 tablespoon soy sauce
- 1 teaspoon rice vinegar
- 1 teaspoon sesame oil

Salad

- 1 tablespoon salt
- 2 teaspoons white sugar
- 300g green (raw) prawns, peeled and deveined
- 1 tablespoon grapeseed oil
- ½ head broccoli, cut into florets
- 2 cups broccolini, cut into 3cm pieces
- 100g shiitake mushrooms
- 1 cup snow peas
- 1 sheet nori
- 1 cup spinach leaves
- ½ cup roasted peanuts
- 2 tablespoons sesame seeds, toasted

Much-admired chef Michael Meredith opened his restaurant Mr Morris in Auckland's fashionable Britomart quarter in late 2020. This recipe dates from 2018, when it was broadcast on *Nine to Noon*.

To make the dressing, whisk the dressing ingredients together in a bowl and set aside.

To make the salad, place the salt and sugar in a saucepan with 2 cups water and bring to the boil. Add the prawns and cook for a minute. Remove the prawns and cool on a plate.

In a frying pan, heat the oil and add the broccoli and broccolini. Cook for a minute. Add the mushrooms and snow peas and cook for a further minute. Remove from the pan and cool.

Heat a non-stick frying pan and toast the nori for a minute on each side, or until crispy. Remove from the pan, leave to cool, then shred roughly into small pieces.

Place the vegetables and spinach leaves in a bowl. Pour over the dressing and toss well.

To serve, place the salad on a serving dish with prawns on top. Sprinkle with nori, peanuts and toasted sesame seeds.

Persian lamb with rhubarb

Serves 6

pinch of saffron threads
½ cup boiling water
1kg boneless lamb shoulder steaks, trimmed of skin and fat
sea salt and freshly ground black pepper
3–4 tablespoons olive oil or clarified butter
2 large onions, finely sliced
1 tablespoon pomegranate molasses, or juice of 1 lemon
2 cups beef or chicken stock
⅓ cup chopped fresh mint
⅓ cup chopped fresh flat-leaf parsley
500g rhubarb, trimmed

Julie Le Clerc's travels in the Middle East and her Syrian family ties position her well to create recipes with a Middle Eastern inflection. This Iranian-inspired recipe was discussed on *Saturday Morning* in 2006, not long after she had published her book *Taking Tea in the Medina*.

Soak the saffron threads in the boiling water for about 30 minutes, or while you prepare the lamb and onions.

Cut the lamb into 3cm cubes and season with salt and pepper. Heat a little oil in a flameproof casserole pan and brown the lamb in 2–3 batches.

Remove the meat and add the onion to the pan, with a little more oil if necessary. Cook the onion over medium heat for 10 minutes, stirring until golden brown.

Return the meat to the pan and add the saffron and soaking liquid, pomegranate molasses or lemon juice, and stock. Bring to the boil then turn down the heat. Cover the pan and leave to simmer gently for 1 hour.

In a frying pan, fry the mint and parsley in a little olive oil to release their flavour, tossing them quickly so they don't burn.

Stir the cooked herbs into the lamb and continue to simmer the stew, uncovered, for a further 30 minutes.

Cut the rhubarb stalks into 3cm lengths. Add to the stew and simmer, uncovered, for 10 minutes to cook the rhubarb without the pieces breaking up.

Serve with rice.

Teriyaki chicken

Serves 4

Teriyaki sauce
75g sugar
150ml mirin
150ml cooking sake
150ml soy sauce

6 boneless chicken thighs
flour for sprinkling
vegetable oil for cooking
spring onion, sliced (optional)

Auckland chef and cooking-school owner Sachie Nomura shared this straightforward and quick-to-prepare recipe with Jesse Mulligan on *Afternoons* in 2011.

To make the teriyaki sauce, place the sugar, mirin and sake in a small saucepan and bring to the boil. Lower the heat to medium and simmer for 2 minutes. Add the soy sauce and simmer for a further 5 minutes or until the sauce has thickened slightly. Remove from the heat.

Mark the chicken with shallow cuts (score) and flatten a little with the back of a sharp knife. Sprinkle (dust) the chicken with flour.

Heat a little oil in a frying pan over medium-high heat and cook the chicken, skin-side down, for 2–3 minutes. Turn and cook the other side for a further 2–3 minutes or until cooked through. (This will depend on the size of the chicken thighs.)

Add the sauce to the pan, stir through the chicken and cook until thickened and lightly caramelised.

Slice the chicken and serve on a plate garnished with slices of spring onion, if you like. Steamed rice and Japanese coleslaw are great accompaniments.

Msakhan chicken

Serves 8

Chicken

8 skin-on, bone-in chicken legs or breasts
3 tablespoons olive oil
1 teaspoon nine-spice mix (to make your own, see recipe opposite)
1 teaspoon sumac
½ teaspoon salt

Flatbreads

8 taboon breads (see recipe on page 229) or alternative (see tip)
¾ cup olive oil
8 onions, coarsely chopped
1 tablespoon salt
1–2 tablespoons sumac
1 tablespoon ground cumin
2 teaspoons nine-spice mix

To serve

4 tablespoons sumac
⅓ cup pine nuts, toasted
olives

In 2019 Phaidon had just published Reem Kassis's magnificent 150-recipe *The Palestinian Table*, drawn from recipes from three generations of her family. She explained how to make this quintessential msakhan on *Nine to Noon*.

Preheat the oven to 190°C. Place the chicken in a large roasting dish and top with the olive oil, spices, and salt. Give it a good rub with your hands, making sure to get some of the marinade under the skin, then arrange the pieces skin-side up and place in the oven for 45–50 minutes or until completely cooked through.

Meanwhile, prepare the topping for the flatbreads. Place the olive oil, chopped onions, salt and spices in a large frying pan over low heat. Cook for 30–40 minutes, stirring occasionally, until the onions have softened and cooked completely. If the onions seem dry or do not release water during cooking, add a few tablespoons of water. When done, remove from the heat and set aside.

Check on the chicken, and if done, remove from the oven and allow to rest for 15 minutes, loosely covered in foil. Pour any juices in the roasting pan over the onion mixture and toss to combine.

Preheat the grill. To assemble the flatbreads, dip the edges of each bread in the oil that sits on the surface of the onion mixture, then lay flat on a baking sheet. Cover each bread with the onion mixture, leaving a border around the edge similar to a pizza. Sprinkle with sumac and toasted pine nuts. Taking 1–2 flatbreads at a time, put on an oven rack and place under the grill for 2–5 minutes to brown the edges and the onions.

To serve, top each flatbread with a piece of chicken. Serve with a bowl of olives on the side.

Tip — Taboon bread is best for this dish, but if you do not want to make it at home you can substitute with a sturdy store-bought flatbread, such as naan or Greek pita bread.

Nine-spice mix

- 6 tablespoons allspice berries
- 6 sticks cassia bark or cinnamon
- 3 tablespoons coriander seeds
- 1 tablespoon black peppercorns
- 1 teaspoon cardamom seeds
- 1 teaspoon cumin seeds
- 10 cloves
- 2 blades mace
- 1 whole nutmeg, crushed

Place all the ingredients in a large frying pan over medium-low heat. Stir with a wooden spoon from time to time to ensure that the spices do not burn, until you begin to smell the aroma of the spices, about 10 minutes.

Remove the pan from the heat and set aside to cool completely, about 1 hour. This step is crucial because if the spices are not cooled properly, they will form a paste when ground rather than a powder.

Place the spices into a heavy-duty spice grinder and grind until you achieve a fine powder consistency. Store the spice mix in an airtight container. It will keep for several months although the aroma will fade with time.

Chicken larb

Serves 4

¼ cup jasmine rice
dash of oil
500g chicken mince
1 cup chicken stock, warmed
2 tablespoons lemon juice
2 tablespoons fish sauce
1 teaspoon dried chilli powder
7–8cm piece of lemongrass, inner stalk only, very finely chopped
¼ cup finely sliced makrut lime leaves
½ small red onion, finely sliced
¼ cup chopped spring onions
¼ cup chopped coriander, plus extra leaves to garnish
1 wedge cabbage, very finely sliced
1 cup sliced cucumber
1 cup sliced carrot

Larb is a sautéed Thai dish that sparkles with brightly sweet flavours. Auckland food writer Connie Clarkson told the *Nine to Noon* audience how to make it in 2008, crediting the recipe to Auckland restaurant Zap 2. Its simple ingredients should be found in the ethnic food aisle of your local supermarket.

To make the toasted ground rice, place the rice in a dry frying pan over a medium-low heat and toss until golden. Remove from the heat and leave to cool. Grind in a spice grinder or a mortar and pestle to a fine powder. You can make this ahead and store in an airtight lidded jar — it keeps for up to 2 weeks.

Heat a frying pan over high heat with a dash of oil and add the chicken mince. Add the stock and cook, stirring to break up any lumps, until most of the stock has been absorbed, about 5 minutes. Remove from the heat and add the lemon juice, fish sauce, 2 tablespoons toasted ground rice and the dried chilli powder. Add the chopped lemongrass, sliced lime leaves, sliced red onion, chopped spring onion and chopped coriander. Toss until well combined.

Serve garnished with the coriander leaves and accompany with the cabbage, cucumber and carrot.

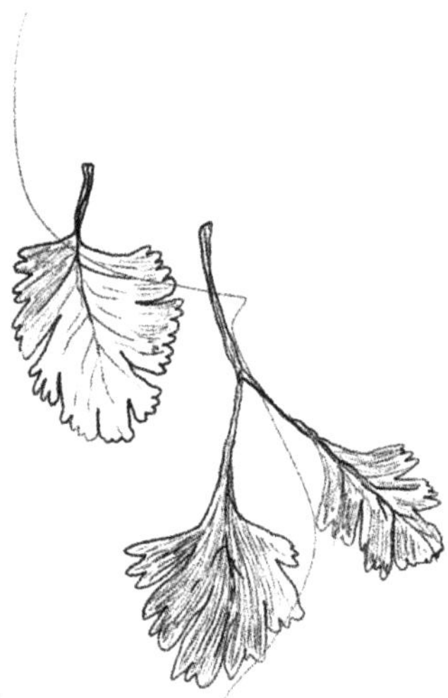

Moroccan braised beef

Serves 6

4 tablespoons olive oil
1kg trimmed topside of beef, shin or chuck steak, cut into 4cm pieces
2 onions, chopped
2 carrots, diced
1 stalk celery, thinly sliced
4 cloves garlic, finely chopped
3 tablespoons toasted cumin seeds
1 tablespoon coriander seeds
1 stick cinnamon
1 teaspoon ground turmeric
1 tablespoon ground ginger
2 small dried red chillies, finely sliced
1 cup pitted prunes
400g pumpkin, peeled, deseeded and cubed
400g can Italian tomatoes in juice, mashed
500ml beef stock
2 cups water
salt and freshly ground black pepper to taste

To serve
steamed couscous
2 tablespoons chopped parsley
2 tablespoons chopped coriander

Former *Cuisine* writer and MasterChef judge Ray McVinnie was on *Nine to Noon* in 2006 to share this North African-style dish made without the usual lamb but with a most New Zealand touch of cubed pumpkin.

Heat the oil in a suitable pan over a high heat and add the beef, in batches, and brown well all over. Remove from the pan and reserve.

Lower the heat and add the onion, carrot, celery, garlic, cumin seeds, coriander seeds, cinnamon, turmeric, ginger, chillies and prunes. Cook gently, stirring occasionally, until the onion is soft.

Add the reserved beef, mix well, and add the pumpkin, tomatoes, stock and water. Bring to the boil, then simmer for 2 hours until the beef is very tender and the mixture has reduced and thickened. (Cover the pan if it is reducing too quickly.) Taste and season with salt and pepper.

Serve on hot couscous and sprinkle with the chopped parsley and coriander.

Tandoori lamb cutlets

Serves 4

- 1½ teaspoons cumin seeds
- 1½ teaspoons coriander seeds
- seeds from 6 green cardamom pods
- 3cm stick cinnamon
- 4 whole cloves
- 3 cloves garlic
- 5cm piece of ginger, peeled and chopped
- ½–1 teaspoon red chilli powder (see tip)
- 1 cup plain unsweetened yoghurt
- 12–16 small lamb cutlets

Cuisine writer Fiona Smith explained the recipe for these Indian-style cutlets on *Afternoons* in 2007. Great as finger food, they can also be served as a main course with rice and vegetables. If you are wanting a meat-free option, try the marinade on thick slices of tofu on skewers.

———

Heat a frying pan over medium heat and dry-fry the seeds, cinnamon and cloves for 1 minute until fragrant. Once cooled, place in a spice blender or mortar and pestle and grind to a powder. Add the garlic, ginger and chilli powder and grind to a paste. Transfer to a bowl and combine with the yoghurt.

Place the lamb cutlets in a non-metal dish and pour the yoghurt mixture over. Stir to coat the lamb well. Cover and leave to marinate for 2 hours at room temperature or up to 24 hours in the fridge.

Heat the grill or barbecue to a high heat, then cook the cutlets for 2 minutes on each side until browned.

Tip — Use 1 teaspoon of Kashmiri chilli powder, which is bright red and mild, or if you have a hot chilli powder, use the lesser amount.

Gujarati fish curry and chapati

Serves 2–3

500g fish fillets, cut into 10cm pieces
6 whole curry leaves, finely chopped
1½ tablespoons lemon juice
½ tablespoon chopped fresh coriander
2 teaspoons minced fresh green chilli
1 teaspoon minced garlic
1 teaspoon minced fresh ginger
1 teaspoon salt
½ teaspoon garam masala
½ teaspoon dried ground turmeric
1½ tablespoons oil
½ teaspoon fenugreek seeds
2 cups blended or pureed tomatoes, canned or fresh

Chapati
Makes 25–30

2 cups white flour
2 cups wholemeal flour
½ cup oil
2 cups boiling water

In 2018 mother and daughter Laxmi and Jayshri Ganda published *A little Bit of This, A Little Bit of That*, their cookbook of everyday Gujarati family recipes. The book went on to win the Best Indian Cuisine Book and Best Spices and Herbs Book at the 2018 Gourmand World Cookbook Awards. They shared this recipe with the *Nine to Noon* audience the same year.

Pat the fish dry with kitchen paper. In a medium bowl, combine the curry leaves, lemon juice, coriander, chilli, garlic, ginger, salt, garam masala and turmeric. Add the fish and combine, then cover and marinate for a maximum of 45 minutes in the fridge.

Heat the oil in a large frying pan on a medium heat. Add the fenugreek seeds and cook for 1 minute or until golden brown. Add the tomatoes and simmer for 6 minutes.

Add the fish and remaining marinade and cook for 2 minutes, then turn the fish, cover and cook for a further 2 minutes or until the fish is cooked through.

Serve hot with chapati, rice and/or condiments.

In a large bowl, combine both flours. Make a well in the middle and pour in the oil and water. Using your hands, knead the mixture into a soft dough for 1–2 minutes. Portion the dough into 1½-tablespoon-sized balls.

Turn the oven grill on and heat a cast iron flat plate or heavy-based frying pan on a medium-high heat.

Place a ball of dough onto a floured wooden board or patli. Dust with flour and press lightly with the palm of your hand into a flat circle. Using a rolling pin, roll into a circle, about 15cm in diameter. Repeat with the remaining balls of dough.

Cook the chapati for 30 seconds, then flip and cook for another minute. Finish by cooking the first side again under the hot grill (or use a jardi) for a further minute or until it puffs.

Serve hot with butter.

Indian lamb shank curry

Serves 4

1.2kg lamb shanks
2½ tablespoons Indian spice mix
2 cloves garlic, crushed
1 tablespoon finely grated fresh ginger
½ teaspoon salt
1 onion
2 carrots
3 tablespoons tomato paste
165ml coconut cream
2 teaspoons soy sauce
1½ cups basmati rice
1 head broccoli
100g baby silver beet
½ tablespoon fish sauce
150g plain unsweetened yoghurt
2 tablespoons sliced almonds

Indian spice mix
2 parts mild curry powder
2 parts beef stock powder
1 part onion powder
½ part ground ginger
½ part ground turmeric
½ part garam masala

Nadia Lim explained her South Asian take on an iconic Kiwi dish on *Afternoons* in 2019, the year she appeared on the TV show *Dancing with the Stars*. As always with lamb shanks, the longer they cook the better, and the dish works just as well in an oven or slow cooker.

To make the Indian spice mix, mix all the ingredients together in a small bowl.

Pat the lamb dry, place in a slow cooker or casserole dish and rub with the Indian spices, garlic, ginger and salt. Thinly slice the onion and cut the carrots into 4cm batons. Add to the lamb, cover and leave to marinate in the fridge overnight or for at least 8 hours.

To cook in a slow cooker: Add 1 cup of water, the tomato paste, coconut cream and soy sauce to the lamb. Cover and cook on low for 9–10 hours or until tender. The lamb will be falling off the bone when ready.

To cook in the oven: Preheat the oven to 180°C. Add 2 cups of water, the tomato paste, coconut cream and soy sauce to the lamb. Cover and cook for about 2½ hours. The lamb will be falling off the bone when ready; if not, cook for a further 30 minutes. Set aside to rest.

To cook the rice, bring a full kettle to the boil. Combine the rice, 2¼ cups boiling water and a pinch of salt in a saucepan and bring to the boil with the lid on. Once boiling, reduce to the lowest heat to cook for 12 minutes. Turn off the heat and steam, covered, for 5 minutes. Do not lift the lid during cooking.

Cut the broccoli into small florets and finely dice the stem. Place in a heatproof bowl and cover with boiling water. Cover with a plate and leave to steam for about 5 minutes, until bright green and tender. Drain well.

Remove the lamb from the sauce and pull or slice the meat off the bone. Return to the sauce, along with the silver beet and fish sauce. Stir to combine and season to taste with pepper. Serve the rice topped with the lamb curry, broccoli, yoghurt and almonds.

Jeyuk (marinated spicy barbecue pork with kimchi)

Serves 4

600g pork loin or belly
1 onion
½ carrot
2 spring onions, trimmed
½–1 cup kimchi, cut into bite-sized pieces
tofu for serving

Sauce

1–4 tablespoons gochujang
1–4 tablespoons soy sauce
1 tablespoon sesame oil
1 tablespoon minced garlic
1 tablespoon ginger juice, or use grated fresh ginger or 1 teaspoon ground ginger
3 tablespoons sugar
ground black pepper to taste
1 tablespoon chilli flakes (optional)

Eunmi Kang brought her cooking smarts from Busan, South Korea, to her popular Miss Kangsta food stall in Wellington. She shared this East Asian gem on *Nine to Noon* in 2014.

In a bowl, add 1–4 tablespoons of gochujang depending on how you want your level of spiciness. Add 1–4 tablespoons of soy sauce to make up 4 tablespoons total. For example, if you prefer a mild taste, add 2 tablespoons of gochujang and 2 tablespoons of soy sauce but the total combination should not be more than 4 tablespoons.

Add the sesame oil, minced garlic, ginger, sugar and a pinch of black pepper.

If desired, add 1 tablespoon of chilli flakes to make it spicier.

Mix all ingredients well and set aside.

For the pork loin, use a meat tenderiser and lightly beat the meat until it is very thin. Cut into bite-sized pieces. For pork belly, cut into bite-sized pieces.

Add the pork to the bowl of sauce, mix and set aside for the meat to marinate for 30 minutes.

Cut the onion and carrot into thin strips, and slice the spring onion diagonally.

In a large frying pan on medium-high heat, stir-fry the pork for about 4–5 minutes.

Add the kimchi and the vegetables to the pan. Cook until the pork is thoroughly cooked.

Place the pork and kimchi stir-fry in the middle of a plate and garnish with crumbled, sliced or cubed tofu.

Spanish rice with lamb ribs and peas

Serves 6

1.2kg lamb ribs
100ml extra virgin olive oil
flaky sea salt
1 onion, finely diced
3 cloves garlic, chopped
1 teaspoon fresh thyme leaves
6 bay leaves
2 green capsicums, finely diced
6 tomatoes, peeled, deseeded, and grated or chopped
300ml white wine
300g bomba (Valencia or paella) rice
200g podded green peas

When the Australian restaurateur Frank Camorra, of Melbourne restaurant MoVida fame, was growing up, his mother kept a Spanish kitchen — and a Spanish kitchen, he told *Nine to Noon* in 2011, the year he published *Rustica: A Return to Spanish Home Cooking*, is not about extravagance.

Take a sharp knife and cut the lamb between each rib to make single ribs with meat on either side of the bone. Alternatively, ask your local butcher to do this. Heat 80ml oil in a 30cm perol pan or large heavy-based saucepan over medium-high heat and cook the ribs, in two batches, for 10–15 minutes or until browned all over. Season with salt while cooking. Remove from the pan and set aside.

Wipe out the pan, and return to a medium heat. Add the remaining oil and the onion, garlic, thyme and bay leaves and season with a good pinch of salt. Cook, stirring occasionally, for 10 minutes or until the onion is softened.

Meanwhile, bring 1.5 litres of water to the boil in a saucepan, then reduce to a bare simmer.

Add the capsicums and tomatoes to the onion mixture and cook, stirring occasionally, for 30 minutes or until thick and pulpy. Add the wine and increase the heat to high. Allow to bubble away for a few minutes, then reduce the heat to medium-low, return the ribs to the pan and add 1 litre of the hot water. Simmer for 1 hour 10 minutes or until the ribs are tender. Add the remaining hot water, increase the heat to medium and bring to a steady simmer. Add the rice, season with salt and cook, stirring occasionally, for 15 minutes. Add the peas and cook for 4 minutes or until tender. The rice should just be a little past al dente but still firm to the bite. Serve immediately.

Kenyan spiced fish

Serves 2

2 tablespoons butter
2–3 cloves garlic, finely chopped
1 small onion or shallot, sliced
pinch of saffron threads
1 teaspoon ground cumin
1 teaspoon ground turmeric
400g firm or flaky white fish, cut into large chunks
salt and pepper
2 tomatoes, peeled and chopped
1 cup coconut cream
squeeze of lemon juice

Lois Daish set out this recipe on *Nine to Noon* in 2005, the year she published her book *A Good Year*, the collection of her favourite recipes from her long-running *New Zealand Listener* column. The cumin brings an earthiness to the flavour while the saffron lifts it towards heaven.

Melt the butter in a frying pan and gently fry the garlic, onion or shallot, saffron, cumin and turmeric for 5 minutes.

Add the fish, season with salt and pepper and pan-fry lightly on both sides. Lift the fish out on to a warm plate and set aside. Add the tomatoes to the pan and cook for 2 minutes, then add the coconut cream and simmer until the sauce is slightly thickened.

Check the seasoning, then put the fish back into the sauce for just a few minutes. Add a good squeeze of lemon juice and transfer to a serving bowl. Serve with plain rice, lemon wedges and a green salad or buttered spinach.

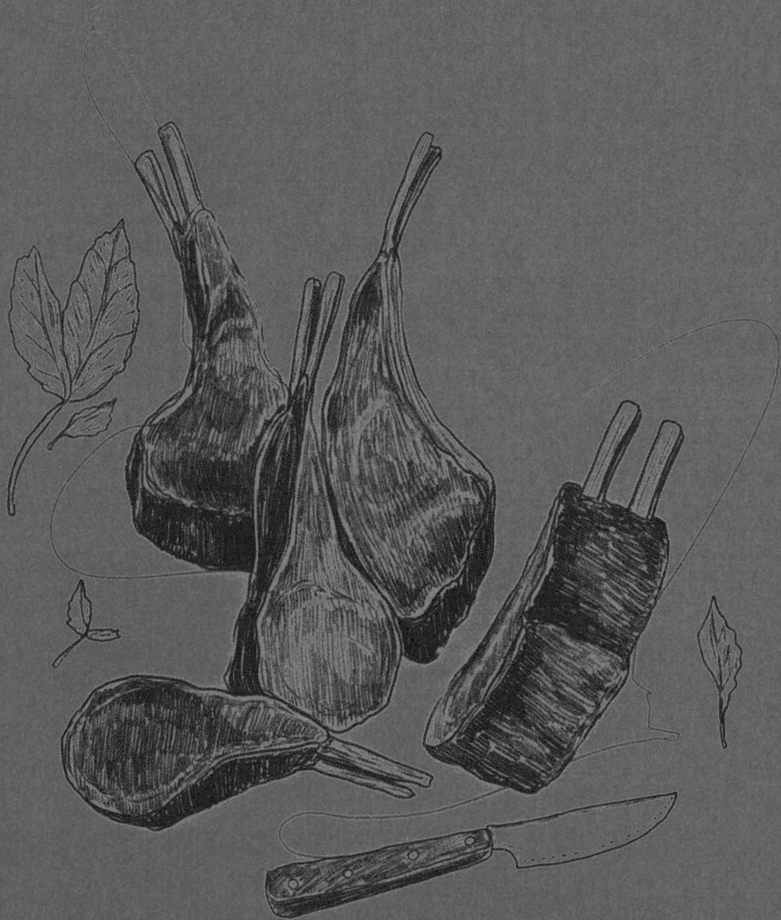

Checkpoint

The take-no-prisoners, early evening current affairs programme *Checkpoint* has been running since 1967 and for all those years, no matter who is behind the microphone, it's been famous for serving up grilled politicians, officials in a pickle or others in a soup of their own making. Great conversations, basically.

These days presenter Lisa Owen is peppy to listen to in gridlocked traffic while you're casting around in your mind for what to cook when you finally get home, or to have on as you chop ingredients for the evening meal. And *Checkpoint* gives you more than a few ideas for dinner conversation later on.

Smoked salmon on herbed pancakes

Makes 16–20 pancakes

1 egg
½ cup milk
1 teaspoon sugar
½ teaspoon salt
1–2 tablespoons chopped fresh dill, chives or basil
¾ cup self-raising flour

Topping
½ cup cream cheese, at room temperature
1 tablespoon horseradish cream
1 tablespoon lemon juice
salt and pepper to taste
about 100g smoked salmon
dill or other herb to garnish (optional)

These savoury pancakes are the creation of the Holsts — Dame Alison and her son Simon — who were on *Nine to Noon* in 2012. They take only about 10 minutes to make, and with a little horseradish cream cheese and smoked salmon, they look fantastic, too.

Put the egg, milk, sugar, salt and the herb of choice in a small to medium bowl, and beat with a fork or whisk until everything is blended.

Add the flour, then mix again until just smooth. Do not mix more than necessary.

Heat a large, non-stick electric or regular frying pan.

Drop the batter off the end of a dessert spoon onto the preheated pan, twisting the spoon as you drop the mixture so that each pancake is as round as possible. Turn each pancake as soon as you see the first few bubbles burst on the surface. Cook the second side until the centre springs back when pressed lightly.

If not serving the pancakes straight away, overlap the cooked pancakes on several layers of paper towel and slip them, towel and all, into a reusable plastic bag to stop them drying out.

Combine the cream cheese, horseradish and lemon juice in a small bowl. Season to taste with salt and pepper.

To serve, spread a little of the creamy mixture on each pancake, then add a slightly 'gathered' piece of thinly sliced salmon and a sprig or shred of whatever herb you choose.

Sashimi Sāmoa

Serves 8

Sashimi

1kg sashimi-quality asiasi (yellowfin tuna)
sea salt and pepper
8 cups trimmed watercress

Miki

4 cups coconut milk, chilled
2 red chillies, finely diced
1 cup finely chopped spring onion
1 cup diced, deseeded tomato
salt

Coconut passion dressing

½ cup passionfruit juice (from about 12 passionfruit; or substitute lime or kumquat juice)
½ tablespoon grated fresh ginger
2 cups virgin coconut oil (or substitute extra virgin olive oil or avocado oil)
salt and pepper

Robert Oliver has spent the last few years championing healthy, traditional Pacific cooking through his cookbooks and 2021 television show *Pacific Island Food Revolution*. This recipe from his award-winning book *Me ʻa Kai* was broadcast on *Nine to Noon* in 2011. The recipe also works well with crayfish, prawns or crab meat.

Chill eight serving plates. Cut the asiasi into logs about 5cm across, as one would for sashimi. Sprinkle liberally with sea salt and pepper.

To make the miki, remove the rich, heavy upper layer of the chilled coconut milk and place in a bowl. Add the chilli, spring onion and tomato, season with salt and gently combine.

To make the dressing, mix the juice with the ginger in a bowl or blender. Slowly whisk in the coconut oil to combine, and season with salt and pepper.

To serve, slice the tuna thinly against the grain, sashimi-style, and place four or five slices on each serving plate, slightly off centre.

Toss the watercress with enough of the coconut passion dressing to moisten, then place next to the fish.

Spoon the miki over the tuna and serve immediately.

Tip — Save the remaining coconut milk to use in smoothies, soups, etc.

Poisson cru à la chinoise

Serves 4, generously

500g sashimi-quality tuna loin, trimmed and cut into 3cm dice
1 cup peeled, deseeded and diced cucumber
½ cup finely minced spring onion
¼ cup lime juice (from about 3 limes)
2 tablespoons sesame oil
2 tablespoons finely minced ginger
2 tablespoons soy sauce
5 tablespoons toasted sesame seeds
hot chillies, chopped (optional)

This recipe is also from Robert Oliver's 2011 book *Me `a Kai* and reflects the many cultural influences on Pacific cuisine.

Mix the tuna, cucumber and spring onion well, and refrigerate in the serving bowl.

Combine the lime juice, sesame oil, ginger, soy sauce and sesame seeds. Dress the fish with this mixture about 15 minutes before serving.

Return to the refrigerator and serve the dish very cold.

Add hot chillies as a garnish if you like.

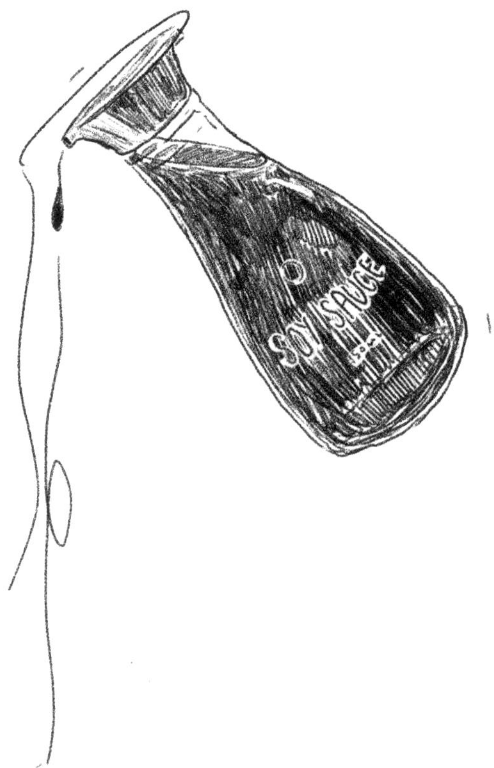

Fried chicken

Serves 4

Chicken
500g organic boneless chicken thighs, cut into bite-sized pieces
500ml chicken stock
80ml soy sauce
40ml fish sauce
40ml oyster sauce
5 star anise
4 cardamom pods
6 cloves
6 peppercorns
pared rind of 2 oranges (use a vegetable peeler)
pared rind of 2 lemons

Crumb
250g self-raising flour
1 teaspoon paprika
1 teaspoon ground black pepper
½ teaspoon ground nutmeg
½ teaspoon salt
egg white, lightly whisked, to coat

To finish
vegetable oil for deep frying

In 2019 James Beck was running Napier restaurant Bistronomy when he told Jesse Mulligan on *Afternoons* in 2019, 'I'm pretty sure that it is world-famous in Napier. The one time I took it off the menu there was a public outcry.'

Preheat the oven to 80°C.

Place the chicken in a roasting dish in a single layer. Place the remaining chicken ingredients in a saucepan and bring to a simmer.

Pour the liquid over the chicken, cover with foil and braise in the oven for about 1 hour. If you have a meat thermometer, check the temperature of the chicken after 40 minutes and thereafter every 10 minutes until the chicken has reached a core temperature of 63°C. Otherwise, cook the chicken until it is firm to the touch.

Cool the chicken in its liquid and reserve.

To make the crumb, combine all ingredients except the egg white in a shallow dish.

Half-fill a heavy-based saucepan with oil. Heat the oil until it is very hot.

Remove the chicken from the liquid and pat dry. Dust individual pieces of chicken in the crumb, coat in the egg white, and dust again in the crumb. In batches, put the chicken into the hot oil and deep-fry until golden brown. Drain on kitchen paper and serve with your favourite dipping sauce.

Oven-grilled mussels with arrabiata sauce and aged cheddar

Makes 60

For the arrabiata sauce
⅓ cup olive oil
2 tablespoons minced fresh garlic
½ teaspoon chilli flakes
½ cup port
½ cup red wine
2 × 400g cans whole peeled tomatoes, blitzed to a purée
2 tablespoons tomato paste
1 tablespoon sugar
25g butter
sea salt and freshly ground black pepper

Mussels
60 live mussels
2 cups white wine or water
400g aged cheddar or similar, grated
½ cup roughly chopped fresh parsley

Al Brown is great with fish, as his award-winning 2009 cookbook, *Go Fish*, demonstrated. He shared this recipe from the book with the *Nine to Noon* audience that year.

Place the oil in a medium-sized heavy-based saucepan over moderate heat. Add the garlic and chilli flakes and stir continuously with a wooden spoon, watching the garlic start to change colour. Once the garlic takes on a nice dark-golden colour, immediately add the port and red wine. Be mindful that as you add the alcohol it will spit and bubble for a few seconds.

Simmer the wine for 5 minutes, then add the tomatoes, tomato paste and sugar. Reduce the heat and simmer for another 15–20 minutes until nice and thick. Remove from the heat, whisk in the butter, then taste and season accordingly.

Cool to room temperature, then refrigerate until required.

Scrub the mussels and pull out the hairy beard between the tightly closed shells. Place the mussels in a large saucepan and add the wine, or water if you prefer. Cover and place over high heat. The mussels are cooked once they open up. Discard any that fail to open.

Strain the mussels through a colander (reserve the cooking liquid for another use), then spread on a tray to cool. Once cold, remove the top half of each shell and discard. Next, carefully prise away each cooked mussel from the white cartilage, place back in the belly of the shell, then lay them all out on a dish or tray.

Spoon a good amount of the arrabiata sauce over each mussel. Top with liberal amounts of grated cheese. Refrigerate until ready to cook.

To cook and serve, preheat the oven grill. Place the mussels on an oven tray, then place under the grill. Cook for 2–3 minutes or until the cheese is melted and slightly golden. Remove the tray from the oven and arrange the mussels on a platter. Sprinkle with parsley and serve to your delighted guests.

Warm potato and pea salad

Serves 6–8

50g unsalted butter
1kg (24–30) small waxy potatoes, washed but not peeled
2 teaspoons salt
¼ teaspoon freshly ground black pepper
1 cup fresh or frozen peas, blanched
140g sugar snap peas, topped and tailed
1 tablespoon finely chopped chervil
1 tablespoon finely chopped dill
1 tablespoon finely sliced chives

Wellington caterer Ruth Pretty shared this recipe on *Saturday Morning* in 2005, the year she was inducted into the New Zealand Restaurant Hall of Fame.

Place the butter in the base of a medium-sized heavy casserole or heavy-based saucepan with a tight-fitting lid. Place over medium-low heat to melt the butter. Add the potatoes, salt and pepper and toss well to coat all the potatoes in butter.

Cover the pan and cook over a medium-low heat for 25–30 minutes until the potatoes are fork-tender. Without removing the lid, shake the pan occasionally to prevent the potatoes on the bottom from burning. Alternatively, place the covered heatproof pan in a preheated 190°C oven and cook for 40–50 minutes until the potatoes are fork-tender and beginning to brown.

Once cooked, turn off the heat, add both quantities of peas and leave to steam for a further 5 minutes or until the peas are cooked. Add the herbs and toss. Serve hot.

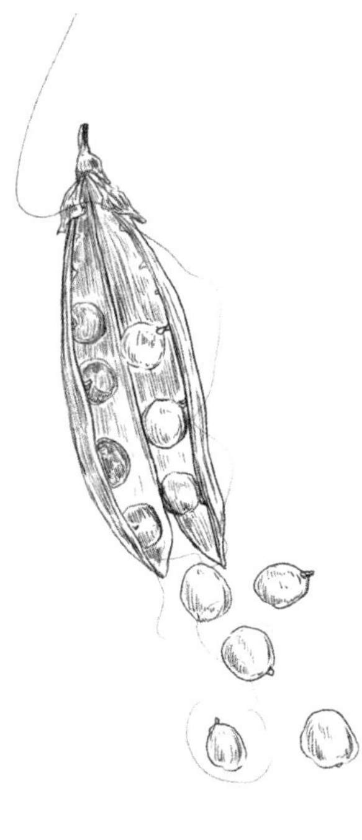

Chicory, blue cheese and sultana gratin

Serves 4 as a side dish

- 4 chicory bulbs, trimmed of any discoloured leaves and halved lengthwise
- 2 teaspoons caster sugar
- 100g butter
- 1 large onion, diced
- 100g sultanas
- 5 tablespoons apple cider vinegar or white wine vinegar
- ½ teaspoon salt
- 125ml cream
- 3 tablespoons water
- 100g blue cheese, crumbled

This terrific recipe from perhaps our most well-known chef, Peter Gordon, is a fresh take on a classic. Gordon discussed it on *Saturday Morning* in 2006, back when he was running The Providores in London and had just opened the tapas bar Bellota in Auckland.

Preheat the oven to 180°C.

Lay the chicory on a chopping board and sprinkle with the sugar.

Heat a wide pan and add half the butter. Once it is sizzling, add the onion and cook, stirring, over a high heat until it's caramelised, then add the sultanas. Cook for a minute or so, stirring frequently, until the sultanas swell a little.

Add the vinegar and salt and continue to cook until the vinegar has evaporated, stirring continuously. Tip into a 2-litre ceramic roasting dish or a similar dish that won't react with the vinegar.

Place the pan back on the heat and add the remaining butter. When it's sizzling, place the chicory in, cut-side down, and cook over a moderate heat until it turns golden. Take the pan off the heat and sit the chicory on top of the onions, cut-side up.

Put the cream, water and cheese in the pan and bring to the boil, then pour the mixture over the chicory.

Seal the dish tightly with foil, place in the centre of the oven and bake for 35 minutes.

Caramelised endive with cheese and Akaroa smoked salmon

Serves 6

- 50g sourdough breadcrumbs
- 100ml cream
- 1 tablespoon finely chopped fresh dill
- 1 tablespoon finely chopped fresh chervil
- a few turns of the pepper mill
- sea salt to taste
- 50g Parmesan, finely grated
- 80g washed-rind sheep's milk cheese, finely diced
- 50g unsalted butter
- 40g caster sugar
- 3 Belgian endive, cut in half lengthwise
- 6 slices smoked salmon
- a little extra virgin olive oil

The Arrowtown restaurant Saffron, run by Pete and Mel Gawron, was one of the great legends of the Central Otago hospo scene. In 2012 Pete published his second cookbook, *The Taste of Central Otago*, and discussed the origins of this recipe on *Nine to Noon* not long after. As with all good chef's cookbooks, the recipe had a great back story: Gawron created it one night after chatting to two guests, whom he eventually realised were Yotam Ottolenghi and Sami Tamimi. Peter Gordon had suggested they eat there.

Preheat the oven to 200°C.

Combine the breadcrumbs, cream, dill, chervil, pepper and salt, and the cheeses in a bowl and set aside.

Heat a large frying pan over medium heat, add the butter and as soon as it begins to froth add the sugar. Stir for a moment, then add the Belgian endive halves, cut-side down, and leave for 3–4 minutes. Place onto a shallow baking tray, cooked-side up, sprinkle with the cheese topping and place in the oven to cook and caramelise for about 10 minutes. Remove from the oven and drape a slice of salmon over each piece of Belgian endive. Drizzle with a little olive oil, return to the oven for a further 5 minutes and serve.

Maomao fillets, mango and banana salad

Serves 2

4 maomao, snapper, tarakihi or kahawai fillets, bones removed
salt
olive oil for pan-frying
4 handfuls of mesclun and watercress leaves
½ mango, pawpaw or rockmelon, peeled, seeds removed, and sliced
1 small red onion, finely diced

Sauce
juice of 1 lime
100ml cream
¼ cup fresh coriander leaves, roughly chopped
2 tablespoons fish sauce
½ red chilli, chopped
1 banana, peeled and chopped

Pete Peeti's television foodshow *Kai Time on the Road* premiered in 2004, the same year he shared this recipe on *Nine to Noon*.

Lightly season the fish fillets with salt.

Heat a frying pan that will comfortably hold the fish fillets over medium heat and add a splash of olive oil. Place in the fish fillets and pan-fry on both sides until lightly golden and almost cooked through. Remove to a plate.

Lower the heat and add the sauce ingredients, except the banana, to the pan. Stir and heat through, then taste for seasoning and adjust.

Add the banana to the sauce and return the fish fillets to the pan to finish cooking.

Divide the mesclun and watercress between the plates. Top with slices of mango, pawpaw or rockmelon and the red onion. Place the fish on top and spoon over the sauce.

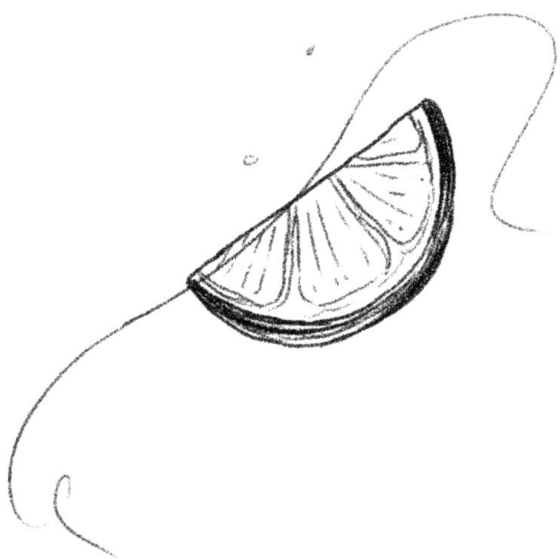

Smoked fish pie

Serves 4, generously

- 4 large potatoes
- 100g butter
- splash of cream
- salt and pepper
- 1kg smoked fish fillets
- 12 smoked mussels, shells removed
- 200g spinach leaves
- 400ml fish stock
- 50ml lemon juice
- 50ml white wine
- 50g plain flour
- 1 tablespoon seeded mustard
- 40g chopped fresh parsley or other fresh herbs

Fleurs Place at Moeraki, on the North Otago coast, has been one of New Zealand's best-loved restaurants ever since it was opened by the legendary Fleur Sullivan in 2002. On a special Queen's Birthday weekend show in 2015, the year the recipe was included in *The Great New Zealand Cookbook*, she chatted about it with host Karyn Hay.

Preheat the oven to 180°C.

Peel the potatoes and cut into even-sized pieces. Boil in lightly salted water until tender, drain and dry off over the heat. Mash the potatoes with half the butter and the cream and season with salt and pepper.

Break up the smoked fish and roughly chop the mussels, and set aside. Wash and chop the spinach leaves.

Bring the fish stock to the boil together with the lemon juice and wine. In a separate saucepan, melt the remaining butter, then slowly add the flour, stirring well and being careful not to burn it. Then gradually add your stock a ladleful at a time, mixing well each time, until you have a smooth, glossy velouté sauce. Add the mustard and herbs.

Mix the sauce with the fish and mussels, place in large ramekins and top with spinach and then mashed potato. Put in the oven and cook until hot, about 20 minutes. Serve hot with salad.

Green seafood curry

Serves 4–6

Paste
½ onion, peeled and roughly chopped
1 clove garlic, peeled
1 red or green chilli
2 makrut lime leaves, or zest of 1 lime
1 stalk lemongrass, sliced
2cm piece of fresh ginger, peeled
2 tablespoons roughly chopped fresh coriander leaves
1 teaspoon fish sauce
1 teaspoon sugar
2 teaspoons water

Curry
1 head broccoli
2 courgettes
1 tablespoon rice bran oil
1 cup light coconut cream
about 200g white fish fillets
12 scallops
½ cup frozen peas
2–4 teaspoons fish sauce
1 teaspoon sugar
1–2 fresh chillies

Journalist, editor and food writer Niki Bezzant detailed how to make this delicious curry on *Nine to Noon* in 2009.

Combine all the ingredients for the curry paste in a blender or processor and blend to a smooth paste. If necessary, add a little more water for a good consistency. (For a vegetarian paste, leave out the fish sauce and replace with salt or soy sauce.) This paste can be made an hour or two ahead, but it will lose its lovely fresh flavour if left much longer.

Slice the broccoli and courgettes. Heat the oil in a large saucepan or wok. Add the courgettes and broccoli and stir-fry for a few minutes until the vegetables are just tender.

Add the curry paste and stir to combine. Add the coconut cream and mix. Bring to a gentle simmer.

Add the fish and cook for 2–3 minutes until it turns opaque. Add the scallops and cook for another 2–3 minutes. Thin with up to ½ cup water if necessary. Add the peas.

Taste before adding the fish sauce, sugar, and chilli if desired.

Serve with steamed jasmine rice and garnish with chopped fresh coriander and sliced makrut lime leaves.

Tip — Here's a variation that works well with beef or lamb: make a red curry, add ½ red capsicum to the paste mixture, and replace the broccoli and courgettes with red capsicums and sweeter vegetables like kūmara and pumpkin.

Spanish meatball bake with smoked paprika and Parmesan

Serves 6

Tomato and red pepper sauce
¼ cup olive oil
6 cloves garlic, finely sliced
1 teaspoon dried oregano
1 tablespoon smoked paprika
3 × 400g cans tomatoes (I love cherry tomatoes for their sweetness)
400g jar roasted red peppers, drained and chopped
salt and pepper

Meatballs
1 cup breadcrumbs or 3 slices of bread blitzed in a food processor (I use stale sourdough bread)
⅓ cup milk
1kg mince (I use half beef and half pork mince)
1 small onion, finely chopped
½ cup Parmesan, finely grated
½ cup chopped flat-leaf parsley
1½ tablespoons smoked paprika
3 garlic cloves, finely chopped
2 teaspoons salt
1 teaspoon freshly ground pepper
⅓ cup olive oil, for frying

To bake
1 cup finely grated Parmesan

Food blogger Gretchen Lowe explained how to make this dish on *Nine to Noon* in 2017.

For the sauce, heat the olive oil in a frying pan over medium-low heat. Add the garlic, oregano and smoked paprika and cook for 1 minute or so, being careful not to burn the garlic.

Add the tomatoes and peppers and season generously. Bring to a simmer then cook, stirring occasionally, until the sauce is thick and the tomatoes have mostly fallen apart, about 25 minutes.

Heat the oven to 200°C.

For the meatballs, put the breadcrumbs in a bowl and pour in the milk. Let stand until the liquid is almost absorbed — a few minutes will do.

In a large bowl, combine all the ingredients, except the olive oil, and form the mixture into about 25 golf-ball-sized meatballs.

Add the olive oil to a frying pan over medium-high heat. When the oil is hot, pan-fry the meatballs in batches, turning occasionally, until golden brown, 5–8 minutes per batch. Transfer the meatballs to a paper-towel-lined plate.

Spoon a thin layer of the sauce over the base of a large rectangular casserole dish. Sprinkle one-third of the Parmesan over the sauce and scatter over half the meatballs. Top with half of the remaining sauce, sprinkle with another one-third of the Parmesan and the remaining meatballs. Finish with the remaining sauce and Parmesan.

Bake for about 35 minutes until golden and bubbling.

Waikanae crab risotto

Serves 4

500g fresh greenshell mussels, scrubbed
300ml white wine (I like to use a Sauvignon blanc)
750ml chicken stock
2 tablespoons butter
1 small onion, finely chopped
1 clove garlic, crushed
250g risotto rice (I like to use Ferron)
300g crab meat
50g butter
25g Parmigiano Reggiano, finely grated
finely grated zest and juice of 1 lemon
salt
2 tablespoons crème fraîche
4 tablespoons chive batons
few sprigs of chervil
1 radish, thinly sliced

Auckland restaurant legend Judith Tabron presided over the famous Soul Bar and Bistro at the Viaduct for 21 years. In 2011, when she explained how to make this dish, she had just published *The Soul Cookbook*.

In a saucepan, steam the mussels in half the white wine until they start to open. Strain the mussels, adding all the juices to the chicken stock. Pick over the mussels, discarding the shells, tough ligaments, the outer lips and the feet. Chop the remaining mussel meat. Reserve.

Bring the mussel and chicken stock up to the boil in another saucepan. Keep this on a very slow simmer as you begin the risotto.

Place 2 tablespoons butter in another medium-sized saucepan, add the onion and garlic and soften them over medium-low heat, stirring occasionally. (Make sure the onion is cooked through before adding the rice.)

Add the rice and seal (toast) for about 5 minutes, then deglaze with the remaining white wine. As soon as the white wine has evaporated, add the stock, ladleful by ladleful, stirring constantly.

When all the stock is incorporated and the rice is cooked (12–15 minutes, depending on the temperature and the size of the pan), remove from the heat. Mix through the crab meat, reserved mussels, 50g butter and the Parmigiano Reggiano.

Finish the risotto by gently stirring in some of the lemon zest and all of the juice, adjust the seasoning by adding salt if needed, and finally stir through the crème fraîche. Garnish with the remaining lemon zest, chive batons, sprigs of chervil and slices of radish. Serve immediately.

Beef stroganoff

Serves 4

450–500g fillet or sirloin steak (a premium cut is needed as the meat is cooked quickly)
1 onion
225g button mushrooms
50g butter
100ml dry white wine
150ml beef stock
salt and freshly ground pepper
150ml sour cream
chopped parsley for garnish
plain boiled rice to serve

Chef Jeremy Jones, then of Timara Lodge in Marlborough, detailed how to create this melt-in-the-mouth stew on *Nine to Noon* in 2008.

Trim the steak and cut into thin strips, about 5cm × 1cm. Peel and finely chop the onion. Trim and slice the mushrooms.

Melt half the butter in a large frying pan and add the onion. Pan-fry gently for a few minutes until the onion is softened, then add the mushrooms and pan-fry for a further 2–3 minutes until cooked. Add the wine and stock and boil rapidly until reduced to about 2 tablespoons. Remove the vegetables and liquid from the pan and keep them warm.

Add the remaining butter to the pan and add the steak. Pan-fry quickly, stirring with a wooden spoon to seal and cook the meat on all sides, about 3–4 minutes. Return the onion, mushrooms and liquid to the pan and season with salt and pepper.

Lower the heat and stir in the sour cream. Reheat thoroughly without boiling.

Sprinkle with the parsley and serve with plain boiled rice.

Moroccan lamb meatballs

Serves 4

100g fresh breadcrumbs
25g flat-leaf parsley (bunch), leaves picked
25g mint (bunch), leaves picked
25g coriander (bunch), leaves picked
2 tablespoons extra virgin olive oil
500g lamb mince
2 cloves garlic, crushed
1 tablespoon harissa
good pinch of ground cumin
salt and black pepper

Sauce
1 tablespoon olive oil
25g butter
1 large onion, finely chopped
3 cloves garlic, crushed
2 tablespoons honey
1 stick cinnamon
finely grated zest of ½ orange
good pinch of ground cumin
good pinch of saffron threads
good pinch of smoked paprika
500g chopped tomatoes

The Sugar Club (in both its Wellington and Notting Hill incarnations) co-founder Ashley Sumner explained how to make these tasty meatballs on *Saturday Morning* in 2006.

Preheat the oven to 180°C.

Place the breadcrumbs, picked herb leaves and olive oil in a food processor and blend to a paste. In a large bowl, mix together the paste with the lamb mince, garlic, harissa and cumin, and season with salt and pepper.

Roll the mixture into medium-sized balls and place in a lightly greased shallow baking tray. Place in the oven and cook for 25 minutes.

In a medium-sized saucepan, heat the oil and butter, then add the onion and garlic and cook, stirring occasionally, over low heat until the onion has softened, about 7 minutes. Add the honey, cinnamon stick, orange zest, cumin, saffron and paprika. Cook for 5 minutes, then add the tomatoes. Increase the heat and bring just up to the boil. Reduce the heat, add the meatballs and juices from the tray and cook slowly for a further 20 minutes.

Pasta alla Norma

Serves 4–6

2 medium eggplants
salt
75ml extra virgin olive oil
2 cloves garlic, finely chopped
2 small bird's eye chillies, crushed
2 × 400g cans Italian tomatoes, mashed
1 tablespoon tomato paste
salt
¾ cup olive oil
500g dried spaghetti
½ cup grated ricotta salata (salted, aged ricotta) or pecorino Romano cheese, plus extra for serving

Julie Biuso talked about the controversy over the origins of this dish on *Afternoons* in 2012: is it a tribute to Sicilian-born composer Bellini and named after his opera *Norma*, or is it just pasta cooked in the 'normal' Sicilian way, with eggplant? Either way, she extolled its deliciousness.

Trim the eggplants and cut into rounds about 5mm thick. Layer them in a colander, sprinkle with salt, and drain after 45 minutes.

Pour the extra virgin olive oil into a saucepan and add the garlic. Cook over a low heat for a few minutes until fragrant then add the chillies and cook for 1 minute. Tip in the tomatoes and mix in the tomato paste and ½ teaspoon salt. Rinse the tomato cans with a little water (use a little less than ¾ cup), and add the tomato water to the saucepan. Turn up the heat and bring the sauce to the boil, then reduce the heat and cook gently, uncovered, for about 30 minutes, or until reduced and pulpy; don't let the sauce reduce over a fierce heat or it will lose its sweetness.

Pat the eggplant slices dry with paper towels. Heat the olive oil in a frying pan over a medium-high heat until just starting to haze. Carefully slide in as many slices of eggplant as will fit in a single layer. Cook, in batches, until a deep golden colour on both sides. Transfer to a plate lined with paper towels and sprinkle lightly with salt.

When the sauce and eggplants are ready (both can be prepared in advance), cook the spaghetti in plenty of gently boiling, well-salted water until just al dente; test it several times throughout and drain it just before it is al dente — it needs to have plenty of bounce left in it to make a memorable dish.

Tip the spaghetti into a large heated serving bowl. Pour over three-quarters of the sauce and add the ricotta salata or pecorino Romano. Toss well, then mix in the eggplant slices and toss again. The eggplant should break apart a bit and the whole dish should look gloriously messy. Spoon the rest of the sauce on top and rush it to the table. Serve with more ricotta or pecorino.

Grilled pork chops with white beans, fennel and spicy sausage

Serves 4

- 100g unsalted butter
- 4 pork chops
- salt and freshly ground black pepper
- 2 cloves garlic, peeled and crushed
- 150g spicy sausage, finely diced
- 2 tablespoons dry sherry
- 400g can white beans, drained
- 2 fennel bulbs, trimmed and thinly sliced
- 300ml cream

In 2008, much-loved Wellington chef Martin Bosley published his cookbook *Martin Bosley Cooks*, full of the at-home recipes he loved to make and drawing on his then regular *New Zealand Listener* columns. He detailed how to make this dish on *Afternoons*.

Melt half the butter in a shallow frying pan until it begins to foam, then add the chops. Cook on one side until golden brown, about 4 minutes, then turn them over, season with salt and pepper and cook for another 4–6 minutes or until the juices run clear.

Remove the chops from the pan and keep them warm.

Add the remaining butter to the pan and cook the garlic until golden brown. Add the spicy sausage and cook, stirring, until fragrant, about 2 minutes, then pour in the sherry and cook for 1 minute.

Stir in the white beans, fennel and cream and simmer until reduced by half and the fennel is just cooked. Taste the sauce and season with salt and pepper.

Serve with the pork chops lying on the beans.

Involtini (baked spaghetti parcels with eggplant and bocconcini)

Serves 4

- 2 medium-sized eggplants (about 600g)
- sea salt and freshly ground pepper
- 2 tablespoons olive oil, plus extra for brushing and for the spaghetti
- 2 cloves garlic, crushed
- 1 tablespoon dried oregano
- pinch of chilli flakes
- 2 × 400g cans crushed Italian tomatoes, or 6 large very ripe tomatoes, diced
- 200g dried spaghetti
- 200g fresh bocconcini or mozzarella in whey, well drained
- handful of fresh basil leaves
- freshly grated Parmesan

Catherine Bell shared this recipe with *Nine to Noon* listeners in 2010.

Preheat the oven to 200°C. Line a tray with baking paper. Lightly grease a baking dish, about 18cm × 26cm.

Trim the stalks off the eggplants and cut each eggplant lengthways into four slices about 1cm thick. This will depend on the size of the eggplants — you need 8 slices. Brush both sides with olive oil and season with salt and pepper.

Place the eggplant slices on the prepared tray and bake for about 25 minutes until tender but not falling apart, turning once during cooking. Set aside.

Make the tomato sauce. Heat the 2 tablespoons olive oil in a saucepan over medium heat, add the garlic, oregano and chilli flakes and cook, stirring, for 1 minute. Add the tomatoes, season and simmer until reduced and thick. Set aside.

Cook the spaghetti in plenty of boiling, well-salted water until al dente. Drain well and toss with a little olive oil to prevent it sticking together.

To assemble, combine the spaghetti and three-quarters of the tomato sauce in a large bowl. Using tongs, twirl the spaghetti around the tongs and place 4 separate mounds in the prepared baking dish.

Tear the bocconcini into pieces and push a couple into the pasta along with 2–3 basil leaves.

Dip the eggplant slices in the remaining tomato sauce and lay 2 slices over the top of each bundle. Top with a couple of basil leaves, more bocconcini, a spoonful of the remaining sauce and, finally, a good grating of Parmesan.

Place in the oven and bake for 20 minutes or until the cheese has melted and the spaghetti is hot.

Pheasant or chicken enchiladas

Serves 4

Tortillas

2 cups plain flour
½ teaspoon salt
3 tablespoons vegetable oil
¾ cup water

Enchilada sauce

2 tablespoons vegetable oil
2 tablespoons plain or gluten-free flour
½ teaspoon mild chilli powder or chilli flakes
¼ teaspoon ground cumin
¼ teaspoon dried oregano
2 cups vegetable or chicken stock

Filling

1 tablespoon vegetable oil
1 red onion, finely sliced
1 clove garlic, crushed
1 red capsicum, deseeded and finely sliced
8 skinless pheasant breasts or 4 small skinless chicken breasts, cut into small dice, about 2.5cm
250g sour cream
1 cup grated tasty cheese, plus ¾ cup for topping
1 tablespoon shredded fresh oregano leaves, or 1 teaspoon dried oregano
1 teaspoon dried parsley

This family-friendly recipe by Whakatāne-based wild food forager Mawera Karetai (Kāi Tahu, Kāti Mamoe me Waitaha ki te Waipounamu) is easy to make in even the busiest of households. She told Jesse Mulligan how to make them on *Afternoons* in 2017.

To make the tortillas, in a large bowl combine the flour and salt, then stir in the oil and water. Combine well and turn out onto a floured surface. Knead for 2 minutes, adding a little flour or water as required to make a smooth dough. Rest, covered, for half an hour.

Divide the dough into 8 and roll into balls. Using a rolling pin, roll out into 18–20cm rounds. In a large, lightly oiled non-stick pan, cook the tortillas over medium heat for 40–60 seconds per side, until lightly browned.

To make the sauce, heat the oil in a small saucepan over medium-high heat. Add the flour and stir together for 1 minute to cook the flour. Stir in the chilli, cumin and oregano, then gradually add in the stock, whisking constantly to remove any lumps. Reduce the heat and simmer for 10–15 minutes until the sauce thickens. Season with salt to taste.

Preheat the oven to 180°C.

To make the filling, heat the oil in a medium-sized frying pan over medium heat. Add the onion, garlic and capsicum and cook, stirring occasionally, until the onion softens. Add the pheasant or chicken and cook, stirring, until the juices run clear. Remove from the heat and stir in the sour cream, 1 cup grated cheese, oregano and parsley. Stir through 150ml of the hot enchilada sauce. Taste for seasoning and adjust.

Brush each tortilla with enchilada sauce. Divide the hot filling between the tortillas. Arrange in a baking dish and cover with the remaining enchilada sauce and ¾ cup cheese. Place in the oven and bake, uncovered, for 20 minutes. Cool for 10 minutes before serving.

Tip — Of course, you can buy the tortillas.

Orange and rosemary chicken

Serves 4

8 chicken thighs, skinned and boned
1 tablespoon olive oil
½ cup fresh orange juice
¼ cup red wine vinegar
1 teaspoon brown sugar
1 clove garlic, crushed
1 tablespoon finely chopped rosemary
½ teaspoon salt
freshly ground black pepper to taste

Food writer Nici Wickes offered this flavourful dish on *Nine to Noon* in 2009, the year she published *World Kitchen: Bringing Great Chicken Recipes Back Home to New Zealand*.

Cut slashes into the chicken meat to allow the marinade to penetrate and place the chicken in a large shallow dish.

Whisk the remaining ingredients together and pour over the chicken. Cover and refrigerate for 30 minutes.

Preheat the oven to 200°C.

Place the chicken and marinade in a large ovenproof dish lined with baking paper and bake for 45 minutes. Baste occasionally with the marinade during cooking if you can be bothered.

Rib-eye roast with Moroccan flavours

Serves 8

1.5kg rib-eye (scotch fillet)
2 tablespoons olive oil
salt

Marinade
100ml olive oil
juice of 2 lemons
2 tablespoons dry white wine or sherry
1 small onion, very finely chopped
½ cup canned Italian tomatoes, mashed
8 pitted prunes, chopped
4 tablespoons chopped coriander
1 tablespoon finely grated fresh ginger
2 teaspoons toasted and ground cumin seeds
2 teaspoons chilli powder
1 teaspoon ground cinnamon
½ teaspoon freshly ground black pepper
1 teaspoon salt

Julie Biuso explained this sensationally spiced dish from her Mediterranean cookbook *Take a Vine-ripened Tomato* to *Afternoons* listeners in 2011.

Trim any excess fat from the beef, remove any silvery skin, then tie it in shape with kitchen string. Mix all the marinade ingredients together in a large shallow dish and add the beef. Turn the beef in the marinade so that it is coated all over, then cover and refrigerate for 3–4 hours, turning the beef occasionally.

Remove the beef from the fridge 1 hour before cooking. Preheat the oven to 200°C.

Scrape off the marinade with a flat-bladed knife and pat the meat dry with paper towels. Heat the olive oil in a roasting pan (choose one in which the meat fits snugly) and when it is hot add the beef. Brown the beef quickly on both sides, then transfer to the oven. Roast for 30–40 minutes, turning once and basting twice with the marinade (cook 30 minutes for rare, 40 minutes for medium-rare).

Remove the beef from the oven and sprinkle with 1 teaspoon of salt. Let the beef rest for 15 minutes, loosely covered with foil.

Meanwhile, put the marinade in a saucepan and cook gently for 10 minutes until softened and pulpy. Tuck paper towels around the edges of a chopping board to absorb excess juices and place the beef on the board. Slice the meat into pieces about 5mm thick. Rest the sliced meat for a minute, mop up the juices, then transfer to a heated serving platter. Serve immediately with the sauce.

Serve with buttered minted couscous and a tossed green salad, or with roasted potatoes or crispy kūmara. The beef is equally good cold (but slice it more thinly). Serve with salads, including a tomato, cucumber and red onion salad, and crusty bread.

Barbecue chicken with green sauce

Serves 4

1 whole chicken cut in half, or 4 legs, skin on

Glaze

2 tablespoons soy sauce
1 clove garlic, crushed
1 teaspoon sesame oil
pinch of chilli flakes
1 teaspoon sugar
salt and pepper

Green sauce

¼ cup parsley leaves
¼ cup coriander leaves
⅛ cup chopped chives
⅛ cup sherry vinegar
⅛ cup neutral-flavoured vegetable oil
2 shallots, peeled and roughly chopped
1 red chilli, roughly chopped

Conor Mertens, of Harvest Deli in Napier, and former chef at Auckland restaurant Orphan's Kitchen and then the pop-up Chimera, was on *Summer Afternoons* in 2020 to explain this dish.

Mix the glaze ingredients together in a small bowl, then rub into the chicken. Set aside, covered, for an hour. Get the barbecue going, preferably charcoal but gas will be fine — just less smoky flavour.

Put all the green sauce ingredients in a blender and blend to a sauce consistency.

When the barbecue is medium-hot, cook the chicken skin-side down until it has nice colour, then flip and cook bone-side down, with the lid closed, until done. The chicken is done when it probes at 65°C or above. Rest the chicken for 10 minutes before serving with the green sauce.

Muttonbird with watercress and kūmara

Serves 3–4

2 tītī (muttonbird)
1 large saucepanful of watercress
6 small freshly dug kūmara, scrubbed
salt and pepper

The Tītī Muttonbird Islands are located in the far, far south of New Zealand, and are named for the traditional seasonal harvesting of the sooty shearwater by Māori. This recipe by Anne Thorp was broadcast on *Afternoons* in 2010, shortly after she published her cookbook *Kai Ora*.

Place the tītī in a large saucepan and cover with water. Bring to the boil, then simmer for 1 hour on a gentle blip-blip simmer. (Leave the windows open when cooking, as there is quite a strong smell.)

Take off the heat, and allow the tītī to sit in the cooking liquid for 1 hour. Remove the tītī and discard enough of the liquid to get rid of the fatty oil. Add enough fresh hot water to make a weaker stock. Return to the heat. Alternatively, you can cook the tītī the day before and skim the oil off the top of the cooled stock.

Bring the stock to the boil and then reduce back to a blip-blip simmer. Place the watercress and kūmara in the stock and cook until the kūmara is soft, about 15 minutes.

The cooked tītī can be grilled under a preheated grill for 10–15 minutes. This not only crisps the skin but also gets rid of more oil.

To serve, arrange a bed of cooked watercress on each plate and place some kūmara on the side. Break the tītī up into segments, place on the watercress and season with salt and pepper if necessary.

Chicken and poppy seed pasta

Serves 4–6

good glug of light olive oil
1 large red onion, finely chopped
4 cloves garlic, finely sliced
200g Savoy cabbage, finely sliced
5 cups dried penne pasta to give 8 cups cooked penne
480g cooked free-range chicken, broken into pieces
2 large carrots, peeled and grated
12 large mint leaves, finely sliced
750ml cream
2 teaspoons flaky salt
few good grinds of black pepper
4 teaspoons poppy seeds
80g Parmesan cheese, grated

Alexandra Tylee, owner of famouse Pipi Cafe in Havelock North, offered this kid-friendly recipe on *Afternoons* in 2016.

Heat the olive oil in a large frying pan on a low heat. Add the red onion to the pan and cook for 10 minutes until the onion is soft but not brown. Add the garlic and stir them both until they just start to colour.

Put the cabbage in a colander and pour boiling water over it to soften. Add the cabbage to the onion and cook until really soft. Then add the penne, chicken, carrot, mint, cream, salt and pepper. Mix together and then let it simmer until the sauce has thickened and the chicken has heated through; this will take about 5 minutes on a gentle heat. Mix in the poppy seeds and half of the Parmesan, and check for seasoning.

Serve with the remainder of the Parmesan on top.

Summer leg of lamb and roasted stuffed tomatoes with butter beans

Serves 8

Lamb
3–4 sprigs of thyme
2–3 sprigs of rosemary
1.5kg leg of lamb, boned but with shank intact, at room temperature
sea salt and black pepper
2 tablespoons olive oil

Stuffed tomatoes
8 medium-sized ripe but still firm tomatoes
2 tablespoons olive oil
1 onion, finely chopped
1 clove garlic, finely chopped
70g fresh breadcrumbs (about 1¼ cups)
handful of flat-leaf parsley leaves, finely chopped
1 red capsicum, roasted, skinned, flesh cut into small pieces
sea salt and black pepper
80g soft goat's cheese

Lamb gravy
2 tablespoons plain flour
splash of red or white wine
500ml beef or lamb stock, or vegetable cooking water
sea salt and black pepper

To serve
800g butter beans, steamed

Private caterer, food magazine writer and food consultant Kathy Paterson shared this recipe with *Nine to Noon* listeners in 2018, the year she published her *Meat & Three* cookbook.

Preheat the oven to 230°C.

Place the herbs in the lamb cavity left from removing the bone, then tie with about 3 pieces of kitchen string at even intervals to hold the lamb in shape. Place in a roasting tin, season with salt and pepper and drizzle with olive oil.

Place in the oven and roast for 20 minutes. Lower the oven temperature to 200°C and roast for a further 40 minutes for lamb that is still a little pink in the centre.

Line a shallow roasting tin with baking paper.

Using a sharp knife, cut about 1cm off the bottom of each tomato, so they will sit flat. Dice the cut tomato ends and set aside. Use a teaspoon to remove the seeds and most of the flesh from the inside of each tomato. The flesh can be roughly diced and set aside. Place the hollowed-out tomatoes in the roasting tin.

Place the oil in a small frying pan and heat over low heat. Add the onion and garlic and cook gently until the onion begins to soften — about 5 minutes. Remove from the heat and place in a bowl with the breadcrumbs, chopped parsley, reserved diced tomato and capsicum. Season and mix to combine.

Divide the goat's cheese and place a piece in the base of each tomato. Fill with the breadcrumb mixture, mounding the top. Place in the oven with the lamb and cook for 20–30 minutes until the tomatoes are tender but not collapsing. Remove from the oven and keep warm.

Remove the lamb from the oven and place on a warmed meat platter. Cover loosely with foil and a clean tea towel and leave to rest while you make the gravy.

Pour off the fat from the roasting tin, leaving about 2 tablespoons. Add the flour and place the roasting tin on the stovetop over medium heat. Stir with a wooden spoon until the flour begins to colour. Add the wine and the stock or water and simmer until the gravy is lightly thickened, stirring continuously. Check the seasoning before straining into a heated jug or gravy boat.

Remove the string and slice the lamb. Serve with the gravy, stuffed tomatoes and steamed butter beans.

Tip — Change up the herbs in the tomato stuffing by adding chopped mint, dill, fennel fronds, sweet marjoram or oregano to the parsley.

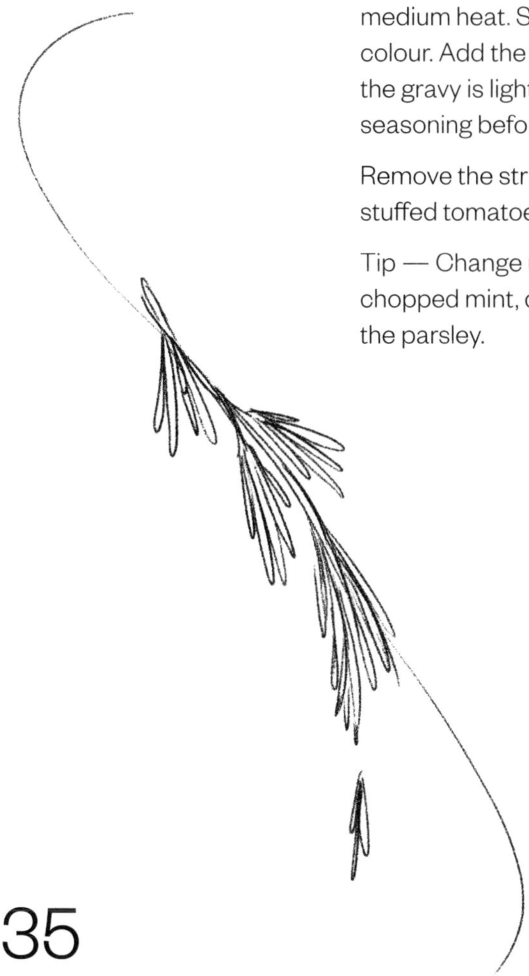

Pork broth, roasted pork shoulder and doughboys

Serves 6

5kg pork bones
2kg chicken bones
olive oil for frying
2 large onions, chopped
2 large carrots, scrubbed and chopped
½ head celery
5 cloves garlic, smashed
small handful of thyme
1 bay leaf
1 tablespoon black peppercorns
2 litres chicken stock
2 kūmara, peeled and diced
2 potatoes, peeled and diced
1 bunch of watercress, leaves picked

Pork shoulder

1 pork shoulder
3 tablespoons olive oil
4 cloves garlic, crushed
salt and pepper

Doughboys

2 cups self-raising flour, sifted
1 tablespoon dried thyme
salt and pepper
½ cup pork broth, cooled

When Monique Fiso opened her Wellington restaurant Hiakai in 2018 it was a revelation. When her cookbook of the same name won an award at the 2021 Ockham New Zealand Book Awards it demonstrated the ground-shifting influence of her indigenous kai focus. Of course, alert RNZ listeners would have been aware of her long before that: she shared this recipe with Jesse Mulligan on *Afternoons* in 2016.

Preheat the oven to 180°C. Put the pork bones and chicken bones in a roasting dish and roast for 30 minutes, or until golden brown.

Set a large saucepan or stock pot over medium heat. Add a dash of olive oil, followed by the onion, carrot, celery and garlic. Cook, stirring occasionally, until lightly caramelised, then add the pork bones and chicken bones. Add the thyme, bay leaf and peppercorns and pour in the chicken stock. Top up with water to cover the bones. Simmer, uncovered, for about 3 hours.

Strain the broth and discard the bones and vegetables. Set ½ cup of broth aside in a small bowl to cool.

While the broth is simmering, cook the pork.

In a small bowl, mix together the olive oil and garlic and season with salt and pepper. Using a pastry brush, spread the mixture all over the pork shoulder.

Place the meat on a rack set into a roasting pan and roast for 20 minutes at 180°C, then reduce the temperature to 120°C. Continue to cook for approximately 2 hours. Remove the pork from the oven and let stand until cool enough to handle, about 30 minutes.

Pull the meat apart in preparation to adding to the pork broth.

To make the doughboys, place the sifted flour in a mixing bowl and stir in the thyme. Slowly add the ½ cup cooled pork broth to the dry ingredients and work into a dough. Be careful not to overwork.

Return the stock pot to the heat and bring to a simmer. Add the kūmara, potatoes and pulled pork shoulder to the broth and cook for 10 minutes. Slowly spoon the dough into the broth and cook for 20 minutes or until cooked through.

When the doughboys are cooked and the kūmara and potatoes are soft, season with salt and pepper and add the watercress. Serve immediately.

Mamma Rosa's polpettine

Serves 6 (makes 12 skewers)

2 small red onions
½ a baguette (French bread)
250g Gruyère cheese, cut into 24 cubes
600g minced veal (or a mix of minced pork and veal)
50g (½ cup) freshly grated Parmesan
50g (½ cup) fresh white breadcrumbs
2 small free-range eggs, lightly beaten
2 large cloves garlic, peeled and crushed
½ teaspoon salt
freshly ground black pepper, to taste
1 tablespoon finely chopped fresh marjoram (or ½ tablespoon dried marjoram)
12 fresh bay leaves
olive oil, for frying

Coating

½ cup plain flour
3 large free-range eggs, lightly beaten with ¼ teaspoon salt
1 cup dried white breadcrumbs or panko crumbs

Julie Biuso learnt how to make these rich and delicious meatball skewers from her Italian mother-in-law and shared them with *Afternoons* listeners in 2015.

Cut the onions in half through the root, then cut each half onion lengthwise into 3 pieces. Slice the baguette into thick rounds and then into 24 chunks about the same size as the cheese cubes. Set aside with the onion.

Put the minced veal in a bowl and add the Parmesan, breadcrumbs, beaten eggs, garlic, salt, pepper and marjoram. Mix thoroughly. Shape into 24 oval meatballs, keeping hands moist with a little water to prevent sticking.

Choose skewers no more than 23cm in length or they won't fit into a large frying pan. Skewer the ingredients in this order: meatball, cube of cheese, cube of bread, piece of onion, bay leaf (folded in two), then meatball, cube of cheese and cube of bread.

When all the polpettine are assembled, dust generously with the flour then brush carefully with the beaten egg and coat with dried breadcrumbs. Transfer to a plate.

The polpettine may be prepared several hours ahead up to this point (it's definitely advisable to do this), covered and kept in the fridge. Note that there is less chance of the cheese melting and burning if it is well chilled.

When ready to cook, heat a 1cm depth of olive oil in a large frying pan over a medium-high heat and cook 3–4 polpettine at a time (you may need to add more oil between batches). When they are golden and cooked, transfer to a rack set over a baking dish and keep warm in a low oven; don't cover them or they will loose crispness. (You may need to skim the oil with a small metal strainer between cooking batches of polpettine to remove any pieces of cheese that ooze out.) When all are done, transfer to a heated serving plate and serve hot.

Tip — The meatball mixture can also be used as a stuffing, or shaped into small balls and roasted in a shallow oven dish in a moderate oven until browned (about 15 minutes) and served with roasted veges — children love them.

Roast sirloin of beef with Māori potato

Serves 6

1kg piece beef sirloin
1 large head of garlic, cloves peeled
fresh rosemary leaves
50g piri piri seasoning
olive oil and butter for cooking
1 large carrot, chopped
1 large onion, chopped
200ml port
2 litres beef stock
1 kg Māori potatoes, washed and cut in half
2 bunches of turnip tops, washed and chopped

This is a localised version of one of the great Spanish staples from Pete Peeti of the TV show *Kai Time on the Road*, which was back for another series in 2007 when he explained this recipe to *Nine to Noon* listeners.

Make cuts about 1cm deep with a small sharp knife all over the beef sirloin. Push garlic cloves into each cut along with fresh rosemary leaves. Season the meat with salt and the piri piri seasoning.

Heat a splash of olive oil in a high-sided frying pan or cast-iron casserole dish over medium-high heat. Place the meat in the pan and seal on all sides. Add the carrot and onion and cook, stirring, for about 5 minutes. Add the port, allowing it to bubble up before adding half the beef stock.

Lower the heat, cover and cook the sirloin to medium-rare, internal temperature 60–65°C. Remove the sirloin from the pan and keep warm.

Slowly add the remaining beef stock to the pan, stirring to extract the flavours from the bottom of the pan. Simmer to reduce the stock to a sauce consistency, or alternatively make a flour and butter paste using equal quantities of both. Whisk into the sauce and continue simmering to thicken and cook out the flour.

Boil the Māori potatoes in lightly salted water until tender. Test with the point of a small sharp knife to see if tender after 10–15 minutes. Drain, then slice and lightly pan-fry in a little olive oil and butter. (You can also add pumpkin and kūmara for colour and different flavours.) Season to taste with salt and pepper.

Bring a saucepan of lightly salted water to the boil. Add a good knob of butter, then add the chopped turnip tops. Cover and cook for 10 minutes or until the turnip tops are soft. Strain the turnip tops. To serve, place the potatoes on a plate, followed by the turnip tops. Slice the meat, place on top of the vegetables, and finish with the sauce.

Braised sausage, leek, pumpkin and potato

Serves 6

12 sausages
5 tablespoons olive oil
3 leeks, trimmed and well washed
500g pumpkin, peeled and deseeded
4 medium waxy potatoes (such as Nadine or Draga), scrubbed
2 cups chicken or beef stock
½ cup chopped mixed fresh herbs (parsley, thyme, tarragon, chives)
salt and freshly ground black pepper

Another evergreen from Lauraine Jacobs on *Nine to Noon* in 2007.

Brown the sausages in 2 tablespoons of oil in a large heated casserole dish. When golden remove from the dish and set aside. Tip off any extra fat from the dish.

Slice the leeks into thick diagonal slices. Cut the pumpkin and potatoes into 2cm dice. Heat the remaining oil in the casserole dish and add the vegetables, tossing well to coat in the oil. Cook over a gentle heat for a few minutes, stirring continuously. Add the stock and bring up to a simmer. Cook for 10 minutes.

Add the sausages so they sit on the vegetables, then cover the casserole dish and simmer for 10–15 minutes until the vegetables are tender and the sausages are cooked through. Add the chopped herbs and season with salt and pepper.

Serve in shallow bowls with some of the vegetable juices and the sausages on top.

Pot-roast chicken with dates

Serves 4

1 large chicken
salt and freshly ground black pepper
butter and vegetable oil for browning
1 onion, finely chopped
1 stick cinnamon
6 whole cloves
1 teaspoon ground turmeric
125ml chicken stock
125ml dry sherry (I like to use Tio Pepe Fino sherry)
2 tablespoons honey
1 tablespoon lemon juice
1 tablespoon Dijon mustard
2 medium-sized garlic cloves, crushed
1 tablespoon finely grated fresh ginger, or 1 teaspoon dried ground ginger
200g pitted dates, fresh or dried
finely grated zest of 1 orange

Leading Auckland chef Simon Gault shared this recipe with the *Nine to Noon* audience in 2004, the year he was helming the restaurant Gault@George in Parnell and had published his first cookbook, *Simon Gault Cooks: Fabulous Food at Home*.

Season the chicken with salt and pepper. Heat a little butter and oil in a saucepan over medium heat and brown the chicken well all over. Transfer to a plate. Add the onion to the saucepan, place over low heat and cook, stirring occasionally, until glazed and golden.

Add the cinnamon, cloves, turmeric, stock, sherry, honey, lemon juice, mustard, garlic and ginger. Place the chicken on top. Cover and cook very gently for 30 minutes. Add the dates and orange zest and continue cooking until the chicken is done — about 30 minutes more.

Transfer the chicken and dates to a warm dish, check the flavour of the sauce and correct the consistency if necessary. Add a little water if it's too thick; reduce by boiling, uncovered, if it is too thin. Pour over the chicken and serve with rice and vegetables.

Rack of lamb with salad and tzatziki dressing

Serves 4

2 racks of lamb (280–300g each), bones cleaned (frenched)
2 tablespoons olive oil, plus extra for drizzling
sea salt and freshly ground black pepper

Salad
500g fresh broad beans, podded
500g fresh garden peas, podded
1–2 red chillies, finely chopped
handful of mint leaves, coarsely chopped
100g firm feta, sliced or crumbled
extra virgin olive oil for drizzling

Tzatziki sauce
½ telegraph cucumber, deseeded and cut into small dice
1 cup plain unsweetened Greek-style yoghurt
1 clove garlic, crushed
handful of mint leaves, coarsely chopped

Palmerston North chef and caterer Hester Guy explained how to make this dish, with its Middle Eastern flourish, on *Nine to Noon* in 2011.

Make the salad: bring a saucepan of lightly salted water to the boil. Add the broad beans and boil for 1–2 minutes, then drain and run under cold water. Remove the outer grey skin and discard, leaving only the bright green beans.

Cook the garden peas in lightly salted boiling water until tender or cooked to your liking. Drain well.

Place the broad beans and garden peas in a bowl and add the chilli, mint and feta. Drizzle with enough olive oil to moisten. Cover and place in the fridge until ready to serve, or leave sitting at room temperature.

Make the sauce: combine all the ingredients together and season well. Cover and place in the fridge until ready to serve.

Preheat the oven to 200°C. Rub the lamb racks with oil and season with salt and pepper. Place in a shallow ovenproof dish or roasting dish, then place in the oven and cook for 10–15 minutes for tender pink lamb. Remove from the oven, cover loosely and leave to rest in a warm spot for 10 minutes before cutting into cutlets.

Place a generous amount of the salad on each plate and top with 3 or 4 carved cutlets of lamb. Spoon over the sauce and drizzle each plate with a little oil. Serve immediately.

Nights

Nights, fronted by Bryan Crump and followed by the indomitable Karyn Hay, bills itself as a four-hour show of fresh ideas and sounds, along with the best radio documentaries and features from here and overseas. Music is always a strong component of the line-up; a perfect background for dessert.

Dark chocolate matcha truffles

Makes 48

- 280g dark chocolate (85% cocoa solids), coarsely chopped
- 1 teaspoon ground cinnamon
- 1 teaspoon vanilla extract
- pinch of Himalayan pink salt
- 1 cup full-fat coconut cream or cream
- 1 tablespoon coconut oil
- matcha green tea powder for coating

In 2016 Belinda MacDonald, joint winner of *My Kitchen Rules New Zealand* in 2014, had just published her gluten-free cookbook *My Green Kitchen*, with Neena Truscott, when she told *Nine to Noon* listeners how to make these truffles with matcha, the highest-quality powdered green tea available.

Line a plate or baking dish with baking paper.

Toss the chocolate in a mixing bowl with the cinnamon, vanilla and salt.

Bring the coconut cream and coconut oil to a slow simmer in a saucepan over medium heat. Pour the hot coconut cream and oil over the chopped chocolate, then stir continuously with a wooden spoon until the chocolate is thoroughly melted and the mixture becomes thick and gorgeously glossy.

Transfer the mixture to the lined plate or dish and refrigerate for 8 hours (or overnight) to harden.

Peel away the baking paper and chop, spoon or cut into irregular-shaped chunks. Toss the chunks with the matcha green tea powder until they are completely coated. Refrigerate until ready to serve. Serve with some fresh berries; the sharpness of fresh blackberries makes a divine combination.

Lemon delicious pudding

Serves 6

4 large free-range eggs, separated
200g sugar
30g butter, melted
40g self-raising flour
grated zest of 2 lemons
½ cup lemon juice
1½ cups full cream milk

In 2012, Dunedin food writer and crockpot cookbook doyenne Joan Bishop had just published *A Southern Woman's Kitchen*, a treasury of her favourite recipes for family and friends, when she shared this recipe for an absolutely delicious traditional dessert on *Nine to Noon*. With the assistance of renowned food historian Helen Leach, she tracked this heritage recipe back to its first publication in the North East Valley Presbyterian Church recipe book *Dainty Recipes* in 1930. Best served at room temperature, it will serve six.

Preheat the oven to 170°C. Lightly butter the sides and base of a deep 7-cup-capacity ovenproof dish.

Beat the egg yolks, sugar and melted butter together until thick and creamy. Stir in the flour, lemon zest and lemon juice. Mix in the milk.

In another bowl, beat the egg whites until they form stiff peaks. With a large metal spoon carefully fold the egg whites into the lemon mixture.

Pour into the prepared dish and place in a shallow pan containing 2cm of hot water. Bake for 50–60 minutes until firm on top and golden brown.

Serve warm or at room temperature as is or with cream or lightly sweetened yoghurt.

Fiji coconut pie

Serves 6

4 free-range eggs
2 cups full-cream milk
1 cup sugar
1 cup desiccated coconut (freshly grated or store-bought, and lightly toasted if you like)
½ cup melted butter
½ cup plain flour
2 teaspoons vanilla extract

Melbourne-born Lynette Mercer arrived in Fiji with her missionary parents in 1941 and as an adult went on to run the famous Plantation Island resort. In 2016 she published a memoir, interwoven with recipes, among them this delicious dessert which she shared with *Nine to Noon* listeners.

Preheat the oven to 170°C. Grease a 6-cup-capacity deep ovenproof dish.

In a medium-sized bowl, whisk all the ingredients together until the sugar has dissolved. Pour the mixture into the prepared dish. Place in the oven and bake for about 40 minutes.

I use my finger to gently press the centre to see if it has set. The flour and butter will have gone to the bottom, forming a lovely soft base, while the eggs, vanilla and milk form the centre custard and the coconut will rise to form the topping.

Serve hot or cold with ice cream or whipped cream, or you could sprinkle with caramelised grated coconut and raw sugar.

Queen of puddings

Serves 4

- 1½ cups breadcrumbs, made from slightly stale white bread
- 2 tablespoons caster sugar, plus 115g (¾ cup) for the meringue
- 15g unsalted butter, plus extra for greasing the dish
- 2 cups milk
- 2 free-range eggs, separated
- ½ teaspoon vanilla extract, or a pinch of ground mixed spice or cinnamon
- 2 tablespoons raspberry jam or more, to taste

Several food writers have offered their version of this classic dessert on RNZ over the years. In 2005 the then Timara Lodge chef Jeremy Jones told *Nine to Noon* how he likes to make it.

Preheat the oven to 170°C. Lightly grease a 1 litre baking dish.

Place the breadcrumbs in the base of the dish. Gently heat the 2 tablespoons sugar, butter and milk in a small saucepan. Lightly whisk the egg yolks using a fork, then whisk into the milk mixture along with the vanilla or spice. Pour over the breadcrumbs, stir to combine and leave to stand for 15 minutes for the breadcrumbs to begin to absorb the liquid.

Carefully sit the pudding in its dish in a larger roasting dish (to make a water bath). Fill the roasting dish halfway with hot water. Put in the oven and bake for 20–25 minutes until just set. Remove from the oven and carefully remove the pudding from the roasting dish.

Spread the jam on top of the pudding. The heat from the pudding should melt the jam so it spreads well.

Reduce the oven temperature to 150°C.

Whisk the egg whites using an electric hand whisk until stiff peaks form. Gradually whisk in the 115g sugar until the meringue is stiff and glossy. Dollop or pipe on top of the pudding. Return to the oven (not in the roasting dish) and bake until the meringue is pale golden and crisp, 15–20 minutes. Serve warm.

Rose-geranium-stewed blueberries with creamed rice pudding

Serves 4

200g fresh or frozen blueberries
1 cup caster sugar
1 leaf and stalk of rose geranium
75g (⅓ cup) arborio rice
1 litre water
seeds of ½ vanilla bean
2 cups milk
1 gold-strength gelatine leaf, softened in cold water, then squeezed to remove excess water
2 cups cream

The Melbourne chef Matt Wilkinson had just published the winsomely titled *Mr Wilkinson's Favourite Vegetables* in 2012, and as part of the book's publicity round he appeared on *Nine to Noon* to share this take on an enduring comfort-food dessert.

Place the blueberries, ½ cup caster sugar and rose geranium in a medium-sized saucepan and place over medium heat. Gently cook for 14–18 minutes or until the blueberries start to break, then remove from the heat. Remove the rose geranium leaf and stalk, cool, then refrigerate until needed.

For the rice pudding, place the rice and water in a medium-sized saucepan and bring to the boil, then remove from the heat and strain. Put the rice back into the saucepan and add the vanilla seeds and milk. Place the saucepan over medium heat and cook, stirring occasionally, for 15–20 minutes or until the rice is fully cooked or all the liquid has been absorbed. Remove from the heat and stir in the remaining ½ cup sugar and the gelatine until dissolved. Spread over a tray or shallow baking dish and refrigerate until set.

Once set, lightly whip the cream until soft peaks form then, using a spatula, fold the cream through the rice. Pour into a serving dish and return to the fridge to firm up, about 30 minutes.

To serve, remove the rice pudding from the fridge and spoon over the blueberries with their juice.

Poke

Serves 6, generously

- 6 large, very ripe bananas
- 2 cups arrowroot, plus 1 teaspoon to thicken the coconut cream
- 400ml can coconut cream (or more to your taste)

Maine Andrew shared this family recipe with Emile Donovan on the summer show *The Weekend* in 2019. Cook Island-born, she hosts a Cook Islands health show on the Auckland radio station Planet FM.

Preheat the oven to 180°C. Grease a 23cm cake tin or a small roasting dish.

Peel and slice the bananas. Place in a saucepan with ¼ cup water. Cook on a low heat until the bananas are very pink. Remove from the heat and allow to cool, then mash (without draining) until very smooth. You should have 4 large cups of cooked banana.

Place the cooked banana and arrowroot in a mixing bowl and mix well to combine. Place in the tin or roasting dish and sprinkle 1 tablespoon water over the mixture. Place in the oven and bake for 1½ hours, until a thin crust forms on the top and the poke is firm to the touch. The cooked poke should be a very dark purple.

Meanwhile, mix 1 teaspoon arrowroot with 1 tablespoon water. Gently warm the coconut cream and add the arrowroot mixture to thicken it a little more, then remove from the heat.

Remove the poke from the oven and leave to cool before scooping out with a spoon or cutting into squares. As you transfer the poke to a serving bowl, top with a layer of the coconut cream. Cover with the remaining coconut cream and serve.

Tip — If the bananas are not very ripe, you may like to add some sugar in with the cooked banana and arrowroot, about ¾ cup.

Nanna Napier's Christmas pudding

Serves up to 12

butter for greasing the bowl
225g raisins
110g sultanas
110g mixed peel
180g shredded suet
1 teaspoon mixed spice
2 tablespoons plain flour
2 teaspoons vanilla extract
1 teaspoon almond essence
finely grated zest of 1 lemon
225g demerara sugar
225g fresh fine breadcrumbs
4 free-range eggs
2 tablespoons milk
120ml brandy

In December 2009 Geoff Scott, then at the helm of famous Auckland restaurant Vinnies, shared this family recipe for the classic Christmas dessert.

Thoroughly grease a standard pudding bowl. Cut out rounds of baking paper and foil larger than the bowl to make a lid.

Bring a large saucepan of water to boil. There should be enough water in the saucepan to come three-quarters of the way up the pudding bowl. Place an upturned saucer or trivet in the bottom of the saucepan for the bowl to sit on. This prevents the bowl cracking.

In a mixing bowl, dredge the fruit, peel, shredded suet and spice in the flour, then add the vanilla extract, almond essence and lemon zest. Mix in the sugar and breadcrumbs.

In another bowl, beat the eggs then add the milk and brandy. Add to the dry ingredients and mix thoroughly.

Press the mixture into the greased bowl. Cover with the paper and foil lid and tie down with kitchen string. Place in the saucepan of boiling water and gently boil for 6 hours. Check the water level from time to time and top up if necessary. The longer you cook the pudding, the darker it becomes.

Serve with custard or brandy sauce.

Whiskey and date steamed pudding

Makes 6

- 1 cup pitted dates, stones removed
- ½ cup dark chocolate pieces
- ½ cup water
- ½ cup orange juice
- 1 teaspoon baking soda
- 40ml whiskey
- 1 cup plain flour
- ½ teaspoon baking powder
- ¼ teaspoon salt or a good pinch
- ½ teaspoon ground cinnamon
- ½ teaspoon ground nutmeg
- 50g butter, softened
- ½ cup caster sugar
- 2 free-range eggs
- 5 sun-dried Turkish figs, roughly chopped

Dariush Lolaiy, of venerable Auckland game restaurant Cazador, discussed this recipe with Jesse Mulligan on *Afternoons* in 2016, the year the restaurant published its award-winning cookbook.

Lightly grease 6 1-cup-capacity pudding moulds or ovenproof ramekins.

Chop the dates and simmer in a pan with the chocolate, water and orange juice for 2 minutes, stirring constantly. Remove from the heat and leave to sit for 5 minutes. Stir in the baking soda and whiskey. Set aside for 20 minutes.

Preheat the oven to 180°C.

Sift the flour, baking powder, salt, cinnamon and nutmeg into a bowl. In another bowl, beat the butter and sugar until light and fluffy. Beat in the eggs one by one. Add the flour mixture to the butter mixture in 3 batches, folding together until just combined. Add the date mixture and fold through along with the figs.

Pour the batter into the moulds. Sit the moulds in a bain-marie with enough hot water to reach halfway up the moulds. Cover the bain-marie with a baking paper and foil lid and carefully place in the oven. Or you could cover the puddings individually.

Bake for 40 minutes, until the tops have risen and are slightly firm and sponge-like to the touch. Remove from the oven and carefully remove the puddings from the bain-marie to prevent them cooking further.

Rhubarb tart

Serves 6–8

Filling
500g rhubarb, sliced into 2cm lengths
175g sugar
2 free-range eggs
50g plain flour
grated zest of 1 orange
150ml cream

Pastry
200g plain flour
pinch of salt
100g butter, diced
3 tablespoons cold water

Glaze
2 tablespoons redcurrant jelly
1 tablespoon water

Jeremy Jones explained how to make this elegant and gorgeous looking dessert on *Nine to Noon* in 2003. The fresher the rhubarb the better, and letting a few pieces protrude above the custard mix adds to the visual appeal. Making the pastry is easy, and Jeremy notes that this dessert tastes just as good, if not better, cold. A couple of days in the fridge gives the flavours a chance to meld.

Place the rhubarb in a bowl, sprinkle with half the sugar and leave, covered, overnight.

To make the pastry, sift the flour and salt into a bowl. Rub the butter into the flour, or alternatively place these ingredients into a food processor and blitz, adding a little water as necessary to bring the mixture together. On a floured surface, form the pastry into a thick disc, wrap and place in the fridge for at least an hour or until ready to use (it can remain in the fridge overnight).

Preheat the oven to 200°C. Roll out the dough on a floured surface and line a greased 22cm non-stick tart tin. Gently fit the pastry to the tin, prick the base lightly with a fork and bake blind for about 10 minutes, until the pastry has formed a light crust.

To make the filling, mix together the eggs, the remaining sugar and any sweet rhubarb juice. Add the flour and orange zest and then stir in the cream.

Place the rhubarb in the pastry case and cover with filling. Return to the oven for 30 minutes or until the custard is cooked through and the rhubarb is soft.

To make the glaze, melt the jelly with the water and brush over the baked tart. Alternatively, sprinkle with icing sugar just before serving. The tart can be served warm or cold.

Rustic tamarillo galette

Serves 6

Pastry

- 250g plain flour, plus extra for sprinkling
- 125g cold butter, finely diced
- pinch of salt
- 1 free-range egg
- 1 tablespoon chilled water

Galette

- 6 tamarillos, stalks and skins removed
- 2 Granny Smith apples, peeled, cut and cored
- 1 teaspoon vanilla extract
- 1 tablespoon caster sugar
- 1 free-range egg yolk, beaten, to brush pastry

This easy dessert is from Auckland cookbook writer (*My Underground Kitchen*, *My Underground Deli*, and *My Underground Everyday*) and foodstore owner Jess Daniell, and was broadcast on *Afternoons* in 2021.

Process the flour, butter and salt in a food processor until the mixture resembles breadcrumbs.

Whisk the egg and chilled water in a small bowl and then, with the food processor running, slowly add the whisked egg and water to the flour mixture. Keep processing until the mixture begins to form large clumps, but stop before it forms a solid ball.

Turn the pastry out onto a clean workbench and gently knead to bring it together. Make a ball, then wrap and refrigerate for at least an hour, or overnight, until needed.

Slice the tamarillos and apples into thin, even wedges and place in a bowl. Add the vanilla extract and sprinkle with sugar, then set aside.

Preheat the oven to 180°C. Line an oven tray with baking paper.

Remove the pastry from the fridge, sprinkle a little flour on your benchtop and roll the pastry out into a rustic circle shape, about 3–4mm thick, then transfer to your lined baking tray.

Starting from the middle, alternately layer the tamarillo and apple slices in a circle, leaving a 10cm border of pastry around the edge. When all of the fruit has been used, fold the sides of the pastry up and over, crimping the overlaps as you go, until you have a fully edged galette. Brush the pastry with the egg wash.

Bake the galette for 25–30 minutes, until the pastry is crisp and golden. Let the galette cool for 10–15 minutes before slicing. Serve with plain unsweetened Greek-style yoghurt or whipped cream.

Maple panna cotta with rhubarb and strawberry compote

Serves 10

Maple panna cotta
750ml cream
250ml milk
1 cup maple syrup
3½ gelatine leaves

Rhubarb and strawberry compote
6 sticks rhubarb, diced
½ cup caster sugar
1 large punnet strawberries, hulled and diced
½ lemon

Vanilla tuiles
4 free-range egg whites
1 cup caster sugar
1 cup plain flour
180g butter, melted
½ teaspoon vanilla extract

Legendary restaurant owner Al Brown showed listeners how to marry these distinct ingredients on *Afternoons* in 2007.

To make the maple panna cotta, pour the cream, milk and maple syrup into a saucepan and place over a medium heat. Bring just up to the boil then lower the heat and simmer for about 10 minutes. Remove from the heat and set aside while you soak the gelatine leaves.

Place the gelatine leaves in a flat, shallow dish and cover completely with cold water ensuring that the leaves do not stick together. Soak for 4–6 minutes until the leaves have softened completely, no longer as this diminishes the setting properties of gelatine. Remove from the water and squeeze out any excess moisture. Add to the still hot but not too hot cream mixture and whisk until dissolved.

Pass through a fine sieve before pouring into 10 individual panna cotta moulds (or dariole moulds or ramekins). Cover and place in the fridge to set overnight.

To make the rhubarb and strawberry compote, place the rhubarb and the sugar in a saucepan and place over a low heat. Cook for 7–8 minutes or until the rhubarb is about half cooked, stirring occasionally. Add the diced strawberries and cook for a further 2 minutes. Remove from the heat and strain off the excess liquid. Let the compote cool then season just slightly with a squeeze of lemon juice.

To make the vanilla tuiles, whisk together the egg whites and sugar, add the flour and beat well. Carefully add the melted butter and fold through. Add the vanilla extract and fold through. Let the batter rest in the fridge for at least 2 hours before using, or preferably overnight.

Preheat the oven to 180°C. Line a baking tray with baking paper. Drop a spoonful of the mixture onto the baking paper and flatten with the back of a spoon into a rough circle, about 8–10cm in diameter. Repeat so you have 4 circles of mixture. Place in the oven and cook for 5–6 minutes, or until a pale golden-brown colour. Remove from the oven and lift off the baking tray. Mould straightaway over a muffin cup, ramekin or glass to make a basket shape. Leave them to cool, then store in an airtight container. Repeat with the remaining mixture. Only cook a few at a time so you can easily remove from the baking tray and mould before they firm up.

To serve, dip the panna cotta moulds in a cup of hot water for 3–5 seconds. Run a paring knife just around the top edge of the mould. Place each mould upside down on a plate and lift to release the panna cotta from its mould. Place a tuile case alongside the panna cotta and fill with the compote. Garnish with a mint tip if you feel it needs it! Serve immediately.

Baked kūmara cheesecake

Serves 8–10

400g kūmara
200g plain sweet biscuits, such as wine or plain digestive biscuits
120g butter, melted
150g caster sugar
250g cream cheese, at room temperature
finely grated zest and juice of 1 lemon
3 free-range eggs
icing sugar for dusting
whipped cream to serve

Pete Peeti's local take on pumpkin pie was detailed on *Nine to Noon* in 2010.

Peel the kūmara and cut into even-sized pieces. Boil or steam until soft, then drain well and leave to cool.

Preheat the oven to 180°C. Lightly grease a 20cm round cake tin and line with baking paper.

To make the base, place the biscuits in the bowl of a food processor and process until finely crushed. Add the butter and process until well combined. Transfer to the cake tin and use the back of a spoon to spread evenly over the base, pressing it gently into the tin. Place in the fridge until required.

Place the cooled kūmara in the cleaned bowl of the food processor and process until smooth. Add the caster sugar, cream cheese, lemon zest and juice and process. When smooth, add the eggs one at a time, processing until combined.

Remove the tin from the fridge, pour in the filling and smooth the top. Place in the oven and bake for 30–40 minutes or until the top is golden and the filling is just set.

Remove from the oven, sit the tin on a wire rack and leave the cheesecake to cool completely before removing from the tin.

To serve, dust with icing sugar and serve with freshly whipped cream.

Dark chocolate, prune and hazelnut torte

Serves 8

300g good-quality dark chocolate, melted
1 cup unsalted butter or coconut oil, softened
¾ cup coconut, rapadura or muscovado sugar
½ cup hazelnut meal (or any type of ground nuts)
1 cup prunes, stones removed
2 teaspoons vanilla extract
6 free-range eggs
pinch of sea salt
icing sugar for dusting
fresh fruit to garnish

Eleanor Ozich, who at that stage had three cookbooks featuring her trademark healthy and rustic yet stylish approach under her belt, discussed this recipe on *Nine to Noon* in the summer of 2018.

Preheat the oven to 170°C. Grease a 23cm cake tin with butter or coconut oil.

Put all the ingredients in the bowl of a food processor and blend until smooth. Tip the mixture into the prepared cake tin and use a spatula to smooth out evenly.

Place in the oven and bake for 20–25 minutes or until a skewer inserted in the middle comes out clean. It can burn easily, so be sure to keep an eye on it. Remove from the oven and leave to cool in the tin.

Once cooled, carefully remove from the tin. If serving immediately, dust with icing sugar and garnish with fresh fruit of your choice.

This will keep in an airtight container for up to 5 days.

Tarte Bourdaloue

Serves 8–10

Short pastry

250g plain flour
125g butter, cut into small dice
25g caster sugar
pinch of salt
1 egg yolk
50ml water

Pears

1 litre water
300g caster sugar
½ lemon
3 firm, ripe cooking pears
40g flaked almonds for topping

Almond cream

100g butter, softened
100g caster sugar
100g ground almonds
2 free-range eggs
1 teaspoon vanilla paste or extract
10g plain flour

This recipe for a pear tart by Florence Jeanblanc-Risler, the French ambassador in Wellington between 2015 and 2017, was broadcast on *Nine to Noon* in 2015, when she was newly appointed to the post. She was often on the radio talking about food during her term.

To make the short pastry, place the flour, butter, sugar and salt in a large bowl. Work together using your hands until the butter is completely mixed with the flour.

Add the egg yolk and water and work until you have a ball of dough. Don't work the pastry too much at this stage, or it will become elastic and chewy. Wrap the dough and let it rest for 20–30 minutes in the fridge.

To prepare the pears, place the water, sugar and lemon in a saucepan and bring up to the boil, then reduce the heat to more of a simmer. Peel the pears, cut in half and remove each core. Add the pears to the sugar syrup and poach for 15–20 minutes until translucent and tender. Remove the pears with a slotted spoon to a large plate and leave to cool.

Preheat the oven to 180°C.

Remove the pastry from the fridge. Roll out thinly to fit a 26cm fluted tart tin, easing it into the corners and trimming away any excess pastry.

Sit the tin on a baking tray. Lightly prick the base of the pastry with a fork, then line the pastry case with crumpled baking paper and fill with baking beans or rice. Return to the fridge to firm up for about 30 minutes, then place in the oven and bake blind for about 20 minutes.

Remove from the oven and carefully remove the beans or rice and paper. Return to the oven for about 5 minutes to bake the pastry a little further. Remove and leave to cool.

To make the almond cream, beat the butter and sugar together until pale. Add the ground almonds and the eggs, one at a time, beating well between each addition. Add the vanilla and beat in. Fold in the flour.

Fill the pastry case with the almond cream, topping with the pears pressed gently into the cream. Top with the flaked almonds. Bake for 35–40 minutes or until the pastry is crisp and golden and the almond cream feels firm to the touch.

Galaktoboureko

Makes 12 pieces

Filling and topping
2 cups milk
½ small vanilla bean, split
½ cup caster sugar
¼ cup fine semolina
2 free-range eggs
30g unsalted butter
½ cup whole blanched almonds
1 tablespoon icing sugar
¼ teaspoon ground cinnamon

To assemble
6 × 30cm sheets filo pastry
125g unsalted butter, melted

Lemon sugar syrup
2 cups sugar
1 cup water
finely grated zest of 1 lemon
1 stick cinnamon

Time for dessert! From award-winning Wellington chef Jacob Brown of Miramar restaurant The Larder, this messy but delicious traditional Greek custard pie has layers of golden-brown crispy filo, sprinkled with melted butter, filled with semolina and bathed in lemon-scented syrup. Brown explained how to make it on *Afternoons* in 2015.

Preheat the oven to 165°C. Butter a fairly deep 12cm × 15cm ceramic or Pyrex baking dish.

Combine the milk, vanilla bean and half of the sugar in a saucepan and bring to the boil. Sprinkle the semolina into the hot milk and return to the boil, stirring constantly. Once it has come to the boil, remove from the heat and stir for 30 seconds as the semolina thickens. Remove the vanilla bean.

In a large bowl, whisk together the eggs and remaining sugar. Pour the semolina mixture into the eggs, stirring constantly. Add the butter and stir until combined.

Pour into the baking dish. Cover with a lid or tray to prevent a skin forming on the custard, making sure the baking dish is deep enough for the custard not to touch the lid when it puffs up. Bake for 30–40 minutes, or until a thin skewer comes out clean. Remove from the oven, allow to cool a little, then refrigerate until cold.

Reduce the oven temperature to 150°C. Toast the almonds on a baking tray in the oven until golden and smelling toasted — keep an eye on them. Set aside to cool, then chop finely and mix with the icing sugar and cinnamon.

When the custard is cold, turn it out of the dish and cut it into 6 large fingers. Brush the filo pastry very generously with melted butter and sprinkle over two-thirds of the almond mixture. Place a finger of custard at one end of each sheet and roll the pastry to form a pastry tube with a custard centre. Brush the tubes liberally with butter, sprinkle over the remaining almond mixture and refrigerate until cold.

To make the lemon sugar syrup, combine all the ingredients in a small saucepan, bring to the boil, then remove from the heat and keep warm.

Preheat the oven to 200°C. Bake the pastry tubes for 10–20 minutes, or until golden brown. Remove from the oven and place straight into the warm lemon sugar syrup for 30 seconds, or pour the syrup over them. Cut each tube in half diagonally and serve immediately.

Lemon cream cake and summer berries

Serves 6–8

Lemon cream
500ml cream
finely grated zest and juice of 2 lemons
100g caster sugar
1 free-range egg, plus 3 egg yolks
20g plain flour

Lemon cake
270g plain flour
1 teaspoon baking powder
5 free-range eggs
375g sugar
150ml cream
finely grated zest of 3 lemons
pinch of salt
100g butter, melted

Summer berries
1 punnet strawberries, hulled (halved if large)
150g raspberries
150g blueberries
150g redcurrants
pinch of caster sugar
a few mint leaves

Paul Bocuse-trained French chef Philippe Mouchel opened the fancy French restaurant The Brasserie by Philippe Mouchel at Melbourne's luxurious Crown Casino complex in 2005 but had left to open his own restaurant, PM24, in Collins Street, just three months before he appeared on *Nine to Noon* in 2010 to talk about his new book *More than French: Recipes and stories*.

To make the lemon cream, bring the cream to the boil, add the lemon zest and leave to infuse for 30 minutes.

Beat together the sugar, egg and egg yolks until very pale. Add the flour and lemon juice and beat again. Strain the infused cream into the mixture and stir well.

Transfer to a saucepan. Over low heat, bring the mixture just to the boil, whisking constantly. Pour into a serving bowl to cool, then cover and refrigerate. Set aside until ready to serve.

For the lemon cake, preheat the oven to 160°C. Butter and flour a 24cm long × 8cm wide × 12cm deep tin.

Sift together the flour and baking powder into a bowl and set aside.

In a large bowl mix together the eggs, sugar and cream. Add the lemon zest, then the sifted flour and the salt, followed by the melted butter.

Pour the mixture into the prepared tin. Place in the oven and bake for about an hour, or until a skewer inserted into the centre comes out clean. Place the cake on a rack to cool, then remove from the tin. Set aside.

Just before serving, mix together the strawberries, raspberries, blueberries and redcurrants and sprinkle with caster sugar.

To serve, arrange the fruit on the top of the lemon cream and place mint leaves on top. Serve the lemon cake on the side, sliced into fingers. Alternatively, spoon the lemon cream on to individual plates. Arrange the fruit on the top and then place a mint leaf on top. Slice the lemon cake and place alongside the lemon cream and fruit.

Tip — You could grill the lemon cake slices, offering a contrast in temperature against the cold cream. To provide an additional element, lemon sorbet can be added. Redcurrants have a short season during summer. If they are not available, add extra blueberries or raspberries.

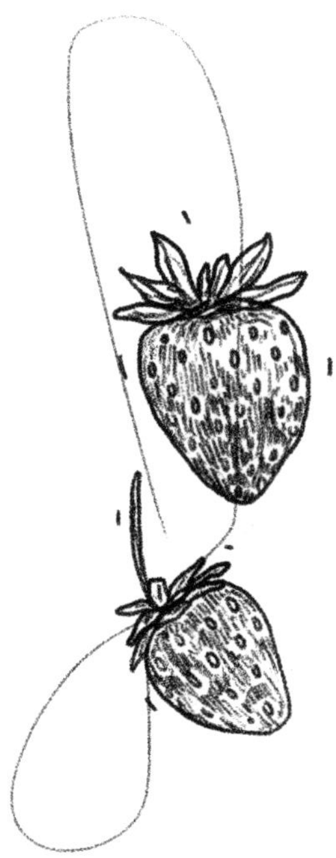

Argentinian crème caramel

Serves 12

Flan de leche
230g raw sugar
6 free-range eggs
½ teaspoon vanilla extract
500ml milk

Orange and mint salad
4 oranges, peeled and segmented (squeeze the juice from the leftover orange flesh into a small bowl and reserve)
60ml extra virgin olive oil
24 fresh mint leaves, finely sliced

Sean Connolly was cooking up a storm as the inaugural chef at SkyCity restaurant The Grill when he shared this recipe on *Nine to Noon* in 2011.

Preheat the oven to 140°C.

Measure 140g of the raw sugar and place in a medium-sized heavy-based saucepan over medium heat. Stir continuously until it has melted and turns to a rich caramel. Remove from the heat before it burns and becomes bitter.

Pour the caramel into a 20cm-diameter flan tin. Carefully tip the flan tin so that the base and sides of the tin are evenly coated in caramel, then set aside to allow the caramel to set.

Place the eggs and the remaining sugar in a mixing bowl and whisk lightly to combine. Add the vanilla and milk and continue to whisk lightly until all the ingredients are thoroughly combined.

Pour the egg mixture into the flan tin, over the caramel.

Boil a kettle of water. Place the flan tin in a deep-sided baking tray. Into the baking tray pour enough boiling water to come two-thirds of the way up the sides of the flan tin. Place in the oven and bake for 45–50 minutes or until the flan is just set. (Top up with boiling water during the cooking process if required.)

Carefully remove the tray from the oven and allow the flan to cool to room temperature. Carefully remove the flan from the baking tray. Cover and place in the fridge to allow to firm up.

Remove the flan tin from the fridge, place a suitably sized plate on top of the tin, invert and carefully remove the tin from the crème caramel.

For the salad, gently combine the orange segments, a little of the orange juice and the olive oil in a mixing bowl. Add the mint and fold through until thoroughly combined.

To serve, cut the flan into 12 slices, place a slice of the flan on a plate and a portion of the orange and mint salad to one side. Drizzle with excess caramel from the flan and serve immediately.

Roast stone fruit salad

Serves 6–8

6 nectarines
6 white peaches
6 apricots
6 tablespoons Demerara sugar
2 teaspoons ground cinnamon
½ cup sweet dessert-style white wine

Lauraine Jacobs offered this easy summer dessert recipe on *Nine to Noon* in 2012.

Preheat the oven to 180°C.

Cut the stone fruit into halves and remove the stones.

Mix the sugar and cinnamon together in a small bowl.

Place the stone fruit in a weighty shallow oven tray or large ovenproof dish skin-side down and sprinkle the spiced sugar over each half. Pop into the oven for about 10–15 minutes, until the sugar melts and the fruit is soft and warmed through.

Remove from the oven and spoon the fruit with its juices into a serving bowl. Drizzle over the wine and gently stir through.

Allow to cool slightly before serving with ice cream, whipped cream or a Greek-style yoghurt.

Tiramisu from Francesca's Italian Kitchen

Serves 10

7 free-range egg yolks
125g sugar
⅓ cup Marsala, plus 1 teaspoon
230g mascarpone, at room temperature
1 cup cream
1 cup hot espresso coffee
30g dark chocolate, chopped
1 teaspoon vanilla extract
4 tablespoons coffee liqueur, such as Kahlúa
20 Savoiardi biscuits (Italian sponge fingers)
good-quality dark cocoa powder, such as Valrhona, for dusting

In September 2018, a couple of years after bringing their delicious cooking concepts from Wānaka to Christchurch, where they opened their second Italian Kitchen, Francesca Voza and James Stapley introduced listeners to this classic dessert on *Afternoons*.

Using a double boiler, heat the egg yolks, sugar and first measure of Marsala to 80°C, whisking all the time. Transfer to an electric mixer and whisk until the bowl is cool to the touch.

In a large bowl, whisk the mascarpone and cream together to form soft peaks. Gently fold this into the egg yolk mixture until just combined.

Mix the hot coffee, chocolate, vanilla extract, second measure of Marsala and coffee liqueur together in a bowl.

Soak each Savoiardi biscuit in the warm coffee mix for 5 seconds and set aside on a clean tea towel. The biscuits should not absorb too much coffee — they should still be crunchy.

Take 10 small glasses or bowls and place 2 Savoiardi biscuits in each, broken in half.

Layer the cream mixture on top.

Cover and refrigerate for at least 1 hour. Dust with the cocoa powder just before serving.

These will keep in the fridge for up to 3 days.

Lemon meringue rolled pavlova

Serves 6

6 free-range egg whites
2 cups caster sugar
1 teaspoon cornflour
1 teaspoon vanilla extract
1 teaspoon malt vinegar
½ cup flaked almonds
1 cup cream, whipped
lemon curd
icing sugar for dusting

Jo Seagar explained how to make this rolled pavlova on *Nine to Noon* in 2010, when she had just published her eighteenth cookbook, *It's Easier Than You Think*.

Preheat the oven to 150°C. Grease and line a 25cm × 35cm sponge-roll or slice tin.

Beat the egg whites in a large metal, china or glass bowl (not plastic) with an electric mixer until really foamy. Slowly, with the mixer still going, add the caster sugar a spoonful at a time until all the sugar has been incorporated and the meringue is thick and glossy white. Fold in the cornflour, vanilla and vinegar.

Spoon into the prepared tin, spreading to the edges, and sprinkle with the flaked almonds. Place in the oven and bake for 25 minutes.

Lay a sheet of baking paper on a flat surface and dust with icing sugar. Turn the pavlova out onto the baking paper, almond-side down. Remove the baking paper from the cooked pavlova and leave to cool completely.

When cold, spread with the whipped cream and dollop lemon curd on top. Using the baking paper to help you, roll up from the long side into a round log shape. Don't worry if the surface cracks. Transfer carefully to a serving platter or board, and dust again with icing sugar before slicing to serve.

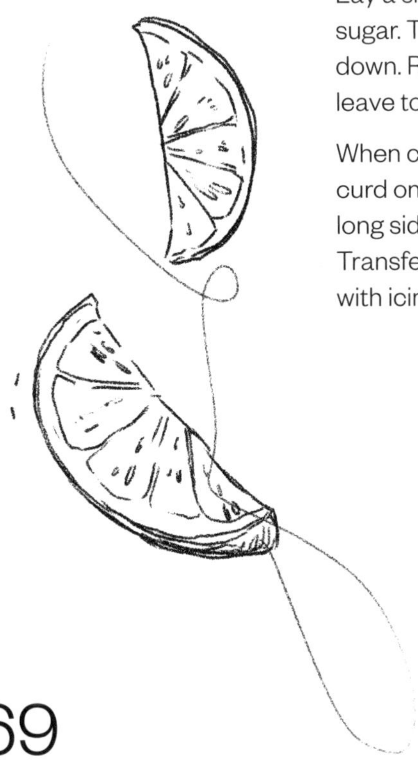

Apple cobbler

Serves 6

For the cobbler dough
2 cups plain flour
1 tablespoon baking powder
pinch of salt
¼ cup sugar
75g butter, cut into small cubes
1 cup cream
1 tablespoon sugar and ½ teaspoon ground cinnamon, for sprinkling

For the apples
2kg Cox's Orange Pippin apples
¾ cup sugar
3 tablespoons plain flour
1 vanilla bean, split

Al Brown explained how to make this classic dessert on *Nine to Noon* in 2010, the year his first cookbook, *Go Fish*, won People's Choice and Best Illustrated Book in the 2010 New Zealand Post Book Awards.

For the cobbler dough, sift the flour, baking powder and salt into a large mixing bowl. Add the sugar and butter to the bowl. Rub the butter into the flour until the mixture resembles coarse breadcrumbs. Using a light touch, stir in the cream to make a soft dough. Set aside to rest.

Preheat the oven to 200°C. Lightly grease a large ovenproof baking dish.

Peel, quarter and core the apples then cut each quarter into 3 slices, placing them into a large bowl as you slice. Add the sugar and flour, and scrape in the vanilla seeds from the split bean. Mix well to combine. Place the apple mixture into the baking dish.

Tear golf-ball-sized chunks of cobbler dough and place them on top of the apple mixture, pressing them down slightly. Leave some space between each ball.

Combine the sugar and cinnamon together and sprinkle over the cobbler.

Place the cobbler in the oven and bake for 45 minutes, or until the apples are tender and the top is golden and crisp.

Serve pronto with a scoop of vanilla ice cream or lashings of fresh runny cream.

15-minute summer tiramisu

Serves 4

250g punnet strawberries, hulled and chopped into 1cm cubes
1 tablespoon caster sugar
squeeze of lemon juice
half a glass or 75ml Prosecco or sparkling wine (for a non-alcoholic option use soda water and elderflower cordial or similar)
200ml cream
1 tablespoon icing sugar or maple syrup
4 tablespoons natural, unsweetened yoghurt
8 Italian sponge fingers (known as Savoiardi or ladyfingers, if store bought)

Nicola Galloway, author of *Homegrown Kitchen* and self-described lover of 'cooking with the seasons', gave *Afternoons* this recipe in 2020.

Combine the strawberry cubes, sugar, lemon juice and Prosecco or sparkling wine in a bowl, muddle around to macerate a little, then set aside.

Whip the cream and icing sugar or maple syrup until soft peaks form. Add the yoghurt and whip again until thick. Spoon half of the cream into 4 serving glasses.

Strain the strawberries in a sieve set over a bowl to collect the liquid. Break the sponge fingers in half and quickly dip into the liquid. Arrange 4 halves into each glass. Top with half of the strawberries followed by another layer of cream, and scatter with the remaining strawberries. Serve immediately or chill in the fridge for up to an hour.

Saturday Morning + Sunday Morning

RNZ's two weekend morning shows — hosted by Kim Hill (Saturday) and Jim Mora (Sunday) — serve up a crisp mix of news, interviews, discussion and recipes, and consistently rate among the highest in terms of listeners. They are the perfect audio to listen to as you prepare or eat brunch.

Pain perdu with warm strawberries

Serves 4

Pain perdu
4 eggs
200ml cream
1 teaspoon vanilla extract
1 tablespoon caster sugar
25g butter
1 tablespoon neutral-flavoured oil
4 thick slices brioche or sourdough bread

Warm strawberries
15g unsalted butter
50g caster sugar
250g strawberries, hulled and halved vertically
1 tablespoon lemon juice
1 teaspoon balsamic syrup or vinegar
1 teaspoon extra virgin olive oil
⅛ teaspoon freshly ground black pepper

Pain perdu, Ruth Pretty explained to *Summer Report* listeners in 2011, is what anglophones call French toast. Listeners may well have been a little envious when she added that she'd last enjoyed this brunch treat at the Champagne house of Laurent-Perrier. The following month Weltec awarded her an Honorary Bachelor in Hospitality Management for her significant contribution to the Wellington region and the wider New Zealand food and hospitality sectors.

Preheat the oven to 100°C. Put in a baking tray to warm.

Place the eggs, cream, vanilla and sugar in a large bowl and whisk to combine.

Heat a large frying pan over medium heat and add the butter and oil.

Put 2 brioche or sourdough slices into the egg mixture for about a minute, then turn the slices over so they soak up the egg mixture for another minute or until thoroughly soaked.

Remove and place in the hot frying pan. Cook for 2 minutes or until golden, then turn over and cook the other side.

Keep warm in the oven while you repeat with the remaining slices of brioche or sourdough.

For the warm strawberries, place the butter in a small heavy-based frying pan set over medium heat and melt. Add the sugar and stir well. Leave the sugar to cook for 2 minutes or until it begins to melt.

Add the strawberries and stir to coat in the butter and sugar. Do not break the strawberries. Cook for 2–3 minutes until the strawberries begin to bleed juice but are still firm to the touch.

Add the lemon juice, balsamic syrup or vinegar, oil and pepper. Gently stir to combine and cook for 1 minute or until the liquids are amalgamated.

Serve the warm strawberries and the pan juices spooned onto the pain perdu.

Tip — You could use milk or a combination of milk and cream; use honey rather than sugar; and add a little finely grated orange or lemon zest.

Salmon fishcakes with poached eggs and remoulade sauce

Serves 4

Remoulade sauce

2 free-range egg yolks
1 teaspoon Dijon mustard
1 teaspoon white wine vinegar
300ml vegetable oil
25g gherkins
25g capers
1 anchovy in oil, drained
1 teaspoon chopped chervil leaves
1 teaspoon chopped parsley leaves
1 teaspoon chopped tarragon leaves
salt and pepper

Salmon fishcakes

400g Agria potatoes, peeled and cut into even-sized pieces
1 tablespoon butter
1 free-range egg yolk
1 teaspoon chopped chervil leaves
1 teaspoon chopped chives
300g salmon fillet, skinless and boneless
salt and pepper

In 2011 Mark Harman, who was in the kitchen at swanky Dine by Peter Gordon, the then signature restaurant in the just-opened Sky City Grand Hotel, taught the *Nine to Noon* audience how to make this light yet filling brunch offering.

For the remoulade sauce, place the egg yolks, mustard and vinegar in a food processor and process for 10 seconds. With the motor running, slowly drizzle in the oil to form a creamy mayonnaise.

Finely chop the gherkins, capers and anchovy. Add to the mayonnaise base along with the chopped herbs. Season with salt and pepper to taste.

For the salmon fishcakes, preheat the oven to 180°C.

Boil the potatoes in lightly salted water until tender. Drain and dry off over the heat, then mash. Using a wooden spoon, beat in the butter and egg yolk. Set aside to cool.

In a large mixing bowl, combine the cooled potato mash and chopped herbs.

Finely chop one-third of the salmon until the consistency of a rough purée. Cut the remaining salmon into 1cm dice. Add the salmon to the potato mix. Mix together and season well with salt and pepper. Shape into 4 even balls, then flatten to a shape and size that a poached egg will sit comfortably on top of.

scant ½ cup plain flour
1 free-range egg, lightly beaten with 2 tablespoons water
1–1½ cups panko breadcrumbs
vegetable oil for pan-frying

To serve
a splash of white vinegar
4 very fresh free-range eggs
microgreens to garnish

Put the flour, egg and panko breadcrumbs in separate shallow bowls. Coat each fishcake in the flour, shaking off the excess. Dip into the egg mixture until well coated, allowing excess to drip off each fishcake. Put each fishcake into the panko breadcrumbs and gently pat down to coat all over.

Place the fishcakes on a tray as you coat and put them in the fridge while you heat the oil. Pour a generous amount of oil into a frying pan and place over medium heat. Once the oil is hot, add the fishcakes and pan-fry until golden on all sides. Transfer to a shallow baking tray and place in the oven to finish cooking for 10–12 minutes. You want your fishcakes to be hot in the middle.

Put a shallow, wide saucepan of water on the heat and bring to a simmer. Add a splash of white vinegar, then poach the eggs until the egg whites have set and the yolks are still runny. Remove the eggs with a slotted spoon and drain off any water on a folded cloth.

Serve the salmon cakes topped with a poached egg and a generous serve of remoulade sauce, and garnish with microgreens.

Spring breakfast spaghetti

Serves 4

250g dried spaghetti
1–2 bunches asparagus, chopped
3 slices sourdough bread, roughly chopped
1 small bunch flat-leaf parsley, chopped
finely grated zest of 1 lemon
4 tablespoons extra virgin olive oil
4 rashers rindless bacon, chopped
1½ tablespoons pine nuts
salt and freshly ground black pepper
juice of ½ lemon
4 very fresh free-range eggs

Nadia Lim told the *Afternoons* listeners about this unusual but easy take on a breakfast dish in 2012, the year she published her first cookbook after winning MasterChef the year before.

Cook the spaghetti in plenty of salted boiling water until al dente, about 10 minutes or according to packet cooking instructions.

With a few minutes of cooking time left for the spaghetti, add the asparagus to the pasta. Drain the spaghetti and asparagus, reserving 2 tablespoons of pasta water.

Put the bread chunks, parsley and lemon zest in a blender or food processor and blitz to a rough crumb.

Heat 2 tablespoons of the extra virgin olive oil in a frying pan and add the bacon. Fry for 3–4 minutes, then add the crumb and pine nuts. Pan-fry for 4–5 minutes or until the breadcrumbs and pine nuts are toasted. Season well with salt and pepper. Set aside.

Put the pan back on the heat and add the drained spaghetti, asparagus, reserved pasta water, remaining olive oil and the lemon juice, and toss together to warm everything through. Season with salt and pepper to taste.

Bring a medium-sized saucepan of water to a gentle boil, reduce to a simmer and carefully crack in the eggs. Poach until the whites are just set but the yolks are still runny.

Divide the spaghetti and asparagus between 4 bowls and top each with a poached egg. Sprinkle over the bacon crumb mixture. Serve immediately.

Veronique's savoury clafoutis

Serves 6

200g mixed vegetables, such as courgettes, capsicum, kūmara
25g butter
30g cornflour
30g plain flour
4 free-range eggs
200ml milk
200ml cream
salt, pepper and freshly grated nutmeg

When Lois Daish discussed this dish on *Afternoons* in 2008 she explained that it was from Veronique Sauzeau, the chef at the French Embassy in Wellington (she is now the proprioter of Le Marché Francais in Wellington). The absence of cheese makes it super light.

Preheat the oven to 210°C.

Prepare the vegetables. Top and tail the courgettes, seed and core the capsicum, peel the kūmara. Cut the vegetables into medium-thin slices.

Melt the butter in a large frying pan over low heat and add the kūmara slices. Cook for a few minutes, then add the courgettes and capsicum, and cook for a further few minutes until the vegetables have softened a little. Put the vegetables in a baking dish.

To make the batter, put the cornflour and flour in a large mixing bowl. Add the eggs and half the milk. Whisk until smooth, adding in the remaining milk and the cream. Season well with salt and pepper and a little nutmeg.

Pour the batter over the vegetables. The baking dish can be filled three-quarters full. Place in the oven and bake for about 40 minutes until puffy and golden brown. Serve hot or warm. (Cold leftovers are also tasty.)

Avocados and prawns with lime and tomato salsa

Serves 4

- 2 medium-sized vine-ripened tomatoes
- 4 tablespoons extra virgin avocado oil (or olive oil)
- 1 tablespoon lime juice
- 4 makrut lime leaves, finely shredded
- 1 spring onion, white and pale green part only, trimmed and finely chopped
- 1 fresh hot red chilli, halved, deseeded and finely chopped
- ½ teaspoon salt
- 12 medium green (raw) sea-caught Australian prawns
- ¼ teaspoon ground turmeric
- ¼ teaspoon ground cumin
- 2 ripe but firm avocados

Julie Biuso outlined this easy dish on *Afternoons* in 2010. Ripe avocados are essential, of course.

Plunge the tomatoes into a saucepan of gently boiling water for 10 seconds. Using a slotted spoon, transfer the tomatoes to a bowl of cold water and peel (if the tomatoes are hard to peel, return them to the boiling water for a few more seconds). Quarter the tomatoes, remove the cores and flick out the seeds. Dice the flesh finely.

In a bowl whisk together 3 tablespoons of the avocado or olive oil, the lime juice, lime leaves, spring onion, chilli and salt.

If the prawns are frozen, thaw them quickly in a sealed plastic bag immersed in a sink of cold water. Twist off their heads, then peel off the shells, leaving the small piece of shell on the tail intact. Using a small sharp knife, slit down the back of each prawn and gently extract the red or black vein. Rinse the prawns, then pat dry with paper towels.

Preheat a barbecue hotplate or ridged grill pan over medium heat.

Put the turmeric and cumin on a plate and roll the prawns in the spices. Halve the avocados, keeping the skin on, and extract the stones. Put the avocado halves on serving plates.

Oil the hotplate or grill pan using the remaining tablespoon of avocado or olive oil. Add the prawns and cook for a few minutes a side until they change colour.

Add the tomatoes to the salsa ingredients and spoon into the cavities of the avocados. Top with prawns. Serve immediately.

Pāua fritters with avocado and wasabi salsa

Makes 30–50, depending on size

Salsa

- 1 ripe but firm avocado, halved, stone removed and peeled
- juice of 1 large lime
- 1 tablespoon finely chopped red onion
- 2 tablespoons olive oil
- 2 teaspoons chopped coriander leaves
- 1½ teaspoons prepared wasabi
- 1 tablespoon sweet chilli sauce
- salt and pepper to taste

Fritters

- 1 cup plain flour
- 1 teaspoon baking powder
- 4 free-range eggs, lightly beaten
- 4 tablespoons milk
- 1kg pāua (shucked weight), minced
- ⅓ cup finely diced red onion
- 3 tablespoons chopped coriander
- 2 tablespoons sweet chilli sauce
- 2 tablespoons lime or lemon juice
- olive oil for frying

In 2007 Steve Logan and Al Brown, the co-founders of Wellington restaurant landmark Logan Brown, had just published a book and made a TV show that was the antithesis of the restaurant's fine-dining style: *Hunger for the Wild*. Discussing this on *Afternoons* gave Steve Logan a chance to discuss the book's freewheeling, living-off-the-land approach.

To make the salsa, cut the avocado into 1cm dice and place in a bowl with the lime juice, red onion, oil, coriander, wasabi and chilli sauce, and mix to combine. Season with salt and pepper. Extra wasabi can be added according to your taste.

To make the fritters, sift the flour and baking powder into a bowl and make a well in the centre. Pour in the eggs and milk and whisk until smooth. Add the minced pāua, red onion, chopped coriander, chilli sauce and lime or lemon juice and mix well. Season with salt and pepper.

Heat a non-stick frying pan or barbecue to medium hot. Add a little oil, then spoon out the fritter mix to the size you would like. Cook until golden on each side, then place on a platter. Consume this first batch with the salsa, then continue cooking fritters so you are eating them straight from the pan or barbecue.

Apple, spinach, fennel and feta crêpes

Serves 4

250g plain flour
2 free-range eggs
1½ cups milk
2 eating apples, coarsely grated
1 small fennel bulb, trimmed and very finely sliced (shaved)
good handful or 2 of baby spinach leaves, sliced
¼ cup feta, crumbled
2 tablespoons chopped fresh garden herbs, such as flat-leaf parsley, chives and mint
butter for greasing the pan

On *Summer Report* in 2012, Chris Fortune, who was then doing a lot of work teaching young people how to cook, declared that even a kid can cook these.

Sift the flour with a pinch of salt into a bowl and make a well in the centre. Place the eggs and milk in a jug and whisk together, then pour into the well in the flour and whisk until the mixture is smooth. Set aside for 20 minutes. If it is too thick, thin with a little extra milk.

To make the filling, place the apple, fennel, spinach, feta and herbs in a bowl and toss to combine. Season to taste with salt and pepper and set aside until needed.

Heat a crêpe pan to a medium-high heat. Lightly grease with butter, then pour in a ladleful of batter and swirl to cover the base in a thin layer. Cook for 1–2 minutes until little bubbles appear and the surface appears dry. Flip and cook for a further minute.

Lay out the crêpes on a benchtop and divide the filling between them. Roll the crêpes up into tight cylinders, then slice into rounds using a very sharp knife.

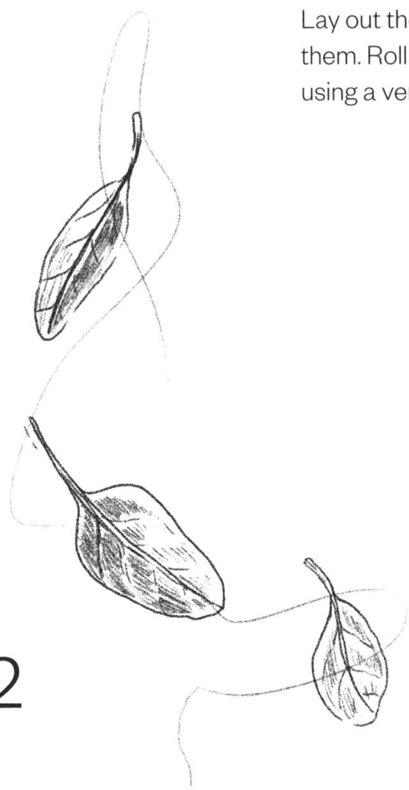

Tuna steak with porcini mushrooms

Serves 6

20g dried porcini mushrooms
2 tablespoons olive oil
½ onion, finely chopped
1 clove garlic
4 anchovies in oil, drained
50g button mushrooms, sliced
½ cup flat-leaf parsley leaves, chopped
1 glass white wine
juice of ½ lemon
salt and pepper to taste
6 × 200g tuna steaks
knob of butter

To serve
steamed fresh asparagus, or spinach wilted with a little garlic

Antonio Cacace, owner of Italian grocer-deli and café La Bella Italia in Petone, Wellington, explained how to make this rich brunch or lunch dish on *Nine to Noon* in 2014.

To make the sauce, soak the porcini mushrooms in hot water for 10 minutes. Then squeeze out the water, reserving this, and roughly chop the porcini.

Heat the oil in a pan over medium-low heat, Add the onion, garlic and anchovies and pan-fry until the onion softens. Add the button mushrooms, soaked porcini, parsley, white wine, lemon juice and enough of the reserved porcini soaking water to moisten. Stir well, then pan-fry until the sauce is reduced by half. Season with salt and pepper and set aside.

Season the tuna steaks and quickly pan-fry, ensuring they're still quite rare in the middle. Place them on a large plate. Reheat the sauce with a knob of butter to make it a bit thicker and shiny. Pour the sauce over the tuna, and serve with some garlic spinach or fresh asparagus.

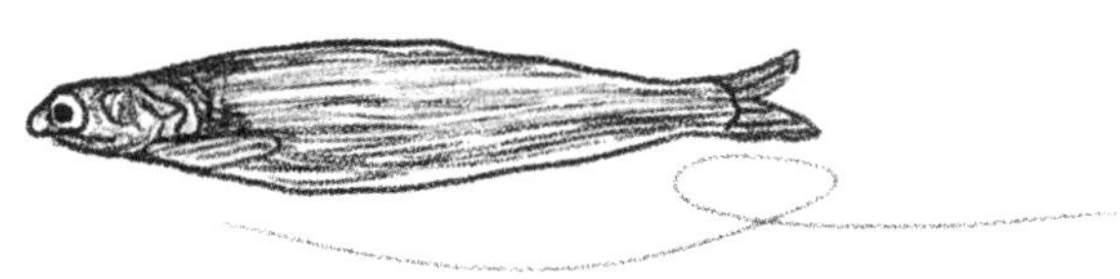

Pea, mint and halloumi fritters with tomato and capsicum sauce

Serves 4

Tomato and capsicum sauce
light smear of olive oil
1 red onion, roughly chopped
1 clove garlic, crushed
1 teaspoon ground cumin
2 red capsicums, deseeded and chopped
400g can chopped tomatoes
1 tablespoon balsamic vinegar

Fritters
½ cup trim milk
2 free-range eggs
½ cup self-raising flour
2 cups frozen peas, thawed
300g courgettes, coarsely grated
100g feta or halloumi, chopped
2 tablespoons fresh chives, chopped
2 tablespoons fresh mint leaves
1 teaspoon finely grated lemon zest
light smear of olive oil

Healthy Food Guide editor Niki Bezzant detailed this vegetarian dish on *Nine to Noon* in 2012, a dish that perfectly aligned with her magazine's mission.

To make the sauce, lightly smear a frying pan with oil and place over medium-high heat. Add the onion, garlic and cumin. Cook, stirring, for 3–4 minutes until the onion has softened. Add the capsicums and cook for 3–4 more minutes, then add the tomatoes and balsamic vinegar. Stir to combine and simmer, uncovered, over a low heat for about 10 minutes. Blend in a processor or blender until smooth.

To make the fritters, whisk together the milk and eggs in a large bowl. Gradually whisk in the flour to make a smooth batter. Stir through the peas, courgettes, cheese, herbs and lemon zest.

Lightly smear a large frying pan with oil and place over medium heat. Spoon ¼ cup of the mixture into the pan, making 3 fritters at a time. Cook for 3 minutes on each side or until golden and cooked through. Continue to make 12 fritters in total.

Serve the fritters with the sauce and a salad.

Chilli-grilled squid on rocket with lime and coriander mayonnaise

Serves 6

Marinade
1 teaspoon dried chilli flakes
2 tablespoons crushed garlic
2 tablespoons finely grated fresh ginger
1 tablespoon sugar
sea salt and freshly ground pepper
3 tablespoons vegetable oil
1kg squid tubes, cut open and scored on the inside

Dressing
1 free-range egg (plus 1 yolk)
finely grated zest and juice of 3 limes
2 handfuls of coriander leaves (2 cups), roughly chopped
1 cup vegetable oil
sea salt and freshly ground pepper
6 good handfuls of rocket leaves
few wedges of lime, to serve

Catherine Bell has been one of the most frequent food-writer guests on RNZ over the years. In 2005 she was on *Nine to Noon* to talk about this dish.

For the marinade, combine all the ingredients in a non-metallic bowl, cover and refrigerate for up to 24 hours.

For the dressing, place the egg and yolk, lime zest and juice and the coriander in a food processor and process until well blended. With the motor running, add the oil in a thin stream until all the oil is incorporated and the dressing is creamy. Season with salt and freshly ground pepper.

When ready to serve, heat a ridged grill or barbecue hotplate until hot. Place the squid on the grill, scored-side down, and hold flat with a spatula or fish slice.

After 1 minute, turn and repeat. When you remove them from the barbecue they will curl up. Slice diagonally into strips.

Arrange the rocket on a platter and lay the squid down the centre. Drizzle with the lime and coriander dressing and serve with lime wedges around the edge of the platter.

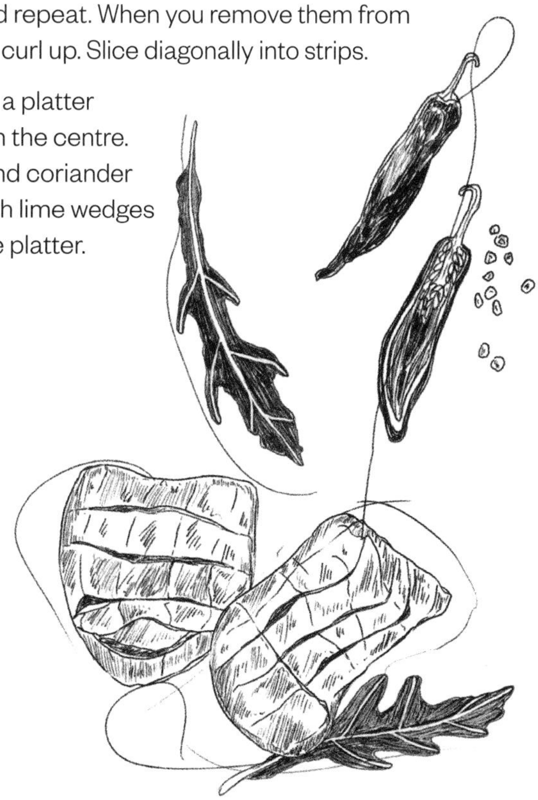

22/03

Essentials

It's the small things that count. We see this in the news, too. Moving a story around a bit is an important radio skill; updating it with splashes of new information or looking for that extra fresh colour to keep the main item essential. Small accompaniments, in other words, that work for you like a sous-chef.

Here's a quick glide across the radio band of tried-and-true accompaniments and base recipes.

Veal or chicken stock

Makes 4 litres

- 2kg veal, beef or chicken bones, rinsed well
- 2 tablespoons vegetable oil
- 2 onions, skin on, halved
- 1 bulb garlic, halved (optional)
- 2 carrots, peeled and chopped
- 2 leeks, chopped and washed well
- 2 stalks celery, chopped
- 2 tomatoes, halved
- 1 teaspoon black peppercorns
- small handful of parsley stalks
- 2 bay leaves
- few sprigs of thyme

Preheat the oven to 220°C.

Place the bones in a roasting dish and drizzle with the oil. Put them in the oven and roast for 20 minutes, then turn the bones and roast for a further 20–25 minutes until browned. Transfer the bones to an 8–10-litre stock pot.

Place the vegetables in the roasting dish and roast for 30 minutes until browned. Transfer the vegetables to the stock pot. Pour off and discard any oil from the roasting dish, then place on the stovetop and deglaze the dish with 1 cup of water, scraping up any caramelised bits. Pour the liquid into the stock pot. Add the remaining ingredients and enough cold water to cover everything.

Bring to the boil over a moderate heat, skimming off any impurities that rise to the surface. Once the stock has come to the boil, reduce to a moderate simmer (do not cover) and simmer for 4 hours for chicken stock or 8 hours for veal or beef, skimming occasionally. Note that the stock will reduce.

Remove from the heat, strain the stock and discard the solids. Allow the stock to settle and cool, then skim off any fat that has risen to the surface. At this point, the stock can be refrigerated for a few days or frozen.

Carl Koppenhagen

Chicken stock

Makes about 2.5 litres

2–3 chicken carcasses
1 onion, skin on and quartered
1 carrot, skin on and roughly chopped
2 stalks celery including leaves, roughly chopped
4 parsley stalks
1 bay leaf
6 whole black peppercorns
about 3 litres water
2 tablespoons apple cider vinegar or lemon juice

Combine all the ingredients in a large stock pot (or slow cooker), making sure all the bones and vegetables are completely submerged. Top up with extra water if needed. If time permits, cover and set aside for 30–60 minutes so that the vinegar can begin to soften the bones to draw out the minerals.

Place over a low heat and bring to a gentle simmer — not a rolling boil, as this can break down the gelatine and other gut-friendly components. (If using a slow-cooker, set it to low.) Skim off any foam that rises to the surface and cook for at least 3 hours on the stovetop (for flavoursome stock) and up to 24 hours for nutrient-rich bone broth (a slow cooker is useful for long cooking times). If the stock level drops below the bones, top up with boiling water to 2cm above the bones.

Remove from the heat (or switch off the slow cooker), and leave to cool completely. Scoop off the fat on the surface (this can be used as cooking fat, like ghee) and strain the stock through a fine sieve. Discard the chicken bones and vegetables.

Pour the stock into glass jars and store in the fridge for up to 5 days, or freeze in portioned containers (named and dated) and use within 6 months.

Nicola Galloway

Yoghurt and saffron marinade

Makes 2 cups

2 cups plain unsweetened Greek-style yoghurt
½ teaspoon saffron threads
1 tablespoon boiling water
1 onion, very finely chopped
2 cloves garlic
1 teaspoon salt
finely grated zest and juice of 2 lemons

Place the yoghurt in a bowl. Put the saffron threads in a small cup, pour over the boiling water and allow the saffron to soak for at least 10 minutes.

Make sure the onion is very finely chopped and add it to the yoghurt. Crush the garlic with the salt and add to the yoghurt with the lemon zest and juice, and the saffron and its soaking liquid. Whisk everything together.

Will keep in the refrigerator for 1–2 weeks. This marinade is superb on fish, chicken and lamb.

Lauraine Jacobs

Chimichurri marinade

Makes 2 cups

½ cup finely chopped parsley
½ cup finely chopped mint
½ cup finely chopped coriander
1 onion, finely chopped
4 cloves garlic, crushed
½ cup extra virgin olive oil
4 tablespoons white wine vinegar
1 teaspoon salt
½ teaspoon dried chilli flakes

Put all the ingredients in a screw-top jar and shake together really well. Store in the refrigerator, and use within a few days as the herbs tend to lose their fresh green appearance quickly.

Marinate beef, lamb or venison with the chimichurri, and you can also serve a little extra as a sauce to pour over the cooked meat.

Lauraine Jacobs

Teriyaki-style marinade

Makes about 1½ cups

finely grated zest and juice of 1 orange
3cm piece of fresh ginger, peeled and finely grated
1 clove garlic, crushed
½ cup soy sauce
¼ cup mirin
¼ cup sesame oil
¼ cup honey
½ teaspoon salt or to taste

Place all the ingredients in a bowl or clean screw-top jar, and whisk or shake well together. Store in the refrigerator for a week or two.

This is an excellent marinade for pork, chicken and all red meats, especially venison and beef. Take care not to cook meat with this marinade over a very hot flame or the high heat of a grill plate, as the honey will quickly burn the surface of the meat.

Lauraine Jacobs

Baba ganoush

Makes about 1½ cups

1 medium-sized eggplant
4 tablespoons olive oil
5 cloves garlic
2 tablespoons tahini
¼ cup yoghurt
salt and pepper

Set oven to 200°C.

Cut eggplant in half lengthways, sprinkle with a little salt and 2 tablespoons of the oil.

Add 4 cloves of garlic to the pan and cook in the oven for 20 minutes or until soft.Turn the eggplant halves once during cooking, so they finish cooking face down. Let cool.

Put the eggplant, skin and all, the roasted garlic, the one raw clove of garlic, the remaining oil, tahini and yoghurt into a food processor and whirr up.

Season with salt and pepper to taste.

Serve as a spread, or as a dip, or even to thicken sauces — it is especially good for thickening curries.

Richard Till

Pesto four ways

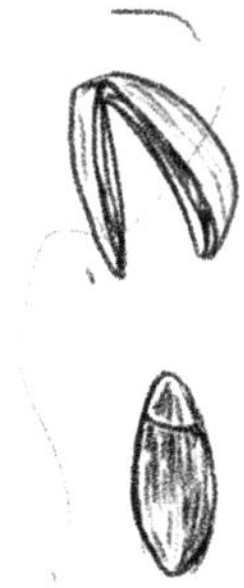

Makes about 1½–2 cups

Kale and walnut pesto
6 large kale leaves
½ cup (50g) walnuts
½ cup (60g) finely grated Parmesan
½ small clove garlic, finely diced
finely grated zest of 1 lemon
½ cup olive oil
salt and cracked black pepper

Pistachio, mint and basil pesto (dairy-free)
½ cup (70g) pistachio nuts
½ cup (15g) tightly packed fresh mint leaves
½ cup (15g) tightly packed fresh basil leaves
½ small clove garlic, finely diced
½ cup olive oil
salt and cracked black pepper

Parsley and cashew pesto
½ cup (70g) toasted cashew nuts
1 cup (25g) tightly packed fresh parsley leaves
8 capers
juice of 1 lemon
½ cup olive oil
¼ cup finely grated Parmesan
salt and cracked black pepper

Spring onion and coriander pesto
¾ cup fresh coriander leaves
1 spring onion, green part only, finely sliced
1 clove garlic, finely diced
juice of 1 lemon
¼ cup toasted pine nuts
½ cup olive oil
sea salt and cracked black pepper

For the kale and walnut pesto, blanch the kale leaves for 1 minute in boiling water before plunging into icy-cold water to halt the cooking and help retain the bright colour. Squeeze tightly to remove as much water as possible. You can then add to the food processor.

For all the recipes, simply place all the pesto ingredients in the food processor and blitz until the desired consistency. Be sure to season generously, as this really helps the pesto to shine.

Kelly Gibney

Walnut pesto

Makes about 2 cups

1 cup walnut halves
4–6 cloves garlic, peeled
2 handfuls of curly parsley
2 tablespoons olive oil
salt and freshly ground pepper

Place the walnuts, garlic and parsley in the bowl of a food processor and blend until combined but still coarse.

With the motor running, pour in the olive oil. Add just enough oil to combine — the mixture should be dry and not overly oily. Season to taste with salt and pepper.

Store in an airtight container in the refrigerator for up to 1 week.

Kim Evans

Syrian hummus

Makes about 2½ cups

250g dried chickpeas
10g baking soda
10g citric acid or the juice of 1 lemon
10g salt
100g tahini
1 cup ice cubes
pinch of dried Aleppo chilli flakes
olive oil, to serve
pine nuts, optional

Place the chickpeas in a bowl and cover with plenty of water. Leave for at least 8 hours, or overnight.

Drain the chickpeas, place in a saucepan and cover with fresh water (4 times the amount of chickpeas). Bring to the boil and cook over high heat. Skim any white foam from the surface.

Reduce the heat and add the baking soda to the chickpeas. Cook for about 1½–2 hours, continuing to remove any foam from the surface, until the chickpeas are really tender.

Remove from the heat and drain, setting aside a handful of chickpeas for decoration. Place the remaining chickpeas in a food processor or blender, while they are still hot, and process until they are completely blended. Put the chickpeas into a container and refrigerate until cool.

Place the blended chickpeas in a bowl, and add the salt, citric acid or lemon juice, and tahini. Mix to combine.

Place the chickpea mixture in the food processor or blender and add the ice cubes. Blend until smooth. If it is dry, add a little iced water or more ice cubes. Keep blending until you achieve a creamy consistency.

To serve, spread the hummus out in a shallow bowl and top with the reserved cooked chickpeas. Dust with the Aleppo chilli flakes and top with a good drizzle of olive oil. Enjoy!

Hasan Alwarhani

Feta and preserved lemon dip with sesame seeds

Makes about 1 cup

150g feta
3 preserved lemon quarters, rind only
125ml sour cream
1 tablespoon olive oil
2 tablespoons fresh mint leaves
1 tablespoon sesame seeds

Crumble the feta into a bowl. Rinse and very finely dice the preserved lemon rind.

Add the sour cream to the feta and use a fork or a small whisk to mix them together — it's fine to still have some lumps of feta remaining. Add the olive oil and continue to gently whisk to incorporate.

Roughly chop the mint leaves, then add them to the dip along with the diced lemon and stir to combine. Scrape into a small bowl.

Finally, toast the sesame seeds in a dry pan until lightly browned (toasted), then scatter over the dip.

Laura Vincent

Pomegranate dressing

Makes a scant ½ cup

4 teaspoons pomegranate molasses
finely grated zest and juice of 1 orange
4 tablespoons olive oil
sea salt and finely ground black pepper
1 tablespoon finely chopped mint

Combine all ingredients.

Fionna Hill

Tarragon cream dressing

Makes about 1½–2 cups

2 free-range eggs
¼ cup caster sugar
6 tablespoons tarragon vinegar
1 cup cream
2–3 tablespoons chopped fresh tarragon

Beat the eggs, sugar and tarragon vinegar together in a heatproof bowl. Put the bowl over the top of a saucepan of simmering water and stir constantly until the mixture is thick. Remove from the heat and cool. (Alternatively, microwave on a medium to high power for 1–2 minutes, stirring occasionally to prevent the egg from scrambling.)

Beat the cream until it just begins to thicken. Fold the cooked egg mixture and the tarragon into the whipped cream. It should have a lovely soft velvety texture.

Refrigerate in an airtight container if not using immediately. The dressing can be made ahead by making the egg mixture and whipping the cream and then combining just before serving.

Tip — Dried tarragon will work fine in this recipe. Use 1 tablespoon, and add it into the vinegar and allow to stand for 5 minutes before beginning the recipe.

Allyson Gofton

Honey mustard dressing

Makes ½ cup

50ml extra virgin olive oil
25ml white wine vinegar
5½ tablespoons honey
1 tablespoon grainy mustard
1 teaspoon flaky sea salt
⅛ teaspoon freshly ground black pepper

Place the oil, vinegar, honey, mustard, salt and pepper in a small food processor bowl fitted with a metal blade. Process until well blended and a thick sauce consistency is reached.

Use immediately or place in a container, cover and refrigerate for up to a month.

Ruth Pretty

Roasted red pepper dressing

Makes about ¾ cup

2 red peppers (capsicums), halved and deseeded
½ teaspoon very finely chopped fresh chilli
2.5cm piece of fresh ginger, peeled and finely grated
2–3 sun-dried tomatoes
½ cup plain unsweetened yoghurt
salt and pepper to taste

Preheat the grill. Place the peppers on a grill rack and roast until the skin has blackened and blistered. Remove to a bowl and cover. Leave to steam and cool, then peel the peppers.

Place the peppers in a food processor together with the chilli, ginger and sun-dried tomatoes and process until smooth. Add the yoghurt and season well with salt and pepper.

Hester Guy

Classic French-style viniagrette

Makes ½ cup

2 tablespoons white wine vinegar
1 teaspoon Dijon-style mustard
pinch of sugar
6 tablespoons extra virgin olive oil
1 teaspoon salt
freshly ground black pepper

Place the vinegar, mustard and sugar in a bowl or small jar and mix well so that the mustard and sugar completely dissolve. Add the oil, salt and a generous grind of black pepper, and whisk or shake the ingredients together until thoroughly combined. Store in the refrigerator in a screw-top jar.

Use this dressing on any classic salad, especially leafy green leaves that have been washed and dried well.

Lauraine Jacobs

Aïoli

Makes about 2½ cups

4 cloves garlic, smashed
2 free-range eggs
1 heaped teaspoon mustard
splash of white wine vinegar
salt and freshly ground white pepper
2 cups grapeseed oil
juice of 1 lemon

Chop the garlic in your food processor. Add the eggs, mustard, vinegar, salt and pepper and process for about 1 minute.

With the motor running, slowly add the oil (you may require a little more oil, depending on the size of the eggs). When it has reached your desired consistency, add the lemon juice.

Adie McClelland

Tahini yoghurt

Makes about ⅔ cup

½ cup plain plant-based or dairy yoghurt
2 tablespoons tahini
1 teaspoon apple cider vinegar
pinch of sea salt
water, to loosen

Place the yoghurt, tahini, vinegar and salt in a bowl and mix to combine. Loosen the sauce with a little water.

Two Raw Sisters

Sauerkraut

Makes 2–3 × 400ml jars

½ medium-sized (450g) green cabbage, outer leaves removed
½ medium-sized (450g) red cabbage, outer leaves removed
5 teaspoons non-iodised salt

Wash your jars with very hot soapy water, rinse under hot water and leave to air-dry.

Cut the cabbage into quarters. Slice very thinly using a sharp knife or a mandolin. Place in a large bowl, sprinkle with the salt and toss.

Massage the cabbage vigorously for 5–10 minutes until it has softened, darkened and released lots of liquid. The longer you massage, the easier it is to pack into the jar.

Pack the softened cabbage and liquid very tightly into the jars, leaving 3cm of space at the top (the cabbage will expand a little as the fermentation happens). There should be enough liquid for the cabbage to be fully submerged when pushed down tightly. Fermentation is an anaerobic activity (without oxygen), so it's important that the cabbage comes into contact with as little air as possible and remains beneath the liquid to avoid contamination. The massaging process should leave you with plenty of liquid.

Place the jar lids on lightly and leave in a cool, dark place. Check the sauerkraut every day during the first week. Use a clean fork to keep the cabbage pushed firmly under the liquid.

After a few days it should get bubbly. After a few more days it will start to smell and taste sour. At the 10-day mark, start tasting it. Once you are happy with the flavour, place it in the fridge and enjoy.

Kelly Gibney

Radish pickles

Makes about 2 cups

2 bunches small red radishes
2 medium-sized fresh chillies, sliced
1 tablespoon peeled and chopped fresh ginger
1 cup water
½ cup white vinegar
2 tablespoons white sugar
1 tablespoon salt
1 teaspoon yellow mustard seeds
dash of brandy

Wash the radishes in cold water, then slice thinly.

Place all the other ingredients in a saucepan and bring to the boil, then remove from the heat and allow to cool.

Pour into a non-metallic bowl or jar and add the sliced radishes. Leave to steep for a minimum of 5 hours or up to a couple of days. Remove from the liquid to serve.

Jacob Brown

Beetroot and redcurrant relish

Makes 1 medium-sized jar

1 large beetroot, grated
2 shallots, finely chopped
1 cup redcurrant jelly
½ cup red wine
3 tablespoons port
1 tablespoon lemon juice
juice of 1 orange
2 teaspoons honey

Combine all the ingredients in a small saucepan and cook for 20–30 minutes or until reduced by one-third.

Once the relish has cooled, spoon into a jar, cover and store in the fridge for up to a week.

Serve with meatloaf, roasted or barbequed lamb or cheese, or use as a spread in a cold meat sandwich.

Catherine Bell

Pickled plums

Makes about 4 jars

1.5kg red-flesh plums, halved and stoned
1½ teaspoons whole cloves
1 teaspoon whole allspice
1 teaspoon black peppercorns
500g brown sugar
2 teaspoons salt
1 tablespoon peeled and very finely chopped fresh ginger
3 cups organic cider vinegar

Bring all the ingredients except the plums to the boil in a preserving pan, stirring until the sugar has dissolved. Simmer for 5 minutes. Gently add the plums and cook until just tender (test with a fine skewer as the cooking time will depend of the ripeness and variety of plum). This may only take 5 minutes.

Remove the plums and pack into hot, dry sterilised jars. Boil the syrup for at least 5 minutes or until it has thickened, then pour over the plums, ensuring they are completely covered. Seal and leave for at least a month before using. Serve with cold meat, a strong-tasting cheese or on an antipasto platter.

Jeremy Jones

Red pepper relish

Makes 4–5 medium-sized jars

10 large red capsicums
2–3 red chillies
2 red onions, very roughly chopped
zest of 2 lemons, finely sliced
zest of 2 limes, finely sliced
½ cup lime or lemon juice
½ cup red wine vinegar
3½ cups sugar
1 teaspoon salt

Remove the stems and seeds from the peppers and chillies. The easiest way to do this is to use your thumb to push the stem of the pepper inwards. You can then pull the pepper apart with your hands and shake out the seeds.

Pulse the capsicums, chillies and onions in a food processor until very finely chopped.

In a large heavy-based saucepan, bring the chopped pepper mixture and remaining ingredients to a simmer over medium heat, stirring often.

Cook for 1¼–1¾ hours, stirring occasionally, until the mixture has thickened and most of the watery liquid that rises to the surface as it simmers has evaporated.

Spoon the hot relish into hot sterilised jars and firmly screw on hot sterilised metal lids.

Alice Arndell

Green capsicum and apple relish

Makes 6 × 400ml jars

- 1kg green capsicums, deseeded
- 500g cored and quartered apples
- 250g onions, roughly chopped
- 100g fresh ginger, peeled
- 40g garlic, sliced
- 4 green chillies, sliced in rounds
- 350ml cider vinegar
- 150ml fish sauce
- 500g sugar

Blitz the capsicums, apples, onions and ginger in a food processor to achieve a consistent paste. Tip into a heavy-based saucepan and add the remaining ingredients.

Bring to the boil, skim off any surface foam and reduce the heat to a gentle simmer. Cook for about 40 minutes or until a jammy consistency has been reached.

Pour into hot, sterilised jars, secure the lids then cool and refrigerate.

Anna Hansen

Brinjal

Makes about 6 x 400ml jars

- 2 large eggplants, about 500g each
- 4 teaspoons salt
- 1 cup vegetable oil
- ¼ cup yellow mustard seeds
- 2 tablespoons fenugreek seeds
- 2 tablespoons coriander seeds
- 2 tablespoons cumin seeds
- 100g crushed garlic
- 100g minced ginger
- 1 tablespoon chilli flakes or 1 teaspoon mild chilli powder, to taste
- 3 × 400g cans peeled tomatoes in juice, chopped, or use canned chopped tomatoes in juice
- ¼ cup tamarind paste
- 1 cup malt vinegar
- 1kg sugar

Slice the unpeeled eggplants into small (5mm) dice. Place in a colander and sprinkle over the salt. Toss well to coat evenly, then set aside over a sink or bowl to drain for 30 minutes.

Heat the oil in a large heavy-based saucepan or preserving pan over medium-high heat. Add the mustard seeds and heat until they start to pop. Remove from the heat and stir in the fenugreek, coriander and cumin seeds followed by the garlic, ginger and chilli flakes or powder. Lower the heat and return the saucepan to the heat. Cook, stirring, for about 4 minutes.

Stir in the salted and drained eggplant without rinsing or patting dry — just shake the colander before adding the eggplant, then cook for 3–4 minutes.

Stir in the chopped tomatoes with juice, the tamarind paste and the vinegar and sugar. Simmer the mixture, uncovered, for about 1½ hours, stirring occasionally. The oil should rise to the surface after an hour. Further cooking produces a medium to thick brinjal, reduced in volume by almost half.

Bottle in hot, sterilised jars with hot, sterilised screw-on lids.

Tip — If you can't find tamarind paste, use tamarind pulp, available from Asian food stores. Break up the tamarind pulp and place in a heatproof bowl. Pour in the hot water and leave to soak for 15 minutes, breaking the pulp up further as it soaks. Once soaked, push it through a sieve and discard leftover fibre and seeds. Measure out ¼ cup tamarind concentrate. Any excess can be frozen for future use.

Rowan Bishop

Tamarillo and raisin chutney

Makes about 3 jars

250g brown sugar
¾ cup cider vinegar
½ teaspoon salt
shake of ground cayenne pepper
100g seeded raisins, chopped
1 large onion, very finely diced
1 bay leaf
5–6 large tamarillos (500–600g)

Put the brown sugar, vinegar, salt, cayenne pepper, chopped raisins, diced onion and bay leaf into a heavy saucepan and slowly bring to the boil.

Simmer quietly while you prepare the tamarillos, by dropping them into a saucepan of boiling water for 1 minute, then draining and slipping off the skins.

Cut the tamarillo flesh into slices and add to the simmering chutney mixture. Continue to simmer for 1–1½ hours, until the chutney is very thick. If it thickens too quickly, add a little water and continue to simmer in order to develop a rich flavour.

Remove the bay leaf and spoon the chutney into 3 heated jars and seal.

Lois Daish

Quick apple purée

Makes 3–4 cups

- 750g–1kg cooking apples or sweet-tart eating apples
- ¼ cup water
- ¼ cup orange juice or extra water
- 2–3 tablespoons sugar (or sugar substitute), to taste

Quarter the unpeeled apples, cut away the central core, and place them in a microwave-proof bowl big enough to hold all the apples with a little space to spare. Add the water and orange juice (if using), cover the bowl with a lid and cook on high for 10 minutes. Stir the apples. If some pieces are not cooked, push them towards the outside of the dish and have the cooked pieces nearer the centre.

Cover again and cook for another 5 minutes. Purée the mixture, skin and all, using a good-quality electric wand or a food processor. The skin should completely disappear.

Add the sugar substitute, mix well and taste, adding extra until you have the flavour you want, or add sugar a little at a time, again until the purée is the desired sweetness. Refrigerate in a covered container for 4–5 days.

Alison Holst

Sweet cherry compote

Makes about 3½ cups

500ml pinot noir
150ml freshly squeezed orange juice
200ml black or redcurrant jelly (seedless jam)
4 tablespoons sugar
800g cherries, pitted (fresh or frozen)
40ml cherry brandy

Pour the wine, orange juice and jelly into a non-reactive saucepan and set over a low heat. Add the sugar and stir until the sugar and jelly dissolve.

Increase the heat and bring to the boil, then reduce the heat and simmer for 10–15 minutes until reduced by one-third and syrupy.

Add the cherries and cherry brandy and simmer for a further 3–4 minutes or until the cherries are just beginning to soften. Cool.

Ruth Pretty

Feijoa jelly

Makes 2 small jars

1.5kg feijoas
water
sugar

Trim the stalks off each feijoa and chop the fruit roughly. Put in a preserving pan or large heavy-based saucepan and add enough water to just cover. Bring to the boil and simmer until soft and pulpy, approximately 45 minutes.

Spoon into a jelly bag set over a bowl and drain for at least 2 hours, or overnight. Measure the juice and add 1 cup of sugar per cup of juice. Boil for 20 minutes or until thick and a lovely pink colour. Put the jelly into hot, sterilised jars and secure the lids.

Tip — Don't be tempted to squeeze the fruit pulp in the jelly bag — it will turn the jelly cloudy. No jelly bag? Use a piece of muslin. Put a bowl under a sieve lined with muslin. Gather up the sides and tie with string. Hang the muslin over the bowl high enough for the juice to drip slowly from it. To provide a flavour twist, add a knob of fresh ginger to the cooking feijoa.

Geraldine Taylor

Strawberry balsamic jam

Makes 3 × 400ml jars

1kg strawberries, washed and hulled
900g sugar
3 tablespoons lemon juice
3 tablespoons balsamic vinegar

Place the strawberries and sugar in a non-reactive saucepan. Stir to combine, then cover and stand for a few hours.

Add the lemon juice and balsamic vinegar and bring to the boil. Boil for 15–20 minutes until setting point is reached. Test for setting point by pouring a teaspoonful onto a cold saucer. Run your finger through the centre — if it wrinkles slightly and doesn't run back straightaway, then the jam is ready.

Allow to stand for 10 minutes, then pour the hot jam into hot sterilised jars and secure the lids.

Mark McDonough

Sugar-free berry chia jam

Makes 1 × 400ml jar

2 cups fresh or frozen berries (strawberries, blackberries, blueberries, raspberries)
8 prunes, stones removed and finely chopped
½ cup water
1 tablespoon chia seeds

Combine the berries, prunes and water in a small saucepan and place over low heat. Leave to cook very slowly for 20–30 minutes, until the berries and prunes are nice and syrupy.

Remove from the heat and stir through the chia seeds. Pour the hot jam into a hot sterilised jar and secure the lid. It will keep for 3 months in a cool pantry, but once opened needs to be kept refrigerated and used within 2 weeks.

Nicola Galloway

Seville orange marmalade

Makes 3 × 400ml jars

4 Seville oranges (about 500g in total), scrubbed
1.7 litres water
1kg granulated sugar

Halve the oranges and squeeze the juice into a large stainless-steel saucepan. Scoop the pips and pulp into a sieve over the pan and squeeze out as much juice as possible, then tie the pulp and pips in muslin.

Shred the remaining peel, either by hand with a sharp knife or in a food processor (a food processor will give very fine gratings rather than strips of peel). Add the shredded peel and muslin bag to the saucepan along with the water. Leave to soak overnight. This helps to extract the maximum amount of pectin from the fruit pulp, which will give a better set. It also helps to soften the peel, which will reduce the amount of cooking time needed.

Place the saucepan over medium heat and bring up to a simmer. Cook, uncovered, for 1½–2 hours, until the peel has become very soft. (The cooking time will depend on how thickly you have cut the peel.) To see if the peel is ready, pick out a thicker piece and press it between your thumb and finger. It should look slightly see-through and feel soft when you rub it.

Carefully remove the muslin bag, allow to cool slightly, then, wearing rubber gloves, squeeze out as much liquid as possible to extract the pectin from the fruit pulp. Discard the bag and weigh the simmered peel mixture. There should be between 775 and 800g; if less, then top up with water to 775g.

Put 4 small plates in the freezer, ready to use when testing for setting point. Add the sugar to the saucepan, then place the pan over a heat. Warm gently so that the sugar dissolves completely, stirring occasionally. Do not boil before the sugar is dissolved.

Increase the heat and bring up to the boil, but do not stir while the marmalade is boiling. After about 5 minutes the marmalade will start to rise up the saucepan (it may drop back and then rise again) and larger bubbles will cover the surface. After 8–10 minutes boiling, test for setting point. Times will vary according to the size of the saucepan — in a large saucepan this takes 7–8 minutes, in other-sized saucepans it may take 12–15 minutes. As setting point can be easily missed, it's better to test too early than too late.

To test the setting point, take the saucepan off the heat and allow the bubbles to subside. Take a plate from the freezer and spoon a little liquid onto the plate, then return to the freezer for 1 minute. Push the marmalade along the plate with your finger. If setting point has been reached, the marmalade surface will wrinkle slightly and the marmalade won't run back straightaway.

If it's not at setting point, return to the heat and boil again for 2 minutes before re-testing. Repeat until setting point is reached. If you have a sugar thermometer, setting point is reached at 104–105°C, but it's good to do the plate test as well.

Leave the marmalade to stand for 10 minutes or until starting to thicken. If there's any scum on the surface, spoon it off. Transfer the marmalade to hot sterilised jars. Cover with a wax disc (wax side down) and seal. When cold, label the jars and store in a cool, dark cupboard. The marmalade should keep for up to a year.

Gus Flower

Plum jam

Makes 3–4 jars

- 2 kg red-fleshed plums such as Omega, Black Doris, Satsuma or damsons, preferably organic, and slightly under-ripe rather than ripe
- ¼ cup water
- 2 teaspoons lemon juice
- 1.8kg granulated sugar (organic granulated 'golden' sugar is suitable)

Prepare 3–4 good-sized jars or a selection of sizes by washing, rinsing, drying and heating in an oven preheated to 110°C.

Wash the fruit, shake off excess water, then cut in half and remove the stones. If the plums are large, chop into quarters or smaller pieces. If the stones are hard to remove, leave them in and scoop out as they rise to the top when you cook the jam.

Place the water in a preserving pan, then add the prepared plums and lemon juice. Set the pan over a low-medium heat and slowly heat the fruit. This draws out the juices and pectin and softens the fruit. Once the fruit starts to bubble, increase the heat to high and let the fruit cook at a good bubble, but watch it so it doesn't turn into a rolling boil. Cook until reduced by one-third, about 25–30 minutes; stir from time to time.

Tip the sugar into a large shallow tin, like a Swiss roll tin. Place the sugar in the oven below the jars to warm for 10–12 minutes while the fruit is bubbling, and put two saucers in the freezer to chill to use later for testing the set of the jam. If you are using a sugar thermometer, warm it in a jug of warm water.

When the fruit is ready, lower the heat, tip in the sugar, and stir with a long-handled wooden spoon until it is completely dissolved. If using a thermometer, shake it dry and insert it into the jam.

Increase the heat under the pan and cook the jam at a brisk but not explosive boil, for about 10 minutes, or until it reaches 104–105°C — the setting point for jam; don't stir during this process. Alternatively, use the saucer setting test (see tip). Once it reaches setting point, immediately remove from the heat and quickly skim off any bubbly scum from the top.

Have the warm sterilised jars ready on either a wooden board or a double thickness of newspaper. Pour the jam into the jars — this is easily done using a jam jar funnel. Wipe the rims of the jars with a clean, hot damp cloth, put on the lids and leave the jam to cool.

When the jars are cool enough to handle, but without moving the jars, wipe their outsides with a damp cloth, then polish with a dry cloth. When the jars are cool, adhere labels and store somewhere cool and dark.

Tip — For the saucer setting test, place 2 or 3 saucers in the freezer to chill. Take the jam off the heat, place a small amount on a saucer and leave to cool. If it wrinkles when you gently push it with a finger, it is done. If not, boil for a few minutes longer before taking the jam off the heat and testing again. Small batches will cook down and reach setting point quickly, preserving the taste, colour and texture of the fruit.

Julie Biuso

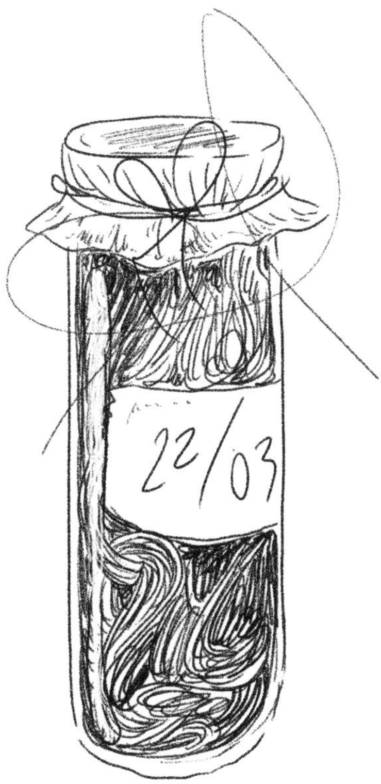

Grandmother's jam recipe

Makes 3 × 400ml jars

900g fresh apricots
900g granulated sugar
juice of 1 large lemon
knob of butter

Begin this the night before you actually want to make the jam. Take a large casserole or small preserving pan and grease the base with a smear of the butter to prevent the jam sticking. Halve the apricots (reserving the stones) and place them in layers in the pan, sprinkling the sugar between the layers.

Add the lemon juice. Cover with a clean cloth and leave them overnight. At the same time, crack about half the apricot stones with a nutcracker and remove the kernels. Blanch them in boiling water for 1–2 minutes, then drain and dry them, and slip off their skins. Reserve the kernels to add to the jam later.

The following day, put 3 small plates in the freezer (this is for testing the set), then place the pan over medium heat. Let the sugar melt and completely dissolve — the mixture must be absolutely clear and free of sugar granules, otherwise the jam will be sugary. Increase the heat to high and let the mixture boil very rapidly for 10–20 minutes, stirring from time to time to prevent sticking.

Use the cold plates to test for a set. Remove the pan from the heat and place a teaspoonful of the jam on a plate. Allow it to cool for a few seconds, then push it with your finger: if a crinkly skin has formed on the jam, then it has set. If it hasn't set, boil it again for another 5 minutes and do another test.

When set, remove the jam from the heat and stir in a trace (knob) of butter, which will disperse any scum that has formed. Add the reserved kernels and let it settle for 15 minutes before pouring it into hot, sterilised jars and sealing. Label the jars when cold.

Tip — To sterilise the jars, wash them thoroughly in warm soapy water, rinse and heat in a moderate oven for 5 minutes. Lids can be immersed in boiling water for 2–3 minutes.

Jonny Schwass

Raspberry coulis

Makes about 2 cups

2 cups raspberries, fresh or frozen
2 tablespoons caster sugar
6 tablespoons water
juice of ½ lemon
1 tablespoon cornflour
1 tablespoon water

Place the raspberries in a large saucepan. Add the sugar, water and lemon juice and bring to a simmer. Blend the cornflour with the second measure of water to make a smooth paste and add to the raspberries.

Bring the mixture to the boil, stirring constantly to prevent it catching on the bottom. Cook for about 5 minutes. Leave to cool, then refrigerate in an airtight container for up to 4 weeks.

Kim Evans

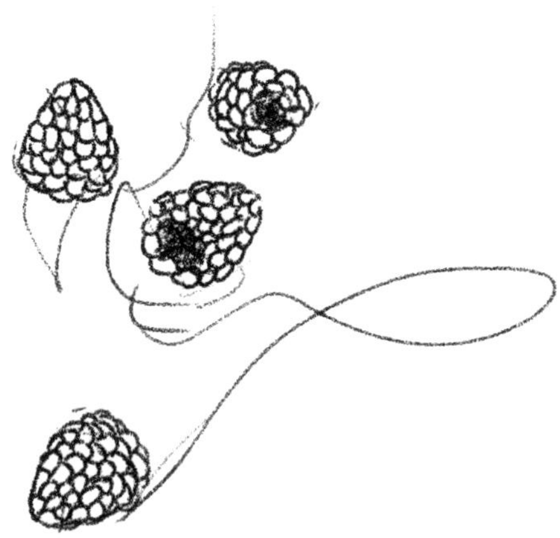

Lemon curd

Makes about 2 cups

125g butter
1 cup sugar
finely grated zest and juice of
3 lemons
3 free-range eggs

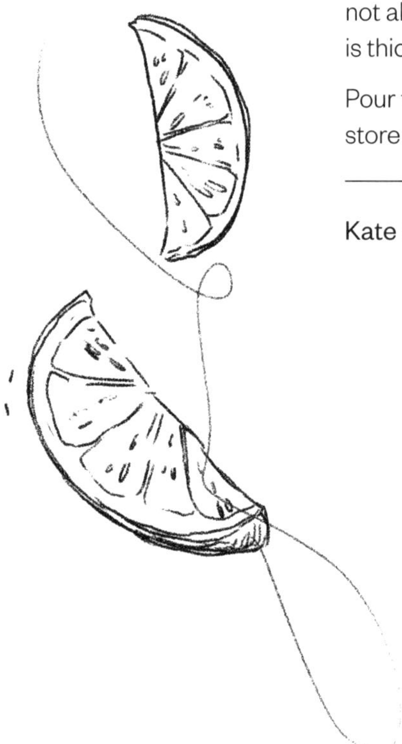

Place the butter, sugar, lemon zest and juice in a heatproof bowl. Set the bowl over a saucepan of barely simmering water, over medium-low heat — be careful not to let the base of the bowl touch the water. Stir continuously until the sugar has dissolved and the butter has melted.

In a small bowl, whisk the eggs together with a fork.

Slowly add the eggs to the hot lemon mixture, stirring continuously over a very low heat until the mixture thickens — do not allow it to boil or it will curdle. The lemon curd is ready when it is thick enough to coat the back of a spoon.

Pour the curd into 1 or 2 hot, sterilised jars and seal. Label and store in the fridge for up to 2 weeks.

Kate Gibbs

Quick Lemon Curd

Makes about 2 jars

- 200g unsalted butter, cut into large cubes
- 200g caster sugar
- finely grated zest of 2 lemons
- 120ml fresh lemon juice
- 6 medium free-range eggs, beaten and strained through a coarse sieve

Place the butter, sugar, lemon zest and juice in a glass bowl and cover. Microwave on high for 4 minutes.

Remove from the microwave, carefully lift off the cover and mix in the eggs. Cook uncovered in the microwave on high for 2 minutes. It will look weird at this stage — the eggs will be puffy and there'll be butter floating around the edges — but don't panic, it will come together! Transfer the mixture to the bowl of a food processor and blend for 30 seconds, or until smooth.

Tip into a container, cool, then cover with a lid and refrigerate.

Julie Biuso

Rich shortcrust pastry

Makes 1 x 23cm pastry shell

1 heaped cup plain flour
pinch of salt
2–3 tablespoons caster sugar
100g cold butter, cubed
1 free-range egg yolk
splash of water

Put the flour, salt, sugar and butter into a food processor and pulse until fine crumbs form. Add the egg yolk and just enough water to form crumbs when pulsed. (Pulse or handle the mixture as little as possible; if the pastry is over-worked, it will be tough.)

Tip out onto a lightly floured bench and quickly bring the pastry together then wrap and rest it in the fridge for ½ hour before rolling out.

Tip — For a plain or non-sweet pastry suitable for savoury fillings, such as a quiche, omit the sugar and egg yolk.

Sophie Gray

Perfect shortcrust pastry

Makes 300g pastry

150g plain flour
good pinch salt
pinch of sugar
115g chilled butter, cut into 1cm cubes
4 tablespoons cold water

Place the flour, salt, sugar and butter in a food processor and blend until the mixture is crumbly. Add the water and continue processing. Within a few minutes the mixture will have formed into a rough ball. Take it out of the food processor, roll into a smooth ball, cover and place in the fridge for a minimum of 1 hour (or overnight).

Tip — When ready to use, roll the pastry out as quickly as possible so it doesn't soften and become difficult to handle. Sprinkle the board and top of the pastry with flour as necessary to stop sticking. Lift and turn the dough as it grows with rolling. The dough should be used as soon as it is rolled out.

Rosie Belton

Flaky pastry

Makes 2 pastry sheets

3 cups plain flour
pinch of salt
450g frozen unsalted butter
180ml iced water

Egg wash
2 free-range eggs
2 tablespoons cream

Sift the flour and salt into a large bowl. Grate 180g of the butter into the bowl and, using your fingers, work into the flour.

Dice the remaining butter into 1cm cubes and add to the bowl. Lightly mix with your hands until the butter cubes are coated with flour mixture.

Add the iced water and mix with your hands until the pastry starts to come together. (The mixture will be studded with large lumps of butter and quite dry at this point.)

Tip the mixture onto a floured bench and gently work together with your hands to form a rough ball.

Roll out to a 30cm × 20cm rectangle. With the long side of the rectangle facing you, fold both short sides to meet at the centre. Then fold in half again.

Wrap and chill in the fridge for at least 2 hours, or ideally overnight.

Roll the pastry into a 30cm × 20cm rectangle and fold as before. Do this twice, then return to the fridge for 30 minutes to rest.

Cut the pastry in half. Roll each half out to 5mm thick to form two pastry sheets. This pastry does not keep and is best used within 24 hours.

For the egg wash, place the eggs and cream in a bowl and whisk until smooth. You can make as much egg wash as you need by using the same ratio of eggs to cream.

Kim Evans

Taboon breads

Makes 8 taboon

- 4½ cups (500g) plain flour, plus extra for dusting
- 2¼ cups (250g) fine wholemeal flour
- 2 teaspoons salt
- 1 teaspoon sugar
- 2 tablespoons olive oil
- 1 tablespoon dry yeast
- 2–3¾ cups (500–900ml) warm water

Place the flours, salt and sugar in a large bowl and mix together. Make a well in the middle and add the oil, yeast and 2 cups (500ml) of the warm water. Mix through with your fingers, gradually adding more water and kneading until the dough comes together. If the mixture feels sticky, leave for 5 minutes then come back and knead again. Repeat this once or twice until you have a very soft ball of dough.

Alternatively, use an electric mixer fitted with a dough hook to mix the dough. Begin with 2 cups (500ml) warm water and gradually add more water as necessary, until the dough comes together in a very soft ball. The dough should be a bit sticky, so use plenty of flour when shaping.

Shape the dough into a ball, rub all over with oil, cover the bowl with a damp tea towel, and set aside until it doubles in size, about 1 hour. Once the dough has risen, gently punch down to release the air bubbles. Divide into 8 portions, shape each into a ball and place on a floured work surface. Set aside to rest for 15 minutes.

Meanwhile, preheat the oven to 240°C (or the hottest it will go) with an oven tray and bone-dry pebbles, if using. Take one piece of dough, flatten it out on the floured work surface, and coat in more flour. Use your hands to flatten and stretch it out to 10–15cm in diameter. Sprinkle with flour, flip, and continue to flatten out until you have a circle 20–30cm in diameter.

If using pebbles, open the oven and pull the oven tray out halfway. Carry the dough between your hands to the oven and lay it over the pebbles, stretching it out slightly into a circular shape. If placing directly on the tray, do not stretch out but use your fingers to make indentations. This will give it a similar shape to having pebbles under it.

Bake for 5–10 minutes, or until the bread develops a light golden top. Remove from the oven and place on a tray lined with paper towels to cool. Repeat with the remaining dough. Store covered for up to 1 day or freeze for several weeks.

Reem Kassis

Hotplate pizza dough

Makes 2 pizza bases

2 teaspoons active dry yeast
1¼ cups lukewarm water
3 cups high-grade flour
2 teaspoons salt

Place the yeast and warm water in a large warm bowl and stir to dissolve. Add the flour and salt, and mix with a wooden spoon until well combined. Ideally, leave the dough for 15 minutes before doing anything else to it; this will let the flour absorb the water and start to form gluten, saving you work and achieving a better result.

If you have a mixer with a dough hook, mix the rested dough for 5 minutes until it is soft and silky. Otherwise, tip the dough onto a lightly floured bench and have fun stretching, rolling and folding it for 5 minutes to develop the gluten.

Place the dough back in the bowl to allow it to rise. Resting your bowl in a bigger bowl of warm water and covered with a cloth creates a nice warm microclimate that is ideal for the yeast to do its magic. If you happen to walk past about 30 minutes after leaving it to rise, you might like to give the dough a 'stretch and fold' to lengthen the gluten. To do this, grab the edge of the dough and stretch it up and away from the middle, folding it back onto itself. Turn the bowl a bit and repeat until you have gone all the way around. Give the dough about 2 hours rising time in total. It should be fine for about 6 hours after you make it.

About 45 minutes before you want to cook the first pizza, divide the dough in half and use your hands to stretch and fold it into 2 nice even rounds. I like to tuck all the sides in underneath to make a nice tight surface on top. Dust each round with flour to prevent them sticking together and place back into the warm bowl. Cover again and leave to rise until you are ready.

To prepare for cooking your pizzas, heat a heavy hotplate over the coals of an outdoor fire, giving it a good scrape and clean as you go.

Sprinkle a board or bit of your table with flour and put 1 round of dough on it. Pull and stretch the dough out to make a wide rectangle. I like to flop it over my hand and use the other hand to tease and pull it gradually wider and wider. If it starts shrinking back too much, just give it a rest for 5 minutes to relax, then finish stretching it. Repeat with the other round of dough.

Check how hot the hotplate is by throwing a little flour on it and seeing how long it takes to brown. If it burns within seconds it's way too hot, and you can cool it down by splashing it with water. It needs to be reasonably hot but not scorching. Have all your topping ingredients ready to go (pre-cooked if necessary, as the hotplate only cooks from below) and any sauce should be preheated so that it will warm the toppings and melt any cheese. Sprinkle the hotplate with a dusting of semolina or coarse cornmeal and transfer the first pizza base onto it. Keep a close eye on it, and once it starts puffing up the bottom will probably be done. Use a barbecue tool to flip it over, then immediately add your sauce and toppings. Allow the bottom of the pizza to cook for about 5 minutes — check how it is going regularly so it doesn't burn. Turn the pizza to even out any hot spots. It is done when the toppings are nicely melted together and the base is brown and crispy — the crunch is what makes this pizza special. If the base is not browning, add a bit of kindling to your fire to create more flame and crank up the heat. Slide the pizza onto a bread board, cut into slices and go for it!

Aaron Brunet

A radio legacy

A brief history of RNZ

1910 — The first radio station in New Zealand opens on 26 July 1911, operating from a tower at the General Post Office in Wellington.

1921 — Professor Robert Jack at the Physics Department of the University of Otago transmits New Zealand's first radio programme from Dunedin.

1922 — Radio broadcasting operations are established in each of the four centres, none of which broadcast for more than a few hours each week. About one in sixty households is thought to own a wireless.

1925 — The Radio Broadcasting Company of New Zealand (RBC) is established to provide a national broadcasting service.

1927 — On Waitangi Day, 6 February 1928, an elaborate pageant of Māori history, song and story is broadcast by all four national radio stations and later repeated for international listeners. The presentation, the country's first in its indigenous language, is considered to be New Zealand's most widely broadcast radio programme up to that time.

1930 — Maud Basham begins 30 years of broadcasting as Aunt Daisy, making her one of New Zealand's radio superstars and one of the best-known local names in home cooking.

1936 — Three broadcasting milestones in one year: the world's first parliamentary broadcast, the first Māori broadcasters, and Jean Batten's speech following her successful solo flight from London.

1939 — Michael Joseph Savage announces the outbreak of war. In 1941 a New Zealand mobile unit records and broadcasts *With The Boys Overseas* — personal experiences of New Zealand troops serving in the Middle East and Italy.

1940 — The first programme entirely in te reo Māori, a 15-minute bulletin about the military fortunes of the 28th Māori Battalion, is broadcast.

1948 — The external services division of RNZ begins broadcasting on shortwave to the Pacific Islands, Australia and Antarctica using two former US army transmitters.

1953 — Acting prime minister Keith Holyoake interrupts coverage of the Queen's coronation to announce that Edmund Hillary has conquered Everest.

1960 — Television broadcasts the first news programme, *NZBS Newsreel*, consisting entirely of British-sourced items but also challenging the media dominance of newspapers and radio.

1967 — *Checkpoint*, the longest-running news or current affairs programme in New Zealand broadcasting history, begins its broadcast.

1975 — *Morning Report* debuts.

1979 — Journalist John Blumsky accompanies a recovery team and reports from the Mount Erebus crash site.

1987 — Māori becomes an official language of the country — and of the broadcaster. RNZ drops its longstanding emphasis on received pronunciation and instead begins promoting regional and indigenous accents.

1990 — Radio New Zealand International officially becomes the offshore broadcast station.

1995 — The Broadcasting Act establishes Radio New Zealand as a standalone Crown Owned Entity comprising National Radio, Concert FM, Radio New Zealand International, and with responsibility for the broadcasting of Parliament.

2001 — Radio New Zealand journalist Rae Lamb delivers breaking news to *Morning Report* from close to the World Trade Center in New York on September 11.

2005 — A new website — a centrepiece of the operation in 2022 — launches Radio New Zealand as a global public-service broadcaster.

The network attempts to axe its signature morning bird call until a dawn chorus of nationwide protest forces a hasty about-face.

2011 — Radio New Zealand National, as the lifeline utility civil defence network, broadcasts special programming for 20 consecutive days following the Christchurch earthquake and Japanese earthquake and tsunami. The interviews are carried live by major international media organisations including the BBC, ABC, CBC, CNN, CBS and ITV.

2014 — Geoff Robinson retires after nearly 40 years hosting *Morning Report*. Jack Perkins retires the following year after racking up 50 years running *Spectrum*.

2015 — Taking a cue from the BBC, CBS and others, the network rebrands its entire operation as RNZ.

2021 — On the back of the Covid-19 pandemic, the network notches up its best-ever ratings across most of the current affairs shows.

A brief history of New Zealand food

1769 — Captain James Cook arrives with kai Pākehā — pigs and potatoes — which will over time complement the Polynesian staples brought by Māori 700 or so years earlier.

1817 — The first vines are introduced by missionary Samuel Marsden and planted in Northland.

1864 — *The English and Australian Cookery Book*, published in London, opens with a zesty chapter on New Zealand fish.

1873 — In Dunedin, Henry Shacklock invents the Orion cast-iron coal range stove.

1882 — Oyster bars are so popular that the seafood needs to be imported from Australia.

1884 — The Chelsea sugar refinery opens on Auckland's North Shore.

1900 — Kellogg's, the country's first dedicated vegetarian breakfast food company, arrives from Michigan and starts making cornflakes.

1902 — The quintessentially Kiwi lamington begins life in, er, Queensland. The recipe will soon feature in a Dunedin newspaper.

1907 — Sure to sell. The *Edmonds Cookery Book*, mainly put together as a way for Thomas Edmonds to sell his baking powder, first appears, before going on to shift more than three million copies by 2021.

— Opening of the vegetarian restaurant the Sanitarium Cafe on Queen Street in Auckland, serving nutmeat pie and vegetarian veal roasts.

1918 — Wellington's future food emporium, Moore Wilson's, begins life as a wholesale merchant.

1920 — Tomatoes appear for the first time in local recipes.

1922 — The Foodstuffs Co-operative is formed in Auckland.

1925 — H. E. Shacklock produces the first electric range.

1927 — The recipe for pavlova appears in *Home Cooker*, for New Zealanders, although since the Russian ballerina Anna Pavlova had not yet visited the Pacific and given her name to our national dish, it goes under the name of 'Meringue with Fruit Topping' for the next couple of years.

1930s — Brussels sprouts, grown by home gardeners for decades, finally make it into fruit and vege stores. Generally boiled to a mush, their reputation with young people as a 'torture food' is repaired in the 2020s, when they are ubiquitous on restaurant menus.

1934 — Radio host Aunt Daisy's (Maud Basham) *Cookery Book of Approved Recipes* is first published.

— Olive Paykel asks her importer husband George to import a refrigerator that she had seen advertised in an American magazine. Their son Maurice starts a company with Woolf Fisher.

1940 — Wartime food rationing is introduced: sugar, tea, butter and meat are kept in tight supply.

1940s — Frosted Foodstuffs begins life in Auckland. All hail the frozen peas.

1948 — New Zealand's first self-service Four Square grocery store opens in Onehunga, Auckland.

1953	Hokey pokey ice cream is invented by Brian Simon at his father's Newjoy Ice Cream Co. factory in Dunedin.
1960s	Capsicum, eggplant, broccoli and courgettes regularly appear on vege store shelves.
	Instant coffee, which was first invented by David Strang in Invercargill in 1881, becomes widely available, signalling the beginning of tea's long decline as the national drink of choice.
1961	Thanks to new legislation, upmarket Auckland restaurant Le Gourmet and nine other restaurants become the first eating establishments since 1917 in which patrons can legally drink.
1965	In gallops Graham Kerr, the country's first celebrity television chef.
1967	Hans Klisser starts to produce Vogel's bread.
1971	The New Zealand Fishing Industry Board is established to encourage people to eat more fish, which had previously been regarded as a 'poor man's food'.
1974	Pizza Hut arrives, followed a couple of years later by McDonald's.
	Wellington's Dixon Street Deli opens. Among its European Jewish offerings: cheesecake.
1975	Jack Forsyth of Turners and Growers starts on his journey to becoming a national institution as New Zealand's 'voice of the vegetables' on National Radio.
	They came. They saw. They bickered. Hudson and Halls begins its 12-year run on local television.

1981 — Auckland city magazine *Metro* begins publishing long restaurant reviews.

1984 — The fourth Labour government relaxes import tariffs, making international specialty foods more available.

1986 — A new immigration Act abolishes nationality preference, and immigration from across Asia surges, bringing with it many now-familiar cuisines.

1989 — *TIME* magazine names orange roughy its 'fish of the decade' (the fish also gets a shout-out on the television soap *Dallas*).

2007 — *Cuisine* magazine is named best food magazine in the world.

2010s — The Middle East comes to Middle Earth: pomegranates are in the stores.

2012 — The launch of My Food Bag kicks off the meal kit home-delivery trend.

2013 — Marmite reappears on local shelves after a year-long absence created by the Canterbury earthquake.

2017 — Prime Minister Bill English is shown putting tinned spaghetti on a pizza — an act described by one American television host as a 'hate crime'.

2018 — A survey finds that twice as many New Zealand men as women are passing off delivered meals as their own.

2020 — A five-week national lockdown to control the spread of Covid-19 leads to flour shortages as New Zealanders embrace baking.

Conversions

The New Zealand standard for measuring cups and spoons is:

- 1 cup measures 250 millilitres
- 4 cups measure 1 litre
- 1 tablespoon measures 15 millilitres
- 1 dessertspoon measures 10 millilitres
- 1 teaspoon measures 5 millilitres

Conversion guide	
1 cup butter	250g
1 cup flour	125g
1 cup sugar	250g
1 cup brown sugar	200g
1 cup icing sugar	125g
1 cup golden syrup	350g
1 cup coconut	90g
1 cup breadcrumbs	70–80g
1 cup dried fruit	150–175g
1 cup nuts (depending on type)	100–140g
½ cup ground almonds	50–60g

About the contributors

Sammy Akuthota has been involved in the family business since his parents founded the successful Satya chain of Southern Indian restaurants in Auckland in 1999. In 2016, he transformed a space behind the Sandringham restaurant into Satya Chai Lounge, a bar and restaurant serving Indian street food, craft beers and cocktails.

Hasan Alwarhani was born in Al-Swaida, Syria. He and his Argentinian partner, Flora, moved to New Zealand in 2013, and established their food business, Damascus, in Wellington in 2017. From working at markets with a single pizza oven, the business has now grown to include catering and a pop-up restaurant inside the Vogelmorn Bowling Club.

Maine Andrew-Ngariki was born in Amuri, Aitutaki, Cook Islands. A social worker, she has long experience in women's and children's health and works in Pasifika peoples' mental health for the Waitematā District Health Board. She is also the deputy chair for Pacific Health and Welfare, and presents the *Cook Islands Health* show on Planet FM.

Alice Arndell, a finalist in season two of *Chelsea New Zealand's Hottest Home Baker*, is the author of *Alice in Bakingland: Delicious, decadent and daring* (2013) and *Bake Me Home: Delicious everyday occasions* (2015).

James Beck spent eight years cooking in top restaurants in Europe, including the Savoy Hotel, Quique Dacosta, Pastorale and Heston Blumenthal's The Fat Duck. After he returned to New Zealand in 2008 he set up his own restaurant, Bistronomy, Napier, in 2015. He sold the restaurant in 2021.

Catherine Bell is a cook, food and travel writer, businesswoman, and co-founder and chair of Garden to Table Trust. She is the co-founder and former editor of *Dish* magazine, founder of the Epicurean Workshop, and the owner of Epicure Trading, which imports and distributes a range of cookware and related products. The Garden to Table Trust teaches children aged 7–10 to grow, harvest, prepare and share good food, and is now involved in over 200 schools across New Zealand. It celebrated its first 10 years in 2019 with the launch of Bell's third cookbook, *Bounty: Cooking with vegetables*.

Rosie Belton is a Christchurch-based writer, drama teacher, director and producer, businesswoman and author. In 2004 she left her professional career in theatre to focus on her passion for home, garden, kitchen, and writing. Rosie lives with her husband, Mark, in the home and garden they created together in Governors Bay.

Niki Bezzant is an award-winning writer, speaker, author and journalist. She is the author of best-selling book on menopause *This Changes Everything* (2022) and has written two recipe books. Bezzant was the founding editor of *Healthy Food Guide* magazine and is a frequent contributor to print, digital and broadcast media on health, food, nutrition and wellbeing. She is now the editor of *Thrive* magazine.

Jan Bilton has spent her working life in the food industry and is the author of 27 cookbooks, including the best-selling *New Zealand Kiwifruit Cookbook* (1981) and *Marlborough on the Menu* (2008), winner of Best Food/Wine Guide at the 2010 Le Cordon Bleu World Food Media Awards. Editor of *Living Today — The Foodtown Magazine* for 16 years, she now syndicates a weekly food column to 10 regional newspapers, is a food photographer and food stylist, and is involved with new product and recipe development.

Kasey and Kārena Bird are the 2014 winners of *MasterChef New Zealand*. After their win, they published the best-selling cookbook *For the Love of . . .: Cooked in New Zealand* (2015). This was followed by *Hungry* (2016). Their cooking series, *Karena and Kasey's Kitchen Diplomacy*, was awarded Best Lifestyle Programme at the 2017 New Zealand Television Awards, and was nominated again in 2018.

Joan Bishop has been writing a food column for the *Otago Daily Times* for 35 years. The former southern territory manager for Sunbeam Appliances, her *New Zealand Crockpot and Slow Cooker Cookbook*, first published in 1985, went on to sell over 125,000 copies.

Rowan Bishop wrote her first cookbook, *The Vegetarian Adventure* (with Sue Carruthers), in 1986. That book became a New Zealand classic. Her enthusiasm for flavours and textures from cuisines around the world has encompassed 30 years, including 10 years as owner and operator of her own catering company in Dunedin. She has written hundreds of newspaper columns and magazine articles, about food travel and general interest. She has published six cookbooks, mainly vegetarian or with a vegetarian bias; a memoir of her family's cancer battles; and has just completed a novel. She lives in Wānaka with her husband, Russell.

Julie Biuso is one of New Zealand's best-known and most respected culinary personalities, with 17 cookbooks to her name and a multitude of awards and honours. In addition to her own television show, she has had regular television gigs and worked as a food magazine editor for 33 years across some of New Zealand's most prestigious publications. She's been a regular guest on Radio New Zealand for more than 30 years. Biuso wrote her most recent book, *Shared Kitchen: Real food from scratch* (2020), with her daughter Ilaria and together they run their award-winning website of the same name.

Martin Bosley is one of New Zealand's best-known food personalities, with over 30 years' experience as a chef-restaurateur, columnist, author and pioneer of New Zealand food culture. One of the co-founders of Wellington's iconic City Market, his food philosophy centres on eating what's in season, what's local and what's fresh.

Al Brown is a best-selling author, chef, presenter, fisherman and restaurateur. The first of his five books, *Go Fish*, won People's Choice and Best Illustrated Book in the 2010 New Zealand Post Book Awards. With Steve Logan he founded the iconic Wellington restaurant Logan Brown. These days his food interests include the award-winning Auckland restaurant Depot, The Fed deli, seven Best Ugly Bagels outlets and a range of food products.

Jacob Brown has run the Miramar, Wellington, restaurant The Larder Café with his partner, Sarah Bullock, since 2009. They had both worked in Sydney restaurants for several years and when they came back to Wellington in 2008, Brown initially worked at The Boulcott Street Bistro. He is a champion of nose-to-tail eating and of supporting local producers, and is a regular guest on RNZ. Early in 2022 Brown and Bullock opened a new Wellington bakery named Myrtle.

Aaron Brunet won *MasterChef New Zealand* in 2013 with his creative and wholesome approach to food. He has supplied recipes for national publications, held cooking workshops and presented food segments on television. Brunet is the author of *Cook with Me: Recipes for enjoying every day* (2014) and has presented on his *MasterChef* experience at a TEDx conference and been a keynote presenter at national food events.

Antonio Cacace and his wife, Luisa, arrived in Wellington from Massa Lubrense, Italy, in 1991 and in 1996 established the Italian food product importer business La Bella Italia in Berhampore. In 2001 the business expanded and moved to Petone, and went on to become an award-winning food destination. Cacace runs guided food tours of Italy, which begin or end in Massa Lubrense, at the family hotel and restaurant La Primavera, where it all began.

Frank Camorra, chef and owner of the famous Melbourne restaurants MoVida, was born in Barcelona and spent his first five years in Córdoba in Andalusia before his parents immigrated to Australia. He was named Chef of the Year at *The Age* Good Food Guide Awards in 2009, and has appeared on several television programmes, including *MasterChef Australia*.

Ros Campbell worked and trained in London as a chef and catering lecturer and qualified at Westminster College, London, specialising in kitchen and larder and patisserie elements. After developing food allergies and intolerances, she returned to New Zealand and began to develop non-allergenic foods; her company Spoilt for Choice supplied breads, pizzas, brownies and dry mixes to cafés, supermarkets and individual consumers. A board member of Allergy NZ, in 2007 she and Jill Macfarlane wrote the *The New Zealand Food Allergy Cookbook*.

Eunmi Clarke (Kang) was born in South Korea and grew up in an orphanage. As a young adult she worked at Samsung while studying food nutrition at university. In New Zealand, she met her husband, Blair, with whom she now has two children. In 2014 they opened the Wellington Korean restaurant Miss Kangsta, where most dishes are wheat free. A new restaurant, Kangsta's Paradise, is planned in 2022.

Connie Clarkson is one of Auckland's restaurant pioneers. She was the owner of The French Café during the mid-1990s and is sought out for her intimate knowledge of Asian cuisine, which tracks back to her childhood in Singapore. She is the author of *Asian Flavours* (2002), which shares stories and recipes from Asia, and the founder of The Kitchen Project, a 26-week programme that helps food entrepreneurs establish thriving culinary businesses. She is now head of business development for Homeland, a cooking school, innovation hub and connector of communities that promotes food and producers from Aotearoa and the Pacific.

Shaun Clouston started working at the award-winning fine-dining Wellington restaurant Logan Brown in the late 1990s after working at Wildfire in Sydney, and is now the restaurant's head chef and a partner in the business with founder Steve Logan. He also oversees the kitchen in their casual Cuba Street eatery Liberty, formerly Grill Meats Beer.

Sean Connolly came to the attention of New Zealand diners when he arrived in Auckland from Sydney in 2011 to open The Grill by Sean Connolly at the SkyCity Hotel. He then set up the Italian restaurant Gusto inside the hotel. Sydney based, in late 2020 he moved to the QT Hotel chain, for whose luxurious new Auckland outpost he designed the signature restaurant, Esther.

Lucy Corry is an award-winning and widely published writer and journalist. In 2022, her first recipe book, *Homecooked*, was named Best Lifestyle Book in the NZ Booklovers Awards.

Jo Crabb and her partner, painter Stephen Allwood, opened Martinborough's well-known Café Medici in 1996. They moved on to run Carême cooking classes at Palliser Estate, and now run The Martinborough Bakery, while still fitting in a few cooking classes. She is the author of *My Two Heavens* (2014), a memoir of her life spent between Martinborough and southern France, which includes recipes from her cooking school.

Judith Cullen is the author of *Judith Cullen's Cooking Classes* (2004) and *Dinner in a Basket: Judith Cullen cooks from the market* (2007). After nine years spent running Dunedin's first café, Partners, she taught cooking classes in her home in St Clair, Dunedin, and throughout the South Island for the following 20 years. She has organised tours to Italy since 2004 and to France, Turkey and Scotland from 2013.

Lois Daish MNZM is a former food columnist at the *New Zealand Listener*, restaurateur, cookbook author and life member of the New Zealand Guild of

Food Writers and has influenced generations of amateur and professional cooks. Her career as a cook and restaurateur started at Downstage Theatre in the late 1960s, and she went on to own Wellington restaurants Number 9 on Bowen Street, the Mount Cook Café and the Brooklyn Café & Grill.

Jess Daniell is the founder of the popular ready-made meal service Jess' Underground Kitchen. The business prepares hundreds of homemade dinners for New Zealanders, with multiple delis in Auckland and an online meal delivery service. Daniell's products are also stocked in independent food stores and supermarkets nationwide.

Buffy Ellen is a qualified nutritionist, naturopath, medical herbalist and founder of the *Be Good Organics* blog and BE GOOD, an online plant-based cooking school and natural health education hub. After experiencing her own healing journey from Graves' disease using plant-based food and medicine, she is now passionate about helping others achieve their best health.

Josh Emett made his name as an acclaimed Michelin star chef, and spent 10 years working for Gordon Ramsay in London, New York, Los Angeles and Melbourne. In 2011, Emett became a judge for *MasterChef New Zealand*, and after five seasons has become a household name. Emett opened his first New Zealand restaurant, Rata, in Queenstown in 2012 with business partner Fleur Caulton, with whom he went on to open restaurant Madam Woo, also in Queenstown, the following year. In 2013 Emett was appointed food director of Britomart precinct restaurant Ostro, and in 2020 he took ownership of the iconic Waiheke restaurant The Oyster Inn and opened Onslow, his first solo venture, in central Auckland, alongside wife Helen. Emett has published three cookbooks, the latest being *The Recipe* (2019).

Kim Evans is the founder of the Little & Friday cafés in Auckland. A sculptor by training, she is a self-taught cook who started selling home-baked goodies at the Takapuna Market. This grew to a commercial-sized kitchen, then to a fully-fledged café. There are now two Little & Friday cafés, in Newmarket and Ponsonby, and three cookbooks, the most recent being *Little and Friday Every Meal* (2016).

Monique Fiso has spent her entire life eating, cooking and dreaming about good kai. Not only is she an accomplished chef, Fiso is also an award-winning author, with her book, *Hiakai*, considered one of the most important contemporary cookbooks in Aotearoa. Fiso and her partner Katie Monteith's restaurant, HIAKAI, has won many awards for its ground-breaking use of indigenous ingredients, and *Time* magazine named it as one the '100 greatest places' in the world. Fiso recently made history as the first wahine chef to be awarded three hats for her restaurant and Chef of the Year at the 2021/2022 *Cuisine* Good Food Awards.

Margo and Rosa Flanagan, Two Raw Sisters, are food entrepreneurs, authors of three best-selling cookbooks, creators of a successful app and passionate cooks. Their mission is to inspire, motivate and educate people on the benefits of plant-based eating, and on creating healthy, sustainable lifestyles that can be maintained and enjoyed. Two Raw Sisters have a unique approach to plant-based living, building delicious meals starting with plants and whole, unprocessed ingredients that are cost-effective and familiar, then recommending that meat, poultry or fish is added as an accompaniment.

Gus Flower was born in Kent, known as the 'garden of England'. After leaving school he became a gardener and remains in the amenity horticulture industry. In 2001 he and his wife, Cathryn, and their son, Sam, moved to Cambridge, New Zealand, where their second son, Josh, was born in 2004. Gus is the operations manager at Hamilton Gardens.

Chris Fortune is a chef, author and educator who got his start at the famous Sugar Club restaurant in London, where he worked alongside fellow New Zealand chef Peter Gordon. He was a founding member of Farmers' Market New Zealand and the Marlborough Farmers' Market, and founder of Teens Can Cook and Kids Can Cook programmes. He now teaches in the culinary arts programme at the Nelson Marlborough Institute of Technology.

Kate Fraser is the author of *Cooking Times: A culinary journey through Kiwi kitchens from the 1930s to the present day* (2009) and is the former editor of the award-winning *Zest* food section of *The Press*.

Emma Galloway is the best-selling author of three cookbooks. A former chef, she is a photographer and the creator of the award-winning food blog *My Darling Lemon Thyme*. Her work has appeared on Oprah.com, Food52, *The Guardian* and elsewhere. She was the recipient of the Tui Flower Award for Best Recipe Writing at the 2019 NZ Food Media Awards. She lives in Raglan with her husband and two children.

Nicola Galloway is an award-winning food writer, chef and author of five cookbooks — including her latest, *The Homemade Table*. Her food focus is on making the most of seasonal produce from the garden and local growers. She has been writing and photographing recipes for 18 years, and has contributed to many online and in-print publications. She also teaches cooking workshops around New Zealand on sourdough bread, fermenting and home preserving. She lives with her family in Nelson.

Laxmi Ganda and Jayshri Ganda are the mother and daughter team behind *A Little Bit of This, A Little Bit of That* (2017). Featuring everyday Gujarati recipes, the best-selling book was awarded Best Indian Cuisine Book and Best Spices and Herbs Book at the Gourmand World Cookbook Awards.

Simon Gault is one of New Zealand's leading chefs. He has worked both in New Zealand and internationally, at establishments including Leiths, London, and the Michelin-star Thornbury Castle, Bristol, and as a personal chef, with clients including Oracle CEO Larry Ellison and Simon Fuller, creator of *American Idol*. Gault is former executive chef of the Nourish Group, and former chef and owner of the Viaduct eatery Giraffe. His business interests include Sous Chef, a fine-foods import, distribution, deli shop and online food company, Gault's Deli & Gault's Cocktails, and his brand Gault's can be found on supermarket and specialty food store shelves nationwide. Simon was a judge on *MasterChef New Zealand*, and the host of popular television series *Chef on a Mission*, *How We Eat with Simon Gault* and *Why Are We Fat?* He has been a food columnist for *New Zealand Woman's Weekly* and the *New Zealand Herald* and is the author of five best-selling cookbooks, including *Homemade* (2012) and *Modern Classics* (2014).

Pete Gawron is an innovative professional chef with a background in Asian fusion style and classical French cuisine. He is perhaps best known for his Arrowtown restaurant Saffron, which after its opening in 1999 quickly gained recognition as a world-class restaurant and featured in *Condé Nast Traveller*'s 'Top 100 Tables'. In 2017 Pete sold his restaurant after 17 years and now focuses on private dining events that celebrate the food and wine of the Central Otago region.

Kate Gibbs is a freelance food and travel writer. A contributing editor at *delicious.* magazine, she is the author of three cookbooks, the most recent being *Margaret and Me* (2015), a memoir of her grandmother, Australian cookery icon Margaret Fulton.

Kelly Gibney is an Auckland-based food writer, stylist, photographer and mother of two daughters. A regular columnist for *Dish* magazine, her writing and photography work has also appeared in *Fashion Quarterly*, *Homestyle*, *Remix*, *Green Ideas*, *Little Treasures* and more. She released her debut cookbook, *Wholehearted: Inspiring real food for every day*, in 2017 and is currently working on a new cookbook. She has worked in hospitality extensively, including in Melbourne, New York and Auckland.

Allyson Gofton has been cooking for New Zealanders for over 40 years. She was the face of the popular television series *Food in a Minute*, has written many best-selling cookbooks, and regularly travels the country hosting charity demonstrations and public-speaking engagements.

Peter Gordon ONZM (Ngāti Kahungunu, Ngāi Tahu, Clan Gordon) and has owned and consulted on restaurants in London, Auckland, Istanbul, New York and Dubai. Peter was Air New Zealand's food consultant for 24 years and, until recently, the UK brand ambassador for Fisher & Paykel. He is also a co-founder of London-based artisan doughnut company Crosstown. After he returned to Aotearoa in 2020, Peter set up Homeland, a restaurant, retail space and cooking school on the Auckland harbourfront, with his partner, Alastair Carruthers. He is the author of eight recipe books, including *Peter Gordon: Everyday* (2012) and *The Sugar Club Cookbook* (1997).

Sophie Gray, former editor of *Food* magazine and food director for Bauer Media, and a regular columnist for *Healthy Food Guide*, *About Kids*, *Food* magazine, *Simple Savings Australia* and *Taste Magazine,* among others, is best known as the 'Destitute Gourmet' behind the food blog of the same name. She is the author of 10 best-selling cookbooks with a focus on fashionable food that doesn't cost a fortune, and is a popular speaker and presenter on food, family life and finances. *Destitute Gourmet* now has a large following on Facebook, Instagram and Tik Tok, and is a comprehensive cooking resource for ordinary people with limited incomes and busy lives who love good food.

Mark Gregory is the first New Zealand chef to be awarded Master of Culinary Arts (MCA) by the Royal Academy of Culinary Arts, and the French Meilleur Ouvrier (Master Craftsman). After a career spanning three decades in top European kitchens, television shows and books, Mark returned to New Zealand and now designs for his chef-wear brand Le Chef, is a director of Denny's, Eveve Software and RestaurantHub and consults for leading New Zealand companies including Lion, Cookie Time and Kenwood. He is also a founding trustee of DineAid, a New Zealand restaurant industry charity that raises funds to help food banks serviced by the Auckland, Wellington and Christchurch city missions.

Hester Guy's cooking career took off in Wellington in the 1970s when she found herself catering, after completing a cordon bleu course in London, for embassies and corporates. Her reputation grew, and her career went on to range from holding fabulous cooking demonstrations and developing a range of fresh meals to pioneering lamb cuts for purchase in supermarkets and hosting her own television show, *Hester Guy Cooks*.

Mark Harman is the chef and owner of catering company Artisan Kitchen in Palmerston North. He has an impressive résumé, having worked in exclusive spots around the world, including the five-star resort Amanyara in the Bahamas, and as Peter Gordon's head chef at fine-dining restaurant Dine at SkyCity. Mark was privileged to both meet and cook for Queen Elizabeth II at Taupō's prestigious Huka Lodge.

Melissa Hemsley is a self-taught chef, food columnist, best-selling cookbook author, real food activist and sustainability champion. She began her food career as a private chef for international actors and bands, including Take That, and has written and co-written five best-selling books, published internationally: *The Art of Eating Well*; *Good + Simple*; *Eat Happy*; *Eat Green* and *Feel Good*.

Fionna Hill is a well-known New Zealand freelance floral designer and author. She has written seven internationally published books; *How to Grow Microgreens: Nature's own superfood* (2011) is available in five languages. A regular travel and garden columnist for various New Zealand magazines, she was also a lifestyle magazine photographic stylist and writer, including for *NZ House & Garden* and *NZ Gardener*. She is now establishing a garden beside her cottage in Wairarapa after high-rise apartment living in Auckland.

Paul Hoather is a former Wellington chef and restaurateur who established three of the city's most notable eateries — the fine-dining restaurant the White House, the bistro Charley Noble and the seafood restaurant Whitebait.

Dame Alison Holst first appeared on New Zealand television in 1965, on the hugely successful *Here's How: Alison Holst cooks*, and went on to become a popular and much-loved television cook with a focus on everyday food. She published her first best-selling cookbook in 1966 and since then has written over 100 cookbooks, with over 4 million total sales, and been a columnist, radio host, food stylist and charity fundraiser.

Lauraine Jacobs MNZM is one of New Zealand's longest-serving food writers, having spent over 30 years writing about everything to do with food, wine, restaurants and culinary travel in *Cuisine*, the *Listener* and in numerous other publications. She is also the author of over 10 food books, and continues to champion all producers of New Zealand food, from start-up artisans and producers to farmers, growers and fishermen.

Florence Jeanblanc-Risler was the Ambassador of France to New Zealand from 2015 to 2018. She is a Knight of the Legion of Honour, the Order of Merit, the Order of Art and Culture, and the Order of Maritime Order.

Alexa Johnston is a writer and independent art curator. Her first book, *Sir Edmund Hillary: An extraordinary life* (2007), was a finalist in the Montana New Zealand Book Awards. An enthusiastic and accomplished baker from a young age, she has published three cookbooks celebrating New Zealand's culinary history. The first, *Ladies, a Plate* (2008), was awarded the Lifestyle & Contemporary Culture Montana New Zealand Book Award.

Jeremy Jones opened one of Wellington's first BYO restaurants, The Sycamore Tree, in 1977. In 1984 he moved to Marlborough with his family and bought an Edwardian villa, converting it into the licensed restaurant The Pepper Tree. In 1997, the family moved to Timara Lodge, near Blenheim, which he and his wife managed and where he cooked for international guests for eight years.

Mawera Karetai (Kāi Tahu, Kāti Mamoe me Waitaha ki te Waipounamu), the 'Wild Cook', is a Whakatāne-based food blogger, pest-management and wild-food champion, mother and educator.

Reem Kassis was born and raised in Jerusalem and is a graduate of the University of Pennsylvania, the Wharton School and the London School of Economics. She worked at McKinsey & Company and the World Economic Forum and became a writer after the birth of her first child. Her award-winning first book, *The Palestinian Table*, was published in 2017 and *The Arabesque Table* was published in 2022. She is a regular writer on food for publications including the *New York Times*, the *Atlantic*, the *Washington Post* and the *Wall Street Journal*.

Sarah Klisser was born into a family very interested in the production and consumption of great food. After her parents emigrated from Holland to Auckland in the 1950s, their small bakery on Ponsonby Road grew into the household name Vogel's bread. After graduating from the University of Auckland with a Masters in Sociology, and a short stint at the Beehive trying to get into the diplomatic corps, she studied at the Cordon Bleu, attaining her Grande Diplôme de Cuisine in London and her Diplôme de Pâtisserie in Paris. She went on to work in New York as an intern at Union Square Café, then ranked by Zagat as the second-best restaurant in the city. She worked in restaurants around the world before returning home to set up New Zealand's first supermarket ready-made meals for Woolworth's. She now cooks with her daughter, who is also an incredible baker and cook.

Carl Koppenhagen has co-owned the award-winning Auckland restaurant The Engine Room, in Northcote Point, with his partner, Natalia Schamroth, since 2006.

Julie Le Clerc is a former café owner and current food editor for *NZ House & Garden*, and has had a strong presence in print media for 25 years, having written and created recipes for various quality magazines and newspaper columns, both locally and in Australia. She is French culinary trained, and years of hands-on cooking in professional kitchens has given her a vast knowledge of ingredients, techniques and cuisines. Her 15 published cookbooks reflect her café and boutique catering background, as well as her extensive travel experience.

Nadia Lim, then a registered dietitian, was the second winner of the *MasterChef New Zealand* contest, in 2011, and has since gone on to be one of New Zealand best-known food personalities and cookbook authors. She is one of the co-founders of the highly successful home food kit delivery service My Food Bag. She was one of the three *MasterChef* judges in 2022. She lives in the mountains above Arrowtown, where she and her husband run a 480-hectare diverse regenerative farm, Royalburn Station.

Steve Logan is one of New Zealand's most experienced restaurateurs. He opened the iconic Wellington restaurant Logan Brown with fellow chef Al Brown in 2006 and 25 years later is still involved in its day-to-day operations as its managing director. He and his business partners opened the casual Cuba Street eatery Grill Meats Beer, now Liberty, in 2014.

Dariush Lolaiy, co-owner with his wife, Rebecca Smidt, of the legendary Auckland restaurant, Cazador, is a multi-award-winning chef, cookbook author and hunter. Influenced by his chef parents, who established Cazador in 1987, as well as by his time cooking in Italy, Greece and London, his specialty is serving game and free-range meats, and fresh, local produce with an emphasis on ethically sourced ingredients.

Laurent Loudeac is executive chef at Tartines Café, Eastbourne, Wellington. Born in Châteaubriant, France, he moved to New Zealand in 1995, and worked first at Puka Park Lodge, in Pauanui, then as sous-chef at the fine-dining restaurant Kimble Bent, and then as the executive chef at Hippopotamus, the fine-dining restaurant in Wellington's Museum Hotel.

Gretchen Lowe is a self-taught cook, food stylist and photographer, who established her blog *My Weekend Table* in 2015.

Belinda MacDonald was the co-winner of *My Kitchen Rules* in 2014 and runs the keto cooking website Flavourbomb. Her cookbook of the same name was published in 2022. Her first cookbook, *My Green Kitchen*, was written with Neena Truscott.

Robyn Martin is one of New Zealand's most experienced cookbook writers and several of her dozens of books have been published internationally. She has a Masters of Science in Home Economics, and her long career in food has included 22 years as the food editor and test kitchen director of the *New Zealand Woman's Weekly* and seven years as the food editor of the *Auckland Star*. As the senior product manager for the Auckland Milk Corporation she launched the Fresh 'n' Fruity yoghurt brand. She and her husband ran a luxury lodge in Marlborough for eight years, and grew pinot noir for 15 years.

Adie McClelland is a widely travelled foodie, chef, tutor, food consultant and private caterer who runs small, intimate cooking lessons around the country. Her two favourite places in the world are the Greek island of Hydra and Mangakuri Beach in Hawke's Bay. She continues to cook and share her food and recipes on her Instagram account, @adiemcclelland.

Mark McDonough was for many years the owner of celebrated Newmarket café and deli Zarbo. During that time he published four cookbooks that expressed the Zarbo ethos. He is now retired and enjoying cooking for family and friends.

Ray McVinnie is a former food editor for *Cuisine* magazine, the *Sunday Star-Times* magazine, and consulting food director for the *New Zealand Herald*'s *Bite* magazine. A professional chef for many years, Ray is an award-winning food stylist and food and travel writer, winning the 2005 NZ Guild of Food Writers Visuals Award; the 2006 New Zealand Magazine Publishers Association award for Journalist of the Year, Home and Food Category; and the 2009 New Zealand Guild of Foodwriters Tui Flower Recipe Award. He was one of the judges of *MasterChef New Zealand*, has lectured in gastronomy at the Auckland University of Technology and is the author of five cookbooks.

Lynette Mercer was born in Fiji, where her parents were missionaries. She and her former husband built Kontiki Lodge (now Korosun) on Vanua Levu and operated the original Namale Plantation Resort for 15 years. She published her memoir of her life in Fiji in 2016. She now lives in Queensland, Australia.

Michael Meredith is one of New Zealand's most acclaimed chefs. After stints at some of Auckland's best restaurants, he opened his award-winning degustation restaurant, Meredith's, in 2007. After taking a three-year break from owning restaurants, he opened the acclaimed Mr Morris in Auckland's Britomart quarter in 2021. He was also a co-founder of the social enterprise Eat My Lunch, which delivers lunches to children in need in low decile schools.

Conor Mertens has worked in restaurants in New Zealand and Tokyo, including Hillside Kitchen & Cellar, Wellington, and Orphans Kitchen,

Auckland. After closing his pop-up restaurant Chimera in early 2020 he moved to Hawke's Bay and is currently involved in Harvest Deli and Bar Teresa in Napier.

Philippe Mouchel trained with Paul Bocuse, and after arriving in Australia in 1991 worked in a number of leading Sydney and Melbourne restaurants before opening Brasserie Philippe Mouchel at Crown, in Melbourne. He now runs the CBD-Melbourne restaurant and wine bar Philippe. His 2011 book *More than French* brought together over 100 recipes influenced by his work experience and travels, especially in Japan.

Sachie Nomura is the founder of the award-winning Auckland cooking school Sachie's Kitchen. Sachie's Kitchen meal kits are available in New Zealand supermarkets and her Kabocha milk is exported to Japan, South Korea and Hong Kong and was a finalist in the World Plant Food Awards 2021.

Robert Oliver MNZM spent much of his chef career working in high-end hotels and resorts around the world before coming back to New Zealand and committing himself to celebrating the healthy traditional home cooking of the Pacific, a mission exemplified in his award-winning cookbooks *Me `a Kai: The food and flavours of the South Pacific* (2010) and *Mea `ai Samoa: Recipes and stories from the heart of Polynesia* (2013). He has been the host of the TV shows *Real Pasifik* and *Marae Kai Masters* and has been a judge for *My Kitchen Rules New Zealand*. He is the founder and executive director of Pacific Island Food Revolution, which aims to return the region to traditional cuisine to curb the Pacific's non-communicable disease crisis.

Eleanor Ozich started her blog *My Petite Kitchen* in 2012 and quickly published two highly successful cookbooks and opened an Auckland café. Now the author of five cookbooks, she runs online cooking courses and events from her home near Piha, on Auckland's west coast.

Peter Peeti is well known in Aotearoa as the face of Māori Television's long-running series *Kai Time on the Road*. Starting his career as a chef, he completed his apprenticeship in Rotorua and worked there as a sous-chef and executive chef in various restaurants before entering the world of television.

Ruth Pretty MNZM and her husband established Ruth Pretty Catering in 1988 in Te Horo, on the Kapiti Coast. The business soon became a major force in catering. The Ruth Pretty Cooking School started in 1993 and by 2009 had expanded to include a kitchen shop and café. She is a regular contributor to radio and television programmes, from 1998–2009 she was a contributor to the *Dominion Post*, and from 2017–2021 she shared her recipes in *New Zealand Life and Leisure* magazine. She is the author of six cookbooks, a member of the New Zealand Restaurant Association Hall of Fame and in 2010 was made a Member of the New Zealand Order of Merit for services to the food industry.

Grace Ramirez was raised in Venezuela and now lives in New York City, but spent four years living in Auckland from 2011. During that time she was a judge for *My Kitchen Rules New Zealand*. She now works as a host on a range of food shows and, among other philanthropic work, with the chef relief team World Central Kitchen, providing people in need with meals during difficult times, and with Chefs' Manifesto, a chef-led project that brings together chefs from around the world to explore how they can help deliver a sustainable food system, through a framework tied to the United Nations' Sustainable Development Goals. She is the author of two books, *The Five Ingredient Electric Cooker Cookbook* and *La Latina*.

Jordan Rondel first experienced the elation of baking as a young girl visiting her grandparents in Paris, and as she grew up the kitchen became her domain. She officially became The Caker in 2010 (later joined by her sister, Anouk), and has grown a cult following for her recipe books, baking kits and made-to-order cakes. Her ethos is informed by her love of home baking and something her grandparents told her when she started, that cakes should taste *even* better than they look, and that is what she has become known for, using quality ingredients and simple decorations, such as a selection of fresh flowers.

Jonny Schwass is one of the South Island's most-experienced and innovative restaurateurs, best known perhaps for his Christchurch eatery and three-time *Cuisine* Restaurant of the Year Awards finalist Restaurant Schwass, which ran from 2007 until the building was destroyed in the 2011 Christchurch earthquake. He now runs Origin Grill, sourcing ingredients from Canterbury producers for catering special events.

Geoff Scott is an acclaimed chef whose unique style of cuisine melds the finest European style of cooking with fresh New Zealand produce. Having trained under the Roux brothers, Alain Ducasse and Michel Rostang, and in restaurants across Europe, he returned to New Zealand in 2005 and ran the award-winning restaurant Vinnies, in Herne Bay, for several years. Geoff now lectures in culinary arts at the Auckland University of Technology.

Jo Seagar MNZM is one of New Zealand's best-known food writers, famed for her catch-cries of 'Easy peasy' and 'Maximum effect for minimum effort'. She trained as a chef at the Cordon Bleu, London, and La Varenne, Paris, before returning to New Zealand and opening the award-winning restaurant Harley's on Anzac Avenue, Auckland, in the early 1980s. Seagar was a columnist for *North & South* magazine and made a number of top-rating television series for TVNZ. She later moved to Oxford, Canterbury, where she set up her popular café and cooking school. She is the author of 21 cookbooks, most of which have been longtime best-sellers, and also wrote for the *New Zealand Woman's Weekly* and the *Australian Woman's Weekly*.

Yael Shochat grew up in the Israeli portside city of Haifa, eating fresh local market foods at home and at the local Arabic and Jewish restaurants. After immigrating to New Zealand in late 1997, she opened the Lunch Box on Shortland Street, which expanded to become Ima (mother in Hebrew) Cuisine on Fort Street. She is the author (with David Cohen) of *Ima Cuisine: An Israeli mother's kitchen* (2016).

Fiona Smith has been almost everywhere during her career in food, from working for the BBC's *Good Food* magazine in London to managing a private chalet in the Swiss Alps. She returned to New Zealand in 2000 and is a sought-after food stylist for advertising, packaging and editorial shoots and a senior food writer for *Cuisine* magazine. She is the author of six recipe books, including *Beets, Leaves and Limes: Great salads and sides* (2009).

Fleur Sullivan is one of New Zealand's pioneering restaurateurs, responsible for the iconic Olivers, in Clyde, the eponymous and famous Fleurs Place, in Moeraki, and, most recently, the boutique function centre and bespoke catering service The Loan and Merc, in her hometown of Ōamaru. She has received numerous awards for her restaurants and in recognition for her contribution to tourism.

Ashley Sumner has had a long career in hospitality that reaches back to the 1980s Wellington restaurant The Sugar Club (with his partner Vivienne Hayman) and its celebrated London sister restaurant of the same name, which opened in Notting Hill in 1995, followed by another in Soho. He and Vivienne later opened The Grocer on Elgin and The Grocer on Warwick, in London.

Judith Tabron is one of New Zealand's best-known restaurant owners. She began her restaurant career in 1977, a rare woman chef in male-dominated kitchens, and worked in London at L'Escargot and then back in Auckland at DeBrett Hotel and Sails. She opened the celebrated Ramses, in Newmarket, in 1989, and then the award-winning restaurant and bar Soul, on Auckland's Viaduct Harbour, in 2001. During her time as its owner she published two cookbooks. She sold the restaurant to new owners in 2018.

Geraldine Taylor has lived on a sheep and dairy grazing farm with her husband in Te Arai, south of Mangawhai, for 50 years. Every year she makes jams, jellies, pickles, relishes and sauce from produce out of her garden and gifted to her.

Anne Thorp is one of the Auckland hospitality industry's veterans. For many years the maître d' at SPQR, where she consulted on many of the recipes, in the early 2000s she moved into private dining, inviting people into her home to enjoy a cultural experience from her cooking and manākitanga. She has shared her food philosophy extensively via television, including her own cooking show *Kia Ora*, from which her cookbook *Kai Ora: Fresh healthy food made with aroha* was published, in 2009.

Richard Till opened a Christchurch restaurant in 1988 and was the host of the popular television series *Kiwi Kitchen* and the author of the 2008 book of the same name. He also had a parallel career in theatre design. A regular at food shows and in the media, he now runs Christchurch meal delivery service Richard's Real Kitchen, but is happiest passing the time with his grandchildren.

Ruth Trevella is an experienced chef and caterer. She and her business partner Amanda Heasley, who also has a background in Canterbury restaurants and cafés, now run the successful Foundation café in Christchurch's landmark new public library, Tūranga.

Sarah Tuck has been the editor of *Dish* magazine, to which she was a longtime contributor, since 2019 and also runs the blog *Stuck in the Kitchen*. Her first cookbook, *Coming Unstuck: Recipes to get you back on track*, was published in 2020.

Alexandra Tylee grew up on a farm in Hawke's Bay, where she loved to help her mother to feed a steady stream of shepherds, shearers, friends and family. She is the owner and chef of Pipi Café, mother to four sons, and the author of three cookbooks, including *Egg and Spoon: An illustrated cookbook* (2020), which won the Elsie Locke Award for Non-fiction at the 2021 New Zealand Book Awards for Children and Young Adults, and one children's story book, *If I Was a Banana* (2016).

Laura Vincent (Ngāti Māhanga) is the author of food blog *Hungry and Frozen*, and her poetry and fiction has been widely published, including in *Peach Mag*, *The Spinoff*, *Shirley Magazine*, *Turbine|Kapohau* and *Queer Life, Queer Love* (2021). Vincent is editing a poetry collection and working on her first novel, and wants nothing more than for someone to tell her they're finished.

Francesca Voza and James Stapley were the team behind the highly successful South Island restaurants Francesca's Italian Kitchen, each now in new ownership. In 2018 they published a cookbook of the same name featuring the restaurants' popular pasta, pizza and traditional Italian dishes and desserts adapted for the home kitchen. James Stapley is now a co-founder of the popular Wanaka eateries Arc and Kika. Francesca Voza now runs three boutique hotels in Christchurch: Miro, Eliza's and Mr Wolf.

Annabelle White is a well-known food and travel writer, cooking teacher and celebrity media cook. White was a food columnist with the *Sunday Star-Times* for over 23 years and a food editor for *NZ House & Garden* and *NZ Woman's Weekly*. She is a regular media/radio presenter covering food, travel and etiquette and is the author of 11 best-selling cookbooks, including *Annabelle White's Best Recipes* (1997), *Seasons* (2002) and *Annabelle Cooks* (1999).

Nici Wickes is a food stylist, recipe developer, food editor and host of the long-running television series *World Kitchen*. She is the author of three cookbooks, the most recent of which is *A Quiet Kitchen* (2022).

Matt Wilkinson is a British chef who, after arriving in Melbourne in 2000, worked in high-profile Melbourne restaurants before opening his own restaurant, Pope Joan. He is now the creative director of Four Pillars Gin and Montalto wines and the author of three cookbooks.

Select bibliography

Alice Arndell *Alice in Bakingland: Delicious, decadent, and daring*. HarperCollins, 2013; *Bake Me Home: Delicious everyday occasions*. HarperCollins, 2015.

Catherine Bell *Everyday Epicurean: Simple, stylish recipes for the New Zealand table*. Tandem, 1999; *Entertaining Epicurean: Stylish seasonal dishes to share with friends*. Tandem, 2000; *Bounty: Cooking with vegetables: 10 years of the Garden to Table Trust*. Epicure Press, 2019.

Rosie Belton *Wild Blackberries: Recipes and memories from a New Zealand table*. Allen & Unwin, 2014.

Niki Bezzant *Beach House Cook Book*. Chanel, 2006; *Eating In: Fabulous food for friends and family*. Chanel, 2009.

Niki Bezzant and Cate Foster *Beach House Cook Book*. Chanel, 2006.

Jan Bilton *The New Zealand Microwave Cookbook*. Whitcoulls, 1984; *The Great New Zealand Cookbook*. Lansdowne Press, 1984; *Summer Food*. Lansdowne Press, 1985; *The New Zealand Dinner Party Cookbook*. Endeavour, 1985; *Fresh & Fancy Fare: The book of the New Zealand television series*. South Sea Visuals in association with Special Projects, 1986; *A Taste of Kiwi*. Hospitality Press, 1987; *Jan Bilton's New Microwave Cookbook*. Pacific, 1989; *The Gourmet Microwave Cookbook: Creative international menus from the microwave*. Viking Pacific, 1990; *Entertaining with Jan Bilton: 25 elegant dinner party menus*. Viking Pacific, 1990; *Easy Asian*. C. J. Publishing, 1996; *Simply New Zealand: A culinary journey*. C. J. Publishing, Viking, 1997; *Everyday Gourmet*. New Holland, 2004; *Dinner's On the Table: Food for families to eat together*. David Bateman, 2008.

Kasey Te Awa Bird and Kārena Te Awa Bird *For the Love of . . .: Cooked in New Zealand*. Self-published, 2015; *Hungry*. Self-published, 2016.

Joan Bishop *The New Zealand Food Processor Cookbook*. Whitcoulls, 1984; *The New Zealand Crockpot Cookbook*. Whitcoulls, 1985; *The New Zealand Electric Frypan Cookbook*. Whitcoulls, 1986; *Joan Bishop's New Zealand Crockpot and Slowcooker Cookbook*. John McIndoe, 2004; *A Southern Woman's Kitchen: Crockpot cooking and more for the family table*. Longacre, 2012.

Rowan Bishop *The Vegetarian Adventure Cook Book: Menus from home and abroad*. Mills Publications, 1988; *The Vegetarian Adventure Cook Book:*

Menus from home and abroad. Mills Publications, 1988; *The Virtual Café Cookbook*. ABA Books, 2000; *Rowan Bishop's Vegetarian Kitchen*. Bateman, 2011; *Rowan Bishop with Relish: Fine chutneys, pickles & more*. Bateman, 2013; *Vital: The almost vegetarian cookbook*. Bateman, 2014.

Julie Biuso *All This and More*. Lindon Publishing, 1986; *Julie Biuso Cooks Italian*. C. J. Publishing, 1989; *Julie Biuso Cooks Vegetables*. Hodder & Stoughton, 1991; *The Long Italian Lunch*. Random House, 1998; *Take a Vine-ripened Tomato*. New Holland, 1999; *Fresh*. New Holland, 2000; *Dancing On my Table: Perspectives on life and food*. New Holland, 2001; *Viva l'Italia*. New Holland, 2002; *Hot Nights Cool Days*. New Holland, 2003; *Sizzle: Sensational barbecue food. New Holland, 2006; Julie Biuso's Never-ending Summer: Stunning barbecue dishes to tempt you all year round*. New Holland, 2009; *Sweet Feast*. New Holland, 2011; *Julie Biuso at Home*. New Holland, 2013.

Julie Biuso and Ilaria Biuso *Shared Kitchen: Real food from scratch*. Bateman, 2020.

Martin Bosley *Martin Bosley Cooks*. Random House, 2008; *Martin Bosley*. Godwit, 2010.

Al Brown *Go Fish*. Random House, 2009; *Get Fresh*. Random House, 2012; *Stoked*. Random House, 2011; *Depot: Biography of a restaurant*. Random House, 2014; *Eat Up, New Zealand: Recipes and stories.* Allen & Unwin, 2017.

Al Brown and Steve Logan *Hunger for the Wild*. Random House, 2007.

Aaron Brunet *Cook with Me: Recipes for enjoying every day*. Random House, 2014.

Frank Camorra *MoVida: Spanish culinary adventures*. Murdoch Books, 2007; *MoVida Rustica: Spanish traditions and recipes*. Murdoch Books, 2009; *MoVida Cocina: Spanish flavours from five kitchens*. Murdoch Books, 2011; *MoVida's Guide to Barcelona*. Melbourne University Press, 2011; *MoVida Solera*. Penguin, 2014.

Ros Campbell and Jill Macfarlane *The New Zealand Food Allergy Cookbook*. Hodder Moa, 2007.

Connie Clarkson *Connie Clarkson's Asian Flavours: An album of memories and recipes*. New Holland, 2002.

Lucy Corry *Burger Wellington: The best burgers from New Zealand's culinary capital*. Wellington Culinary Events Trust with Mary Egan Publishing, 2018; *Homecooked: Seasonal recipes for every day*. Penguin Random House, 2021.

Jo Crabb *My Two Heavens: A life in French food, from Martinborough to Montjaux*. Random House, 2014.

Judith Cullen *Judith Cullen's Cooking Classes*. Longacre Press, 2004; *Dinner in a Basket: Judith Cullen cooks from the market*. Longacre Press, 2007. *Otago Fonebook*. Self-published, 2017 (with Michelle Chalklin-Sinclair).

Lois Daish *Good Food: Recipes from the Listener*. New Zealand Listener, 1989; *Dinner at Home*. Bridget Williams Books, 1993; *Fuss-free Food for Two*. C. J. Publishing, 1997; *A Good Year*. Random House, 2005.

Jess Daniell *My Underground Kitchen*. Random House, 2015; *My Underground Deli: 100 favourite recipes from Jess' Underground Kitchen*. Eat Shop Do, 2017; *My Underground Everyday: Over 100 inspiring recipes from Jess' Underground Kitchen*. Eat Shop Do, 2020.

Josh Emett *Cut*. Random House, 2013; *Josh's Backyard BBQ*. Random House, 2014; *The Recipe: The world's finest chefs and the essential classic recipes for anyone who loves to cook*. Upstart Press in association with Blackwell & Ruth, 2019.

Kim Evans *Treats from Little and Friday*. Penguin, 2012; *Little and Friday: Celebrations*. Penguin, 2013; *Little and Friday Every Meal*. Penguin, 2016.

Monique Fiso with Lucy Corry and Tracy Berno *Hiakai: Modern Māori cuisine*. Godwit, 2020.

Rosa Flanagan and Margo Flanagan *All Eaters Welcome*. Bateman, 2020; *Two Raw Sisters: Changing perceptions of plant-based food*. Bateman, 2019; *Salad: 70 delicious recipes for every occasion*. Allen & Unwin, 2021.

Chris Fortune *Pick, Preserve, Serve: Enjoying local and home-grown produce year-round*. Bateman, 2008; *The Kiwi Sizzler Smoking Book: A how-to guide to smoking food*. Bateman, 2010; *The Kiwi Sizzler Portable BBQ Book: Grill food anywhere*. Bateman, 2015.

Kate Fraser *Cooking with Zest*. Fairfax New Zealand, 2006; *Food from Friends*. Henry Elworthy, 2007; *Cooking Times: A culinary journey through Kiwi kitchens from the 1930s to the present day*. HarperCollins, 2008.

Emma Galloway *My Darling Lemon Thyme: Recipes from my real food kitchen*. HarperCollins, 2014; *A Year in my Real Food Kitchen*. HarperCollins, 2016; *My Darling Lemon Thyme: Every day*. Harper Collins, 2021.

Nicola Galloway *Alive: Food for health and vitality*. Alive Foods, 2004; *Cooking for your Child: From first foods to school lunches*. Craig Potton, 2006; *Feeding Little Tummies: A guide for New Zealand parents & caregivers*. Craig Potton, 2011; *Homegrown Kitchen: Everyday recipes for eating well*. Potton & Burton, 2017.

Laxmi Ganda and Jayshri Ganda *A Little Bit of This, a Little Bit of That: A Gujarati Indian cookbook for Aotearoa*. The Land of the Long Red Sari, 2017.

Simon Gault *Simon Gault Cooks: Fabulous food at home*. Random House, 2004 (with Noelle Knottenbelt); *Nourish*. Random House, 2008; *Homemade*. Penguin, 2012; *Modern Classics*. Penguin, 2014; *Summer with Simon Gault*. Penguin Random House, 2019.

Pete Gawron *Saffron: Food from the Central Otago heartland*. Godwit, 2008; *The Taste of Central Otago: More recipes from Arrowtown's Saffron*. Godwit, 2012.

Kate Gibbs *The Thrifty Kitchen*. Random House, 2009 (with Suzanne Gibbs); *After Toast: Recipes for aspiring cooks*. Allen & Unwin, 2013; *Margaret and Me: Recipes for life from my grandmother's kitchen*. Allen & Unwin, 2015.

Kelly Gibney *Wholehearted: Inspiring real food for every day*. Beatnik, 2017.

Allyson Gofton *The Great New Zealand Baking Book*. Bateman, 1994; *The Next Book of Fabulous Food*. Viking, 1996; *Food in a Minute: Recipes from the popular TV series*. Viking, 1997; *Food in a Minute: All new recipes from the popular TV series*. Viking, 1998; *Food in a Minute: Food for the family*. Hodder Moa Beckett, 2000; *Food in a Minute: The cookbook*. Hodder Moa Beckett, 2001; *Flavours*. Hodder Moa Beckett, 2003; *Food in a Minute: Casual cooking*. Hodder Moa Beckett, 2004; *Taste Favourites*. Random House, 2006; *Food in a Minute Favourites: Celebrating 10 years*. Hodder Moa, 2006; *Allyson Gofton's After Work Cookbook*. Penguin, 2008; *Cook: Delicious recipes for family & friends*. Penguin, 2009; *Bake: Favourite home-made recipes*. Penguin, 2009; *Country Calendar Cookbook*. Penguin, 2011; *Good Food Made Simple: More than 150 quick-smart recipes and meal solutions*. Penguin, 2013; *Recipes from my French Kitchen*. Penguin, 2015; *Country Calendar Homestead Baking*. Penguin Random House, 2016; *Slow Cooked*. Penguin Random House, 2017; *The Baker's Companion*. Penguin Random House, 2019.

Peter Gordon *The Sugar Club Cookbook*. Hodder & Stoughton, 1997; *Cook at Home with Peter Gordon*. Hodder & Stoughton, 1999; *A World in my Kitchen*. Hodder Moa Beckett, 2003; *Vegetables: The new food heroes*. Quadrille, 2006; *Salads: The new main course*. Quadrille, 2006; *Fusion: A culinary journey*. Jacqui Small, 2009; *Peter Gordon: Everyday*. HarperCollins, 2012.

Sophie Gray *Destitute Gourmet: Stunning food from small change*. Cumulus, 2000; *Destitute Gourmet: More stunning food from small change*. Bateman, 2002; *Everyday Smart Food for the Family*. Bateman, 2003; *Enjoy!* Random House, 2007; *Delicious*. Random House, 2008; *Live well, Spend Less: Easy ways to save money in every part of your life*. Random House, 2009; *100+ Tasty $10 Meals*. Random House, 2010; *Feed the Family for $15 or Less*. Random House, 2012; *Fill the Tins: Easy baking for home*. Random House, 2014; *Destitute Gourmet: Over 80 affordable and tasty new recipes plus fan favourites*. Penguin Random House, 2021.

Mark Gregory *Mark Gregory's Cuisine*. Century Hutchinson, 1988.

Anna Hansen *The Modern Pantry Cookbook*. Ebury Press, 2011.

Melissa Hemsley *The Art of Eating Well*. Ebury Press, 2014 (with Jasmine Hemsley); *Good + Simple*. Ebury Press, 2016 (with Jasmine Hemsley); *Eat Happy: 30-minute feelgood food*. Ebury Press, 2018; *Eat Green: Delicious flexitarian recipes for planet-friendly eating*. Ebury Press, 2020; *Feel Good: Quick and easy recipes for comfort and joy*. Ebury Press, 2022.

Fionna Hill and Jo Seagar *Celebrations: Stylish food & decorating ideas*. Random House, 2001.

Alison Holst *Meals with the Family*. Hicks Smith and Sons, 1967; *The New Zealand Radio & Television Cookbook*. Hamlyn, 1974; *Alison Holst's Family Cookbook*. Reed Methuen, 1987; *Alison Holst's Complete Cooking Class*.

Beckett Publishing, 1989; *Kitchen Diary Collection*. Inprint, 1991; *The Best of Alison Holst*. C. J. Publishing and Beckett Sterling for Premier Books, 1991; *Everyday Cookery*. Moa Beckett, 1993; *Alison Holst's Family Favourites*. C. J. Publishing, 1993; *Alison Holst's Good Food*. C. J. Publishing for Premier Books, 1995; *The Ultimate Collection*. New Holland, 2000; *Alison Holst Cooks Cool Food for Warmer Days*. Hodder Moa, 2006; *The Best of Alison Holst: Over 1000 of her favourite recipes and tips*. New Holland, 2015.

Alison Holst and Simon Holst *Alison Holst's Meals without Meat: Vegetarian recipes*. C. J. Publishing, 1990; *Best Ever Muffins, Breads, Biscuits, Slices & More*. Hyndman, 2000; *The Ultimate Vegetarian Collection*. New Holland, 2012; *The Complete Home Baking Collection*. Hyndman Publishing, 2015.

Lauraine Jacobs and Dean Brettschneider *Taste: Baking with flavour*. Random House, 2005.

Lauraine Jacobs, Ginny Grant and Kathy Paterson *The New Zealand Vegetable Cookbook*. Random House, 2010.

Lauraine Jacobs *The Confident Cook*. Random House, 2006; *A Treasury of New Zealand Baking*. Random House, 2009 (editor); *Comfort: Food for sharing*. Random House, 2010; *Everlasting Feast: A treasury of recipes and culinary adventures*. Random House, 2013; *Always Delicious: Favourite recipes from the New Zealand Listener*. Potton & Burton, 2018.

Alexa Johnston *Ladies, a Plate: Traditional home baking*. Penguin, 2008; *A Second Helping: More from ladies, a plate*. Penguin, 2009; *What's for Pudding?* Penguin, 2011; *Ladies, a Plate: Jams and preserves*. Penguin, 2013.

Reem Kassis *The Palestinian Table*. Phaidon, 2017; *The Arabesque Table: Contemporary recipes from the Arab world*. Phaidon, 2021.

Carl Koppenhagen and Natalia Schamroth *The Engine Room: No. 115*. Godwit, 2012.

Julie Le Clerc and John Bougen *Made in Morocco: A journey of exotic tastes & places*. Penguin, 2004.

Julie Le Clerc and Peta Mathias *Hot Pink Spice Saga: An Indian culinary travelogue with recipes*. Random House, 2014.

Julie Le Clerc and Vic Williams *Vineyards of New Zealand Cookbook*. Viking, 2001.

Julie Le Clerc *Simple Café Food*. Penguin, 1999; *More Simple Café Food*. Penguin, 2000; *Little Café Cakes*. Penguin, 2001; *Simple Deli Food*. Penguin, 2002; *Café @ Home*. Penguin, 2003; *Feast @ Home*. Penguin, 2004. *Viva Food: Four seasons of sensational flavours*. Penguin, 2005; *Taking Tea in the Medina*. Penguin, 2006; *New Zealand Woman's Weekly Cookbook: Seasonal favourites from our kitchen to yours*. Penguin, 2008; *@ Home, with Love*. Penguin, 2008; *Made by Hand: Natural food to nourish and delight*. Penguin, 2010; *Julie Le Clerc's Favourite Cakes*. Penguin, 2011.

Nadia Lim *Nadia's Kitchen: Fresh, tasty recipes from MasterChef NZ winner Nadia Lim*. Random House, 2012; *Nadia Lim's Good Food Cookbook: Simple, healthy & delicious food for busy people*. Random House, 2013; *Nadia Lim's Fresh Start Cookbook: Over 100 delicious everyday recipes for lasting good health and weight loss*. Random House, 2015; *Easy Weeknight Meals: Simple, healthy, delicious recipes*. Allen & Unwin, 2015; *What's for Dinner?* Allen & Unwin, 2016; *Let's Eat!* Nude Food, 2017; *Dinnertime Goodness: 85+ fresh, seasonal meals*. Penguin Random House, 2017; *Fresh Start, Feel Good!* Nude Food, 2018; *Family Favourites*. Random House, 2018; *Vegful*. Nude Food, 2019; *Yum!* Nude Food, 2022.

Dariush Lolaiy and Rebecca Smidt *Cazador: Game, offal & the rest*. Cazador, 2016.

Belinda MacDonald *My Green Kitchen: Nourishing food for New Zealanders*. Bateman, 2016 (with Neena Truscott); *Flavourbomb: Fast, fresh, fun keto for Kiwis*. Penguin, 2022.

Robyn Martin *New Zealand Woman's Weekly Best of the Test Kitchen*. Random House, 2003; *Robyn Martin's Best Recipes for Crockpots & Slow Cookers*. Chanel & Stylus, 2007; *Robyn Martin Bakes*. Chanel & Stylus, 2008; *Quick & Easy Cupcakes, Slices, Macaroons, Biscuits, Cakes & More*. Chanel & Stylus, 2011.

Adie McClelland *Black Dog Cottage Cookbook*. Phantom House, 2009; *The Second Black Dog Cottage Cookbook*. Phantom House, 2012.

Mark McDonough *Zarbo: Recipes from a New Zealand deli*. Random House, 2002; *More Recipes from Zarbo: A New Zealand deli*. Random House, 2003; *Zarbo Zest*. Random House, 2005.

Mark McDonough and Dean Brettschneider *The Cook & The Baker: Sensational recipes from Mark McDonough & Dean Brettschneider*. Random House, 2010.

Ray McVinnie *The New Zealand Fish Cookbook*. Reed Methuen, 1986; *Cooking the Catch: Fresh New Zealand seafood recipes*. Reed, 1997; *The Modern Cook*. New Holland, 2001; *Eat*. New Holland, 2003.

Lynette Mercer *Fiji Recipes and Memories*. Self-published, 2013.

Michael Meredith *Food for Good*. Allen & Unwin, 2017.

Philippe Mouchel with Rita Erlich *More than French: Recipes and stories*. Slattery Media Group, 2011.

Sachie Nomura *Sachie's Kitchen*. HarperCollins, 2014.

Robert Oliver *Me'a Kai*. Godwit, 2010; *Mea'ai Samoa: Recipes and stories from the heart of Polynesia*. Godwit, 2013.

Eleanor Ozich *My Petite Kitchen Cookbook: Simple wholefood recipes*. Murdoch Books Australia, 2014; *Sweet Delights*. Eleanor Ozich, 2016; *The Art of Simple: Recipes and ideas for a calmer way of life*. Penguin Random House, 2017; *Homemade*. Penguin Random House, 2019; *Simply Food: 80 delicious wholefood recipes for everyday living*. Penguin Random House, 2021.

Kathy Paterson *Meat & Three*. Kathy Paterson in association with Beef + Lamb New Zealand, 2018.

Kathy Paterson and Annabelle White *Simply the Best: Good honest cooking*. New Holland, 1999.

Peter Peeti *Kai Time: Tasty modern Māori food*. New Holland, 2008.

Ruth Pretty *The Best of Ruth Pretty*. Penguin, 2001; *The Ruth Pretty Cookbook*. Penguin, 2002; *Ruth Pretty Cooking at Springfield*. Viking, 2003; *Ruth Pretty's Favourite Recipes*. Penguin, 2006; *Ruth Pretty Entertains*. Viking, 2008; *Ruth Pretty Cooks at Home*. Penguin, 2012.

Grace Ramirez *La Latina: A cook's journey through Latin America*. Random House, 2015.

Jordan Rondel *The Caker: 50 new and unusual cake recipes*. Random House, 2013; *The Caker: Wholesome cakes, cookies & desserts*. Beatnik, 2015.

Jo Seagar *Jo Seagar's New Zealand Country Cookbook*. Tandem, 1993; *You Shouldn't Have Gone to So Much Trouble, Darling*. Random House, 1997; *Jo Seagar's Easy Peasy Summer Entertaining*. Cumulus for Whitcoulls, 1998; *Pearls from Jo Seagar's Kitchen*. Random House, 1999; *Sugar & Spice with Jo Seagar: A selection of the best recipes from the Chelsea Sugar Great New Zealand Bake-off*. Random House, 2000; *Jo Seagar's Nifty Tricks for Entertaining: Magic menus, hints and recipes*. Random House, 2001; *All Things Nice with Jo Seagar: New Zealand's baking experts' best ever recipe collection*. Random House, 2002; *The Chelsea Café*. Random House, 2005; *Jo Seagar Cooks*. Random House, 2006; *Jo Seagar: The cook school recipes*. Random House, 2008; *Everyday Cooking: Easy, simple recipes for everyone*. Random House, 2009; *It's Easier than You Think*. Random House, 2010; *Italia: Recipes from the Italian cook school*. Random House, 2011; *A Bit of What You Fancy*. Random House, 2013; *Jo Seagar Bakes*. Random House, 2014; *Elbows off the Table, Please: Recipes to make any occasion special*. Penguin Random House, 2016; *Better than a Bought One: Clever recipes and ideas for home-grown celebrations*. Penguin Random House, 2018.

Yael Shochat *Ima Cuisine: An Israeli mother's kitchen*. Penguin Random House, 2016 (with David Cohen).

Fiona Smith *Dim Sum: Delicious finger food from China and South-East Asia*. Ryland Peters & Small, 2001; *Fondue*. Ryland Peters & Small, 2002; *Easy Sushi Rolls and Miso Soups*. Ryland Peters & Small, 2004; *Pâtes & Terrines*. Ryland Peters & Small, 2007; *Beets, Leaves and Limes: Great salads and sides*. Ryland Peters & Small, 2009.

Fleur Sullivan with Nathalie Brown *Fleur: The life and times of pioneering restaurateur*. Random House, 2011.

Fleur Sullivan, Graham Warman and Paul Sorrell *Fleurs Place: Simple, fresh, naturally good food*. Penguin, 2008.

Judith Tabron *Soul: Recipes from Judith Tabron & friends at Soul Bar & Bistro*. Random House, 2005; *The Soul Cookbook*. Random House, 2011 (with Gareth Stewart and Lauraine Jacobs).

Anne Thorp *Kai ora: Fresh, healthy food made with aroha*. Random House, 2009.

Richard Till *Kiwi Kitchen*. Renaissance, 2008; *Richard Till Makes It Easy: Illustrated step-by-step recipes for delicious everyday food*. Renaissance, 2009; *Kitchen Sink: The best of Richard Till's columns from the Sunday Star-Times*. Renaissance, 2010; *Leftover Gourmet*. HarperCollins, 2011; *One Pot Cooking*. HarperCollins, 2013.

Sarah Tuck *Coming Unstuck: Recipes to get you back on track*. From the Kitchen, 2017; *Stuck Together: Recipes to share with the people you love*. From the Kitchen, 2020; *Dish: Fast*. ICG Media, 2021.

Alexandra Tylee *Pipi: The cookbook*. Random House, 2012; *Pipi at Home*. Random House, 2016.

Alexandra Tylee and Giselle Clarkson *Egg & Spoon: An illustrated cookbook*. Gecko Press, 2020.

Laura Vincent *Hungry & Frozen*. Penguin, 2013.

Francesca Voza and James Stapley *Francesca's Italian Kitchen: Delicious Italian recipes made in New Zealand*. Penguin Random House, 2018.

Annabelle White *Best Recipes*. C. J. Publishing, 1997; *Annabelle Cooks*. Penguin, 1999; *Seasons: A year of fabulous food*. Penguin, 2002; *Annabelle Cooks Healthy*. Penguin, 2008; *Casual Cooking: Recipes for good times in the kitchen*. Penguin, 2012.

Nici Wickes *World Kitchen: Bringing great chicken recipes back home to New Zealand*. New Holland, 2009; *Cook, Eat, Enjoy: Tasty dishes from my travels to your kitchen*. HarperCollins, 2013.

Nici Wickes and Carole Wickes *My Mum's Kitchen: Beautiful baking, desserts & preserves by Nici & Carole Wickes*. Bauer Media Group, 2019.

Matt Wilkinson *Mr Wilkinson's Favourite Vegetables*. Murdoch Books, 2012; *Mr Wilkinson's Simply Dressed Salads*. Hardie Grant Books, 2015.

Matt Wilkinson and Sharlee Wilkinson *Mr & Mrs Wilkinson's How It Is at Home: A cookbook for every family*. Hardie Grant Books, 2017.

Acknowledgements

There are many fine people to thank for this cookbook. It could not have happened without the early support of RNZ chief executive Paul Thompson and then the advice and input of head of strategy Stephen Smith and head of content Megan Whelan. *Afternoons* host Jesse Mulligan agreed at once to write the foreword. RNZ's website team has, over the years created a treasure trove of recipes, and it was our privilege to explore it and make our selection from it.

We are so grateful to the chefs and food writers — New Zealand's food heroes — who agreed that we could publish their recipes. We thank them for their enthusiasm for the project and for checking the recipes again, and, in many cases, updating them.

We are grateful for the permissions granted by the publishers of the international chefs who have appeared on RNZ to talk about food and cooking over the years.

Thanks are due to Pippa Keel for her whimsical line drawings and to Kate Barraclough for the design.

May every day in the kitchen with RNZ on the radio be a great one!

About the editors

David Cohen is a Wellington journalist whose work appears frequently in New Zealand media. Overseas, he has been published in *The Spectator*, the *Daily Telegraph* and the *New York Times*, among others. He has reviewed restaurants in Ireland and Italy, attended cooking schools in South Africa and written widely about wining and dining in Aotearoa. A writer by day, fledgling chef by night, he has a longstanding personal passion for Persian cuisine. Among his previously published titles — there have been six — is a co-authored cookbook, *Ima Cuisine*, chock-full of Middle Eastern recipes from the Auckland restaurateur Yael Shochat. He works as a senior producer on *Morning Report*.

Kathy Paterson is a writer, recipe developer, food stylist and photographer. A plentiful herb garden and a trial-and-error vegetable garden give her the starting place for her recipes, along with her love of the classics with a modern twist. Her latest projects include the successful cookbook *Meat & Three*, a book showcasing New Zealand food and encouraging readers to cook with premium meat and seasonal vegetables, along with taking the lead on *Cosy*, a Food Writers New Zealand digital publication produced during the first lockdown in New Zealand, with all the proceeds going to city missions and food banks through the organisation Meat the Need.

Everybody Eats is a multi-award-winning charitable dining concept that aims to solve three huge problems: food waste, food poverty and social isolation. It transforms food that would otherwise go to waste into three-course restaurant meals, served by volunteers and enjoyed by customers on a koha or pay-as-you-feel basis. The model is inclusive, allowing people who can afford to pay for a meal to do so, and perhaps to contribute to future meals while giving more vulnerable people an opportunity to enjoy a dignified experience without feeling guilt or stigma.

The concept was first trialled on Auckland's Karangahape Road, where guest chefs from top Auckland restaurants prepared up to 400 meals on Monday nights. It then expanded to Onehunga, Papamoa and Wellington. Everybody Eats now has two permanent locations, on Dixon Street, Wellington, and in Onehunga Mall, Auckland. They hope to continue growing to reach other communities in Aotearoa.

To dine, volunteer, donate or for more information, please visit www.everybodyeats.nz

Index

MASSEY UNIVERSITY PRESS

RNZ TE REO IRIRANGI O AOTEAROA

First published in 2022 by Massey University Press
in association with RNZ
Private Bag 102904, North Shore Mail Centre
Auckland 0745, New Zealand
www.masseypress.ac.nz

Design by Kate Barraclough
Illustrations by Pippa Keel

A catalogue record for this book is available from the National Library of New Zealand

Printed and bound in China by Everbest Printing Investment

ISBN: 978-0-9951135-4-1

A portion of the royalties from the sale of this book goes to the food charity Everybody Eats.